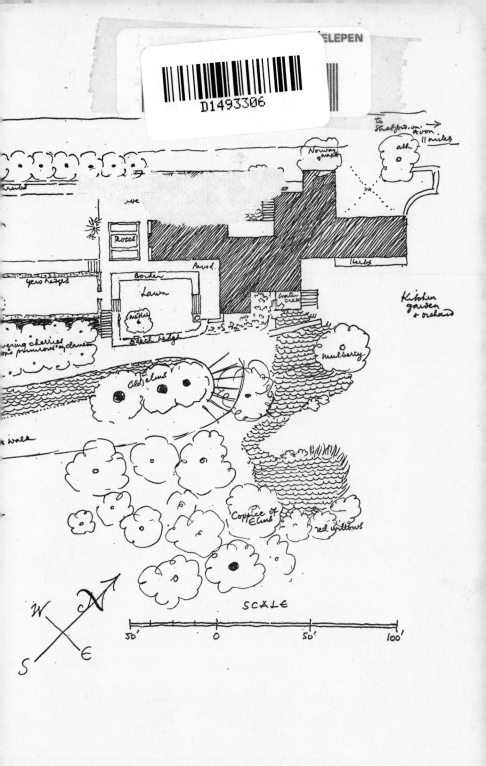

to
Stratford-on-Avon
11 miles

Norway maple

ath

hw

shrub

ive

Roses

Paved

Herbs

Kitchen
garden
& orchard

Border

Yew hedges

Lawn

medlar
6

Beech hedge

Water
cress

flowering cherries
roses primroses & dames

mulberry

Old Elms

e walk

Coppice of
Elms

red willows

SCALE

W   N
    E
S

50'   0   50'   100'

Designer's Trade

THE LYGON ARMS, BROADWAY, WORCESTERSHIRE

Designer's Trade

*Autobiography of
Gordon Russell*

London · George Allen and Unwin Ltd

PRINTED IN GREAT BRITAIN
in 13 pt Perpetua type
BY SIMSON SHAND LTD
LONDON, HERTFORD AND HARLOW

To my dear long-suffering wife who has cheerfully aided and abetted many curious ventures

An artist is not simply a person with ideas. He is a person who has the skill to make his ideas manifest.

ERIC GILL

FOREWORD

On December 4, 1944, I find a note in my diary 'Started Designer's Trade', so I suppose it is not un- reasonable to add, as Gibbon would have done, that on August 8, 1967, the anniversary of our wedding day, I finished it.

During the last war I was working at the Board of Trade and saw a good deal of an old friend of mine, Noel Carrington, who was then with Penguin Books. Talking of Broadway one evening, he remarked how in- terested he was in what my family had done there and urged me to write about it, as it was the kind of thing that could not possibly happen again. I found the idea of writing a book somewhat daunting, but he said it ought not to be too difficult to make a list of possible chapter headings and when I had half-an-hour write a bit under any of them, getting the material together while I remembered it and arranging and polishing it later. I pondered over this advice, thought of a possible title and wrote fifteen chapters within six months. Then it was put away for over twenty years, during which time a great deal happened in England and to me. I wonder whether the same treatment accorded to a bin or two of port might have been more rewarding!

Gordon Russell —

Kingcombe
Chipping Campden, Glos

ACKNOWLEDGMENTS

I wish to thank those who have read the whole or part of the manuscript and given valuable help and advice so that, to my astonishment, the book was at last completed: my wife, whose encouragement and support made the story possible, my brothers Don and Dick, John Gloag, Nikolaus Pevsner, Philip Unwin and Rosamund Hogg for her critical appraisal and tireless efforts in digging out information, collating and typing.

My thanks for the illustrations are due to the British Travel Association for the frontispiece; Michael Russell plates 15 (bottom), 19 (top), 21 (top); Michael Wickham plates 14, 15 (top), 21 (bottom), 22; Sam Lambert plates 13 (bottom), 16 (bottom), 19 (bottom), 20, 23; the Council of Industrial Design plate 18 (bottom); Roger Mayne plate 10 (top); the Evesham Journal plate 16 (top); Gordon McLeish & Associates Ltd. plate 17 (top); P. W. & L. Thompson plate 17 (middle); John Maltby Ltd. plate 17 (bottom left); and Barratts Photo Press Ltd. plate 18 (top).

CONTENTS

ILLUSTRATIONS

ILLUSTRATIONS IN TEXT *taken from drawings
by Gordon Russell made before 1914*

PART I

The Birth of an Idea
1892-1919

CHAPTER I

Early Years

My grandfather, Henry Russell, was born in London and lived all his life there. I never saw him, but I have a photograph, and what I have heard of him indicates an active, versatile and choleric person. He married three times and left a large family somewhat ill provided for. His last wife, Ellen, was much younger than he was and outlived him by more than sixty years, to within a few months of her centenary. At one period, my grandfather managed the Cotton estate in Mile End and lived there in a house which I have seen and which had until recently the remains of a pleasant walled garden. In the eighteen-sixties, open country was quite close. He was fond of the sea and I have a map he made in 1866, and signed in a fine, clear hand, of lighthouses on the north-east coast, apparently for the Board of Trade. He would have been amused by his grandson's link with the Board, as appears hereafter. Several of his sons became sea captains in the Merchant Navy, others went into banks, counting houses and suchlike jobs: I cannot remember hearing of any professional men among them. I should say he came of good, racy, hardworking stock which probably, for leaven, had the odd pirate and trollop a few generations back. Some of my friends may think this an underestimate in numbers and overestimate in time!

My uncle Barnabas was the family genealogist. He knew that his mother's family had come from Deptford, where there had been a considerable naval dockyard, so he spent some days searching the local registers and examining tombstones. He said he found one of a woman of his grandmother's family who had a daughter but there was no mention of a husband or father.

He then worked out a theory that she was a beauty and had been the mistress of an Admiral, 'perhaps of Royal blood'. He retailed this story at some length and with great relish to his sister Ada in Buenos Aires. As she had snobbish inclinations and was a pillar of the English church there we could never discover whether she felt that this insubstantial family skeleton should be concealed or paraded!

My father, Sydney Bolton Russell, was born on March 28, 1866. He was the second of four children—Ellen, Sydney, Ada and Barnabas—by my grandfather's third wife, Ellen. In 1880 my grandfather died and the family fortunes were such that my father, then fourteen, was withdrawn from school and set to earn a few shillings a week in a coal-merchant's office. Although in later life he had a comfortable income, it was always earned with a feeling of strain occasioned, I think, by too much responsibility at a tender age. After a few years he went into the London and County Bank (now the Westminster) and as a clerk with a salary of around £150 a year he married Elizabeth Shefford on June 8, 1891. They went to live at Cricklewood in a small, semi-rural cottage. Here I was born, and was christened Sydney Gordon. My father was then in the Knightsbridge branch of the Bank, and I feel sure that my arrival on May 20, 1892, must have occasioned a lot of extra work for him, for I have heard that at about this time he started to keep the books of several small firms who were customers at the Bank. At least one connection he formed in this way proved to be of great value to him later on.

My mother came of farming stock at Winkfield, near Windsor. I remember hearing of a vast farm kitchen with a beam dated 1599 in the ceiling although I don't think I ever went there. She never, to my knowledge, evinced much interest in maintaining contact with her family so that her background remains to me half-legendary, slow, feudal and delicious, in sharp contrast with the smart, hard, ugly and monotonous little suburban house where I first remember her. No. 35 Tooting Bec Road, to which my parents had moved, was like thousands of other houses which, year by year, ate up the countryside around London. No slightest hint of the emotions which building had once stirred in the breasts of men obtruded itself anywhere. But it faced the sun, had large windows and, wonder of wonders, it looked out upon a considerable field with real cows in it. This pleasant sight was made even more attractive by being seen through a row of fine Lombardy poplars, known to me as 'fumblers' for some reason I cannot remember. Could they perhaps have been aspens, which Sir Herbert Maxwell says were anciently called 'tremblers'? These trees seemed to stir a breeze in the hottest weather, they dappled the road with shade and their leaves rustled in that almost metallic way common to their tribe, which to this day I find infinitely soothing.

These were the first trees whose peculiar attributes I remember, and I think this must have been the first time I took any notice of texture and pattern—without, of course, realizing that I was consciously becoming aware of their existence. I believe I did get pleasure from the constantly changing pattern of sunlight and shadow on pavement and road and this perhaps led me to observe all kinds of flooring and paving more closely. The ground a child walks on is near his eyes and I came to realize that quite different materials were used indoors from those outside. It may have been about this time that I observed how greatly the weather affected the paving. The rain gave the London pavements of York stone a very special kind of beauty in addition to washing them clean. This attained an exquisite quality as the lamplighter went his rounds during a winter evening, and the flickering gaslight was reflected from the wet stones, which had a faintly irregular face from cleaving and wear. In some of them one could make out a slightly rippled surface rather like the sand on the shore at low tide at Littlehampton, where we had spent a holiday one summer. Then there was the infinite variety of size in these natural stones. I remember the excitement of finding occasional ones which spanned the full width of the pavement and gave a special quality to the whole street. I felt a personal sense of loss when I saw the stone being replaced by concrete slabs—uniform, dull, lifeless and without texture or character, like nearly all the building of the time. Since then, even where the stone has not been replaced, it has been broken to insert new lighting standards, parking meters and so on.

Before his marriage, my father had taken up photography with great gusto and he took particular delight in recording old buildings. When I was popped into a tall basket and photographed I too became interested and although I never became a photographer it was quite natural that, as I took readily to drawing, I should try to illustrate a building. I have a drawing of Walmer Castle dated 1900 and several of steam locomotives, for which I early developed a taste which I have never lost. I suppose it must have been my fascination in observation and analysis which led me on the paths of design for, as I shall record, I had no formal training but was indeed fortunate in my background, which I think tremendously important. I am not sure how this works out in my own case, in view of what I have said about the house we lived in, but there were the compensating advantages I have noted and Tooting Common was a pleasant spot. In any case, we did not live there long. On returning to look at it many years later I found that the pleasant field had been covered with the worst kind of building.

A curious and unrelated sequence of other memories assails me. Of my brother Donald, nearly two years younger than myself, and how surprised I was that his forehead bled when I led him into a lamp-post with his eyes closed, pretending to be a blind man. Of my father, cutting the privet hedge in front of the house, or sticking flags on pins into a map to explain the course of the Boer war, or his Sunday morning routine of winding the clocks, which were one of his few mechanical enthusiasms. He had been in the Volunteers until he married, but my mother couldn't imagine how he could possibly carry a rifle without blowing his head off. Sometimes, however, I sensed that he viewed that possibility with equanimity—even as a welcome risk—compared with the fixed routine of the Bank. Of Queen Victoria driving in an open carriage to lay a foundation stone and of the personal sense of loss when her death brought black-edged papers into the house. Of my father telling of the first motor-bus he had seen, of going on that sulphurous inferno called the Underground and of the opening of the electric tube railway. Of hearing how he had taken dear old Whatman, a farmer with whom he had stayed as a boy at Burwash in Sussex, to see 'the tube' on one of his rare visits to London and how, having penetrated as far as the platform with many misgivings, he positively refused to go down a 'rat's hole'. Of my grandmother putting knives under the tablecloth in a thunder storm and the sense of security it gave me. Of the relief of Mafeking, the noise of fireworks and the beginning of a new century whose first day seemed oddly like the last day of the old one and gave no hint of the horrid upheavals that were brewing. Of eating grapes and mulberries in an aunt's garden and so perhaps acquiring a taste for exotics which has persisted. And of the visits of sundry aunts, uncles and cousins. My uncles Joe and Harry, both at sea, vied with one another in telling highly improbable stories of the sort of things one might expect to find inside a shark. Barnabas not only sang well but showed great prowess in bicycle racing and business. George was a partner in a well-known firm of silver-smiths in Orchard Street and was reliable and conventional. He used to talk of heraldry sometimes, heraldry as a science not an art, but best I liked to hear how he was visited by my uncle Hamilton and his wife, Hattie. Hamilton, George's exact opposite, had no respect for convention, although his job was humdrum enough, as cashier in a bank in the lovely little Sussex town of Rye. His infrequent visits to London were most popular with Don and myself as we were presented with a bright half-sovereign each, a delight unknown to modern youth who have hardly seen a gilded windvane let alone a disc of gold. Hamilton preferred an old policeman's cape to an overcoat, and his wife Hattie, one of the kindest souls, found her husband's boots so comfortable for the long hours she worked in her garden that she came to prefer them on all occasions. So attired, with Hamilton carrying a large carpet-bag full of apples, the pair bore down on George's smart place of business, to his consternation but to the delight of the clerks and assistants and the astonishment of the fashionable customers.

Our yearly holiday was usually spent on a Sussex farm, near Warbleton—the 'War-bill-in-tun', that is a pike stuck through a barrel, the local inn sign. My father knew this countryside well for he and my mother used to ride bicycles, quite a daring thing for a woman to do at that time. I remember how her brake failed on a hill and she came off at speed, cutting her face so badly that it had to be stitched. There was only one brake, which engaged the front tyre so that a puncture put it out of action. I shall not forget the delight of going to the flat lead roof of the tower of Warbleton church to see the view, and of making a drawing of the church from the churchyard. How delightful it was to see the massed ranks of spiders' webs studded with dewy pearls in the early morning, to listen to the cocks crowing and the hens clucking, to watch the pigs guzzling fruit with live wasps in it, to search for mushrooms with clothes baskets which were soon filled, to help with the harvesting—perhaps help is hardly the right word—and to listen to the droning cockchafers as we returned to a table well spread with home-made delicacies in a cosy room lit by an oil lamp. Then to bed, in a low-raftered room whose walls were covered with a rose-patterned wallpaper and through whose small casement the moonlight streamed, whilst an owl hooted in a nearby tree. These were simple pleasures indeed but how real, how rich, how abiding.

To a highly-strung boy coming from the noise and bustle of London—a London in which one could, none the less, still observe human beings instead of just dodging machines—the quietness and slower tempo of the country were most soothing. And then in 1901 we were told we were going to pack up and leave the house in Tooting and instead of visiting the country for a few weeks each year we were going to live there, in a Derbyshire village called Repton. This sounded like heaven indeed!

CHAPTER 2

Cockney to Countryman

I count myself fortunate that neither my grandfather nor my father cared to stick in a groove, and took up new work with surprising energy and abandon, and I hope I may claim to have inherited these enlivening characteristics. My father was thirty-five and had already spent seventeen years in the Bank when Mr Stewart—better known as Sir Charles Stewart for his later work as the first Public Trustee—offered him the post of agency manager of Samuel Allsopp and Sons, the brewers at Burton-on-Trent. It appeared that Stewart, who I believe was a customer at the Bank, had been called in to advise on the reorganization of the firm owing to difficulties following the Boer War.

The house we moved to was Askew Cottage, Repton, which stood by itself on the outskirts of the village. The back part was of some age and several rooms had been built on to the front, but architecturally it was not of much greater interest than the house we had left, although it was more seemly and its utterly different situation made it seem quite romantic to us. A short drive from the road led to a stable and outbuildings in which a pony and trap were housed and which were the domain of an Irishman named Kelly who looked after the outside work. There was a garden with a small lawn between house and road, which was some six feet below floor level. On the other side of the road was a good kitchen garden and behind the house an orchard which abutted on a lane. There were fields nearby with pools in them, there were lots of trees and hedges full of birds and not far away was quite wild country through which the backwaters of the Trent meandered. There were even hermits' dwellings hacked out of the pudding-stone. Moreover, the new secretary and the accountant of Allsopp's had also moved to houses in Repton and as they both proved most congenial to my father we did not lack a certain amount of society from the start. The Grammar School to which we went in Burton boasted a master who was a keen student of natural history. Occasionally, on Saturdays, he would come to tea with us and, with exemplary generosity, would take us out to explore the neighbourhood. Having been born in London we could not have left that city at a more impressionable age.

We spent three years at Repton—three years that seem so short in my recollection of them that I am sure they must have been very happy ones. I remember King Edward VII visiting Burton to go over one of the breweries and the splendid view we had from the top of a mountain of barrels; and how we were shown over the brewery too and even given sips of a most delicious 'barley wine' which was said to have been brewed on the occasion of an earlier Royal visit, though somehow I can't quite picture Queen Victoria in a brewery!

My father's job entailed a good deal of travelling as Allsopp's owned a great number of public houses up and down the country and it was part of his duty to inspect them. Many, I believe, had been bought at ruinously high prices about the time of the South African War on valuations based on sales of beer and spirits artificially boosted by groups of licensees who visited each other's houses in turn, drank like fishes themselves and treated all and sundry. My father hated the idea of being forced to drink when he had no wish to do so, but to visit a pub without ordering something for the good of the house was not done at that time by a member of the brewer's staff. However, he generally managed to find somewhere to put his drink—a spittoon, fireplace, garden bed or flower pot. Aspidistras, being plants he always disliked, came in for much strong nourishment, not entirely to their lasting benefit. But in one pub he was stumped. There was neat whisky in his glass —not a vast quantity even in those days—and it seemed there was nowhere to put it. Suddenly the extreme coldness of his feet gave him a clue and, choosing his moment with skill, he tipped the liquid into one of his boots. A most heartening and pleasant glow presently suffused that foot, so hastily ordering another whisky, he repeated the dose on the other foot and from that moment the aspidistras were safe! This experiment had unexpected results for during the First World War I was sent every week from home a parcel of all kinds of acceptable things among which there was always a bottle marked 'Foot Lotion' as men in the ranks were not supposed to have spirits.

It was on one of his visits of inspection that my father saw for the first time an old house, then belonging to Allsopp's, of which he had read in J. J. Hissey's *Across England in a Dog Cart* —the Lygon Arms at Broadway, Worcestershire, at the foot of the Cotswold hills. He wrote a report to the firm urging them not to treat this house as an ordinary inn: he felt it would never have a large beer trade as it was in a village in an agricultural district, but it was a splendid piece of Cotswold architecture and he advised that it should be developed carefully for people to stay in. The firm was quite unimpressed. Talking over the matter with an old friend he said he was somewhat piqued at the lack of interest and he would like to make an offer for it himself as he found it quite irresistible. His friend, who was somewhat alarmed by such harum-scarum notions, urged him to try once more to get Allsopp's to take his advice before making an offer. This he did, but with the same result. So without any experience of running a business of his own, little knowledge of innkeeping or catering, very little capital (but with all the zest which the amateur so often brings to a new job) and financial backing from R. C. Drew, a businessman with hotel interests whose books he had kept when working at the Bank, he decided, at the age of thirty-seven, to change his work again. To my mother the whole business must have seemed an extraordinary cock-and-bull story, but his enthusiasm, coupled with an assurance that she would not be asked to do anything in the business, won the day. He made Allsopp's an offer, which they took—possibly because sales of beer were small there—and we were told of another move.

For weeks beforehand we talked of nothing else. Twenty times a day we looked up Broadway on the map. We found out that there was a tower on top of Broadway Hill, that the nearest station was Evesham, that Stratford-on-Avon, Cheltenham and Worcester weren't very far away, and that the villages nearby had pleasant English names—names which haunt one when far from England: Childswickham, Aston-sub-Edge, Willersey, Hidcote Bartrim, Mickleton, Saintbury, Chipping Campden, Didbrook, Winchcomb. I was twelve, Don was ten, and Dick, my youngest brother, about six weeks old. On January 26, 1904—my mother's birthday—my father took over the Lygon Arms, and we were to join him as soon as he had made some preparations.

The great day came at last, February 1, 1904, cold, grey and I believe rainy, and we set out, 'we' being my mother, a charming Scots nurse who became a dear friend and we three boys. We went to Burton and then via Birmingham to Evesham. I still remember that first impression of the infernal regions through which the train entered and left Birmingham: they haven't changed much. At Evesham station we were met by Charlie Jarrett driving a brougham as the railway line from Honeybourne to Cheltenham via Broadway was then being built and was opened the following year. (Now it is closed to local traffic and Evesham is, once again, the nearest station for the North.) One had time to see things when behind a horse, and we enjoyed the six-mile drive to Broadway. The road had a pleasant, remote air which it has quite lost. I think the Sandys Arms inn and a stonebuilt farm called Whitechapel were then about the only houses. Just as it was getting dusk we drove up to the splendid doorway of the Lygon, where my father was waiting to meet us. He took us upstairs to a room where he said that Oliver Cromwell had slept before the Battle of Worcester in 1651, and pointed out to us the beautiful carved stone fireplace and rich plaster ceiling (see Plate 4). A large

tea was all ready, with ham and cakes, as my father imagined
we should be ravenous after our journey.

Everything was most absorbingly original to us. The loud
buzz of conversation and laughter heard through a partition in
the bar was quite new, as also were the delightful and untidy
dens inhabited by members of the staff referred to vaguely as
'The Boots' or 'The Ostler'. Don and I shared bedroom
number eight. It was a new experience to have a number on
our door and, when we opened it, to find that we had to go
down several steps. There were stone mullioned windows
with small leaded panes of greenish glass.

The next morning we awoke before we were called, but we
found we could not open the iron latch on the door, of which
we had never seen the like before. There were, of course, no
electric bells but several furious jerks of the bell-pull—whose
wires could be heard hissing and rustling outside—at length
brought a tousled youth, the under-boots, to the door and we
were released. His dishevelled appearance led my father one
day to ask him whether he did undress o'nights and he replied
proudly, 'I allus looses meself.' Directly after breakfast we
started to explore the great old house, which as far as I
remember had no visitors staying in it. We went into the oak-
panelled room where Charles I was said to have met his local
supporters, into the 'Glory Hole', which went up through two
floors and was said to have been used for smoking bacon, into
the 'Bogey Hole', very dark and mysterious, with doors at odd
places in the walls leading to attics, and into all sorts of bedrooms, every one different from the last. It was a most wonderful and rewarding morning, ending with the discovery of the
glorious hay-lofts above the stables which were to be a great
source of delight to us for several years to come. In the afternoon we were taken out, again by Charlie Jarrett in the
brougham, for a short drive round the village and surroundings. Within a few miles of Broadway four counties met at
one point and there were even islands of one county inside
another. Jarrett pointed out to us where the boundary
between Worcestershire and Gloucestershire crossed the

road and we were surprised there was no bump as we passed over it.

We were to come to know Charlie Jarrett very well. A coachman of the old school with the smell of the stable about him, his particular delight over the next few years was in baiting the drivers of motor-cars. Describing to us how on a pitch-black night he was driving from Evesham 'feasible like'—whatever that may have been intended to mean—he had reached the highest point where the wind roared over the road. 'There was one of they newfangled moty-cars there with 's cesalene [acetylene] 'eadlights full on so I pulls up just for to show courtesy like. And at first I couldn't see nothing at all. I were fair blinded with the glare, I were. And then I sees a pair of boots sticking out from under the carriage and I sez to me-self, I sez, ''Jud [dead] as perishing mutton!'' So I hollers to them boots, ''Air you admiring the view?'' But you know he weren't, sir, he were fair wallowing in 'is luxury, but what 'e said to me it wouldn't do no good neither to you nor to me for to repeat it. No it would *not!* It were what my old dad's brother who were a policeman in Birmegum were wont to call unseen language.' Charlie's aversion to bad language was skilfully assumed for the benefit of the young: he could swear in a picturesque and unbridled cascade, and he could drink to the undoing of lesser men.

I shall never forget that first day at Broadway, which was then a most beautiful village, of a kind I had never seen before. Years afterwards I came across George Gissing's description of his first visit to Chipping Campden—having been brought up in an industrial town—and I know what it must have meant to him.

CHAPTER 3

Schooldays in Chipping Campden

Within a few weeks we were lucky enough to be sent to the Grammar School at Chipping Campden, one of the loveliest little towns that can ever have been built by men. How fortunate to spend the formative years of one's life in surroundings such as these. Here I was able to walk quietly, or even noisily, along a street which I still think among the best in Europe. I never cease to be grateful to my unknown but deeply revered teachers, the builders of these little Cotswold towns and villages. I came to them to learn, and they taught me many things for lack of which the world is the poorer today. They taught me that to build beautifully is quite different from beautifying a building. They taught me how to handle fine materials with respect. They taught me to employ direct, workmanlike methods and to try to apply the searching test of honesty to all work and actions. They taught me to go to the quarry to look at stone, to go to the coppice to look at trees. And I don't think there was a tool used by them of which I wasn't aware and most of these I later learned to use myself, though seldom with the same skill.

In spite of considerable Victorian rebuilding, the school, too, was beautiful. It had been founded by John Ferreby in 1487 and the big schoolroom was an excellent example of seventeenth-century work. Great beams spanned the ceiling and at one end was an immense open fireplace with a bust of Ferreby above, somewhat defaced by generations of scholars. Round the walls were fixed benches with narrow fixed desks in front of them, and through the great mullioned windows which opened on to the pavement came the rich burr of Gloucestershire voices, little polluted as yet by urbanized education and quite untouched by the films or the BBC which have so greatly affected later generations. Of course, as the Board of Education was soon to point out when they made a grant to this and other Grammar Schools, it was out of date. Why, even the light didn't come from the left! I don't dispute that such matters are important, but that beauty is an extra and comes far down the list of necessities is a wicked heresy that has grown up with the industrial revolution. It appeared to me that everything the Board did to the school detracted from its interest and it was obvious that in their opinion environment had nothing to do with education. This wrongheadedness persists and many of our new school buildings, even today and even here in Chipping Campden, are lamentable if one compares them with the best, which in England can be very good indeed.

We were fortunate in that only a few months previously C. R. Ashbee, architect and designer, had brought the Guild of Handicraft down to Chipping Campden from Essex House in the Mile End Road. This was a tremendous operation. There were about sixty craftsmen altogether including silversmiths, blacksmiths, enamellers, sculptors, wood-carvers, joiners, printers, etc. Many remained my friends for years—Will and George Hart, Alec Miller, Harold Pyment, Thornton and Downer. It pleases me to think that years later I introduced Bob Welch, an interesting young silversmith, to George Hart, who let him part of his workshop where he now designs for both hand and machine production. There is no doubt at all that the Essex House group has had a constructive and beneficial influence on local workmanship and to have witnessed the impact of these enthusiastic 'foreigners' on the local people was a rare event, although I didn't appreciate it fully at the time. All this surging activity of skilled handwork grafted on to the fine Cotswold tradition of building in the little town was highly stimulating.

Looking back on the Arts and Crafts movement I cannot help feeling how unfortunate it is that such a lusty and promising youngster never really grew up. This was, I think, largely because its parents dissociated it from the main stream of the life of its own time. They were conscious of rectitude as hand-workers and scorned the machine. I have found both immensely interesting and I don't believe we shall get really first-rate handwork again until we alter the outlook both of those using machines and of craftsmen. In Germany, the founding of the Werkbund gave the movement a link with industry which the Arts and Crafts Society never possessed here. I do not suggest that it did not affect industry here, but the impact was oblique; it was perhaps greatest in printing. There can be little doubt that the great improvement in the printing trade which we have witnessed in our time has been brought about largely by the immense prestige and influence of the small hand presses. The work of the Kelmscott, Ashendene, Doves, Nonesuch, Gregynog, Essex House, Alcuin, Arden and other Presses became widely known and set a standard of fine quality which was of value to the whole trade. But there was a second impact. When W. R. Lethaby, then in charge of the Central School of Arts and Crafts in London, asked Edward Johnston to form a class in calligraphy in about 1900 he took a most important step and it was not long before Johnston had founded a school of writing based on sound principles which he had rediscovered. Unfortunately, this is not being carried on today as enthusiastically as it should be. I regard it as a useful discipline for students. When Frank Pick later asked him to design a standard form of letter for use on London's underground railways the reaction on lettering everywhere was to be immense. Apart from that, one of Johnston's earliest pupils was Eric Gill who, from cutting letters beautifully in stone in a way which has to some degree affected inscriptions everywhere, went on to design founts of type for the Monotype Corporation. I mention this to show that hand and machine design are closely connected and one forgets or ignores this at one's peril. William Morris, that

C

grand, virile, outspoken person, saw it in his later years, and it is unfortunate that so many of his well-to-do socialist disciples should have had so little understanding of the needs of the common man.

Like the scholars at all good grammar schools, those at Chipping Campden were a cross-section of the community, including the son of a colonel, one or two doctors' sons, farmers' sons, tradesmen's sons and so on. Some of the boys of the guildsmen started to attend and a brisk trade was done in silver cuff-links, fountain-pen clips and such like. It seems curious to me that my first recollection of the Guild should be of these insignificant products, but at any rate I realized that something was being made which I could use and that was important. I was aware, too, that much more work was going on in the old silk mill, renamed Essex House, which had become the Guild's home. Part of an old building which we used as a school woodwork shop was also taken over by Ashbee. In it were housed glass cases with plaster-casts of all kinds of things from the Victoria and Albert Museum and I often dallied to look at them. It would have been an excellent thing if small parties of boys could have had the objects explained to them or have been taken to see the craftsmen at work, but although the headmaster, F. B. Osborne, was a man of sturdy character who was to remain my friend until his death twenty years later, he was a Philistine in such matters. He disliked what he called the 'Cockney invasion' and was complacently unaware of what the Guild was trying to do. I don't think Ashbee can have been very tactful, but he was certainly sincere, and it was largely due to his stimulating personality that many old things were preserved and much new work was done in a way which was far ahead of that of the pre-Guild period. He pointed out to Campden people how good Campden was. Years later I used to meet him occasionally at the Art Workers' Guild, to which I was elected in 1926 and of which he was Master in 1929. I feel grateful to him, although I never knew him well.

It seems odd to me now that in such a promising background there was no conscious attempt to introduce any visual education. Our drawing lessons consisted of illustrating perspective by means of cubes, spheres and cones, which we were expected to shade conscientiously. Or we were set to copy what was described as 'a piece of decoration'. It was obvious that our teachers were as bored as we were by these exercises, and having never looked critically at Campden street themselves, it did not occur to them to send us out to make a drawing of one of the houses and find out what we could about it. I remember I did make a sketch from my dormitory window of the delightful little market hall built by Sir Baptist Hicks in 1627, but in school my chief drawing interest was in the making of maps and I recollect the pleasure I got from the patterns formed by carefully drawn contours. I started to look at old maps and was struck by the value of symbols and the skilful way different kinds of lettering were used to give information such as the size of a town.

Our woodwork instructor, George Badham, was an excellent workman and under his guidance I made my first piece of furniture, a small set of bookshelves (which I still have) out of old oak floorboards from the school. Planing these was a heavy task as the wood was nearly as hard as iron, with many nails, and the dust of centuries had been ground into it.

In the town there were several blacksmith's shops, a saddler's, basket maker's and so on, the loss of which has been grievous. It was common to see a mason at work, or a slater repairing one of the stone roofs which are so typical of Cotswold building. Then there were the local worthies. There was the retired solicitor, who wore an oilskin and sou'wester even in the summer and who often stood at his gate to pass the time of day with townsfolk. It was reported that one old farmer never went to that end of the town in daylight for fear of being put down for 6s 8d, the regulation fee for a consultation. And there was old Dolphin, who kept his small front room full of potting earth and could sometimes be seen in an ancient postman's hat and coat cleaning the front of his house with a tooth-brush and bucket of water, in which somewhat laborious operation he was usually encouraged by a ring of ribald small boys. There was Malin, the saddler's boy, who used to get under his bench when we looked through the window, and Sykes, who started as a medical student and ended up driving cattle. An old farmer, who rode to hounds on an ancient nag, wore curiously outlandish clothes and a leather belt with a brass buckle. There was the vicar's wife— thin, kind and always in a tearing hurry, so known as the galloping hair-pin; the old man who was reputed to have grown his own tobacco and nearly killed himself smoking it. There was a rumour that gardeners who had greenhouses used to inveigle him into paying them a visit as the effect on green-fly was miraculous, but the difficulty must have been to keep him in the right place long enough without either being nearly asphyxiated oneself whilst whiling away the time with talk and blandishment, or losing the effect by remaining out-side unsuffocated and attempting to keep the conversation going through a slightly opened door, a ticklish problem, whichever way you look at it.

And there was Fred Griggs, trained as an architect in C. E. Mallows' office but better known for his book illustration and etchings, whom I met just about this time and who be-came a close friend. He came to Campden to see the Guild and stayed for over thirty years. He loved Campden with a passionate devotion, and I think that even today few people living there realize how much they owe him. On many occasions he fought for big issues, but he also safeguarded many points which, although small in themselves, were in the aggregate of immense value. It was mostly his efforts which preserved unspoiled Dover's Hill, the Conygree (coney green —rabbit field) and a number of old houses. He designed the beautifully-placed war memorial above the High Street and it is a sad commentary that, even quite recently, it was suggested locally that in making an alteration to this it was 'a waste of money to employ an architect'. It is curiously significant that visual appreciation in this country is so rare that the years of training necessary to give form, convenience and beauty to the things we all use and look at should often be reckoned an extra, a luxury, indeed an unnecessary extravagance. And it is right and proper that in welcoming the change from what was euphemistically called 'the common sense point of view' —certainly it was common enough but it displayed little sense —the work of artists like Griggs should be recalled. There have been few men from whom I learned so much, or whose friendship and criticism I valued more.

I suppose work went on much as in other schools, but looking back it seems a pleasant, sunny, unhurried period. Don and I were weekly boarders, for Campden is about four and a half miles from Broadway over Fish Hill. We started to walk home on Saturday mornings to the tune of 'The Blue Bells of Scotland' from the Church tower, and we were met by mother driving the pony cart. We seldom got very far—there were so many things to investigate on the way, such as men at work on various interesting jobs, birds' nests, cider making, or even smoking an occasional Woodbine, then five for a penny. It was a notable expedition, however often it was repeated. On Mondays, Don and I had our legs pulled by the Headmaster, who loved reading about the latest rumpus my father had started over gas or water supply, or litter on the green. 'Well, Don, what's the latest news from Broadway? No knives, I hope—just ''Councillors call each other liars'' again!' This was a headline in the local paper. But that didn't prevent his walking down to lunch with us on Sundays, and my father kept the wine he liked in 'Mr Osborne's bin'.

I now see that all this was a valuable part of my education. To begin to discriminate in what one eats and drinks, for instance, seems to me essential if one hopes to live a civilized life. I have met a number of people who said they did not notice what they ate, either because they lived in a rarer atmosphere than I did or because they hadn't time for such trifling matters. There is no surer way of getting bad food and worse drink. The kind of education which seeps into one when good conversation is combined with the unhurried consumption of an excellent meal is often more lasting than that which is consciously hammered in.

CHAPTER 4

South American Interlude

I left school at the end of the Christmas term 1907 and by a singular stroke of good fortune my uncle Joe, who was then a Captain in the Lamport and Holt Line, persuaded my father to let me go with him as Purser on his next voyage to South America. His ship, the S.S. *Veronese*—anglicized—did not normally carry such an officer, so the position was somewhat of a sinecure. This was perhaps as well, for I was hardly experienced enough to tackle unknown duties with distinction. Anyway, I was fitted out with a uniform and I still have a photograph of myself in it, looking slightly astonished. We left Liverpool for the River Plate on January 11, 1908, and within a few days were basking in sunshine. It was a marvellous trip and, for me, exactly at the right stage in my development. I had not been abroad before, I was not in the least blasé and I already had enough practice in looking at things, especially buildings, to make me a voracious gazer.

We put in at Corunna and Vigo and then went on to Montevideo and Buenos Aires. Here we stayed a month, the hottest of the year, and I spent part of it with my aunt Ada and her husband at San Rosario. He, Tom Miller, was an engineer on the Central Argentine Railway and his great grandfather had been the designer of one of the very first steam ships. The planning of their house appealed to me, with its loggia connecting all the rooms and the central patio with its large figtree, then in fruit. And what figs they were! We came back up the coast of Brazil, calling at Santos, where I had a cousin, at Rio de Janeiro and Bahia. I have always wanted to go back to Brazil, of which I have most lively and pleasant recollections.

38

I have been greatly interested in the recent revival of good architecture in that country, the remarkable gardens of Burle Marx and the fact that so many of the younger architects paint. The things which I remember so vividly are that quite a number of buildings remained from the Spanish and Portuguese colonization of the sixteenth century and that they acquired a special character through the intense brilliance of the sun, which led to the adoption of a proportion of fenestration quite different from its European prototype: small windows, and these mainly in the south or cool wall, immense spaces of wall, usually plastered and whitewashed, and perhaps a fine baroque doorway—its rich and deeply cut carving showing up in the most splendid and jewel-like way against the white wall. The roofs were usually of pantiles, with a flattish pitch and very wide overhang, which gave a long cool line of blue-black shadow. At Santos we went inland and saw some of the coffee plantations and also a little of the fringe of the forest, a story-book country of great trees alive with monkeys, with humming-birds so small and butterflies of such immense size that one rubbed one's eyes in amazement. We spent a day at Rio, which has been greatly extended since then, but I cannot believe that the marvellous bay with tropical vegetation climbing the steep hills behind the city can have been spoiled. After the filthy water in English ports I was delighted to see dockside water so sparkling and clear that a small coin could be seen twenty feet down. On the other hand, I noticed that a couple of negroes sitting in the sun were amusing themselves by spitting on their own bare feet, a form of entertainment fortunately unknown at home.

To hardened travellers, our journey was on a great trade route but to an imaginative boy, seeing it for the first time, it was as if I had grasped the hand of Cortez. We called at Las Palmas and Tenerife before reaching Southampton. There I found, to my delight, that the ship was going on to Hamburg and Rotterdam before putting in at Middlesbrough to load rails. The passengers, about thirty in number, mostly disembarked at Southampton but I stayed aboard.

I remember that Rotterdam struck me as being the first really clean northern port I had seen and this gave it an air of great efficiency. There were no straggling heaps of paper and rubbish in corners and even the flotsam and jetsam on the water appeared to have been collected. The people were neat and tidy, with little sign of actual poverty, and gave one the impression that they were proud of their city. With many centuries of sailing tradition behind them they seemed to have found a way of being shipshape on land too.

Going up the river to Hamburg gave a vivid impression of the approach to a great port. It was all there for one to see— not only shipping and warehouses, but the great shipbuilding yards of Blohm and Voss and little tugs snorting around every-where. Canals lined with mediaeval warehouses went under the main streets and we journeyed about the town by water. Most of the new buildings had a harsh and pompous air of efficiency which I found unpleasant. Going back after the 1914-18 War, I saw that much of the old city had been pulled down and there were many new buildings like the Ballin Building and Chile Haus, in a rather unpleasant brownish brick. Now, following the Second World War, I suppose nearly all of it has been rebuilt.

It snowed while we were in Hamburg and the wind seemed more bitter because of our recent sunning. In the diary I kept are several entries of mornings spent sketching, especially of locomotives at various docks. Under April 23, 1908, appears: 'Passed Cuxhaven about 10.20. At 11 we were ordered to anchor for two hours as the forts were having a little gunnery practice.' Little did I realize that this was a prelude to blow-ing my pleasant, well-ordered world into smithereens.

I had added a new dimension to my experience and by attempting to discover what each country did best I had acquired a rudimentary yard-stick which was to prove valuable to me at home. I became fascinated by shipping and ports. It seemed to me that London was not nearly as proud as she ought to be of her splendid river. To land at Tilbury and then take a train whose route seemed to have been planned to view the

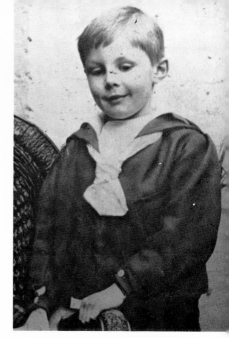

My mother, Elizabeth Russell,
c 1900

Myself, *c* 1896
Photograph by S. B. Russell

With my father, S. B. Russell, *c* 1902

3   The Lygon Arms, Broadway, in 1905. On the right is the 1869 Assembly Room

A meet of the North Cotswold Hunt, showing the Great Hall of 1909 which replaced the Assembly Room

Interior of the Great Hall. Architect: C. E. Bateman

The Cromwell Room with early seventeenth-century fireplace and plasterwork
described by Lord Torrington in 1787 (see page 59)

5   Early designs by Gordon Russell: an oak single bed, *c* 1911, silver buttons for
the head porter and handwritten statutory notice, 1912

IMPORTANT NOTIFICATION FO[R]
GUESTS AT THE LYGON ARMS

Chapter LXI. Anno Vicesimo Sexto et Vicesimo Septimo
Victoriae Reginae.
An act to amend the Law respecting the Liability of Inn[keepers]
keepers, and to prevent certain frauds upon them.
13th. July. 1863

NO Innkeeper shall, after the passing of this
Act, be liable to make good to any Guest of
such Innkeeper any loss of, or injury to, Good[s]
or Property brought to his Inn, not being a horse or
other live animal, or any gear appertaining thereto, o[r]
any Carriage, to a greater amount than the sum of
Thirty Pounds, except in the following cases, that is
to say :-
(1) Where such goods or property shall have bee[n]
stolen, lost or injured through the wilful act[,]
default or neglect of such Innkeeper or any
servant in his employ :
(2) Where such goods or property shall have bee[n]
deposited expressly for safe custody with such
Innkeeper :

PROVIDED always that, in the case of such deposi[t]
it shall be lawful for such Innkeeper, if he think
fit, to require, as a condition of his liability, that
such goods or property shall be deposited in a box o[r]
other receptacle, fastened and sealed by the person de[-]
positing the same.

squalid backyards of an endless number of dreary little houses was hardly an imaginative approach to one of the great cities of the world.

When I got home the head waiter at the Lygon, who liked making little speeches, was not far wrong when he told my mother: 'I have no doubt, madam, that Mr Gordon, returning from the Southern Hemisphere, will find a disconcerting change in the atmospherical conditions.' He was right. It wasn't easy to believe that the navel oranges I had brought from Bahia were growing in the open a few weeks before.

CHAPTER 5

The Lygon Arms, Broadway
A Family Business

When I returned home in April 1908 I started on such jobs as
seemed to need attention without any very clearly defined
plan. In fact, I may be said to have come near to rivalling Mr
Polly's efforts at the Potwell Inn. I took spells of duty in the
office of the Lygon, made out bills, booked orders for the
station bus—sometimes, I remember, from small girls in the
form of 'Mother says will you please to tell the buzz to call at
Fleabank'—and, as the bus was run by the Lygon, sometimes
I booked in the day's takings from Harry Walker, the driver.
Being extremely thin, he suffered a good deal from the cold
and as he burst through the front door in March he would say:
'It's a full top-coat colder this morning!' There was a book
labelled POSTING, into which, day by day, all items of horse
and carriage hire were entered. At first these were quite considerable. On one occasion, being unable to send a trap to
meet a customer at Honeybourne station, we asked John Eva
at the local inn over there to send a telegram if he could
manage it. The customer stuffed the telegram—'Will meet
you station 9.15 Eva'—into his pocket and had to take his
wife to Honeybourne later on to reassure her by reading the
landlord's name on the board outside! I roasted coffee and
helped with the bottling of fruit. I took down my father's
letters in shorthand, which I taught myself, and typed them,
slowly and painfully. I typed and duplicated the menus. I even
designed lettering for letterheads and wrote advertisements,
for which I also did the drawings. I helped to keep the books

42

and marked most of the stock of the small business in antiques which my father had started the previous year. The show-rooms were in a cottage next to the Lygon, and with a certain amount of trepidation I showed people round and learned a good deal from their questions and comments. I made sketches of antiques to send to customers both here and in America.

The first workshop – a loft over the coach-house at the entrance to the Lygon yard, 1904

Later that year my father bought a small de Dion car and I was told to find out how it worked. The answer was simple—not always it didn't! Our hills were too much for its single-cylinder engine, although it was a good performer on the level. It had a door at the rear and when the engine started to stall on a hill I issued 'Abandon ship and push' instructions, which had to be obeyed by all! Shortly afterwards it was replaced by a slightly less unreliable vehicle called after the mythical bird, Phoenix, and I remember thinking this must be because it might go up in flames. It was a game little car, however, and in the hands of one of its designers, a Dutchman named Huydonk—always known to us as Van Hoodwink—it could do wonders. The arrangement of the engine was novel and people were surprised to see us lift the bonnet and take out

The Work-shop.
Lygen Cottage.

The second workshop, 1907

vegetable marrows or other merchandise. It had a separate radiator on each side to each cylinder and on one occasion when I collected it from the works near King's Cross they had omitted to put water in one of them. When the car gradually ground to a halt I discovered that one cylinder was a glowing red. Seizing the starting handle I turned it until my face was a similar colour. At last it cooled, and filling the neglected radiator with water and myself with beer, we set out once more. But oh what a shock! This car also proved too temperamental for our limited knowledge of mechanics. When my

44

father installed one of the first local electric light plants he took on a man named Grant to run it. He did a certain amount of chauffeuring too and looked after a Sunbeam which proved wonderfully reliable for years. I seem to remember that tyres were responsible for much trouble—but perhaps I recall this as I always detested changing them! They were Palmer cords and had steel studs which got very hot under certain conditions. About 1910 a Scout car was added and Grant appeared in a fine new overcoat and peaked cap. True to the Lygon tradition of jacks-of-all-trades he was quite a good woodworker in his spare time!

Apart from mechanical duties, on occasion I put barrels of beer on the tram, as the stillage with its two wooden rails for barrels in the cellar was called. I could tap and vent them and even take a sip when the beer had settled to see that it was all right. A thirty-six-gallon barrel is heavy and one must know exactly how to handle it. This was a pretty art, I always thought, and could be done almost effortlessly by a master like the brewer's drayman. I flattered myself that I became pretty good at it, but it certainly needed an expert, like moving a grand piano or making an omelette. At this time the brewers all had stables of splendid horses who were given a ration of beer each day and were always turned out in beautiful condition, faultlessly groomed and with all the brasses on their harness shining. The drayman, too, was physically an excellent specimen and wore a kind of nightcap which was brilliant red and most becoming. He also had his ration of beer and I was interested to hear that in breweries the rare case of drunkenness was treated as proof of theft. The whole outfit—horses, drayman and dray loaded with barrels, themselves admirable examples of design, so perfectly adapted to requirements that they had altered little through the centuries—was a sight I shall not forget.

I was also put in charge of the workshop where three or four men repaired old furniture and did a variety of other jobs. The foreman here was Jim Turner, a local man of about forty who was born at Snowshill, the next village to Broadway, and had been a carpenter on the Middle Hill estate. He walked with a curious, slouching swing, and behind a rather gruff manner, he had a warm heart. During our schooldays Don and I used to spend hours in the workshop at weekends and holidays, making all kinds of models. We were blissfully ignorant of the damage we must have done to the tools, which were the men's own property, but there is no doubt in my mind as to the value of this experience to us! Anyhow, I think it must have made Jim view me with some suspicion. When I appeared with a very crude working drawing—till then unknown in the shop— and full of enthusiasm and suggestions, not all of the most practical nature, he must have thought I needed 'to be took down a peg or two'. So he put the drawing, which he had great difficulty in reading anyway, upside down on the bench and started firing off questions, protests and advice—this wouldn't work, that couldn't be done. The other men's work gradually came to a halt so that they could enjoy such interludes and I learned from them, albeit painfully. My respect for his practical knowledge and experience grew as I came to know him better and in time he came to see some value in my theories. He had a sound working knowledge of building too and when we wanted to move into a larger workshop in 1907 it was Jim who squared up the existing stone walls, framed the roof, laid the tiles, did a bit of plastering and set the stove. He was a sound, conscientious workman who hated scamped work. A favourite expression of his was, 'That 'ull make a job on it', and these words have often kept me going against discouraging odds. He spoke the Cotswold dialect with rich and humorous whimsicality. To hear him use the plural 'housen' or 'eyen' took one back at a bound to Saxon England. He would say to his son Edgar: 'Turn all that tack out of my bag and put in a rip-saw. Not that 'un, silly monkey, I aren't zharped 'e. Ay, that 'un 'ull do. And a mallet and a fey-oh [few] chisels. Better take an 'ommer, I s'pose, and two or three bits. There's no telling what us might have to do afore night.' Indeed, there was no telling, as he was called on for a great variety of jobs. He always talked of casements as 'cagements' and ceiling joists were 'sailin' jysts'. A piece of furniture not standing level was 'all of a giggle' and brittle timber was 'doaty' or 'carroty'.

On Saturdays the wages were put out in neat little piles, with the few gold coins on top, and the men came up to collect them at the office window, always in the same order. There were so few of them that there was no need to name the piles. When, in 1908, health insurance was introduced it was necessary to put the money into wage envelopes showing the name, deductions and total on the outside. It seemed sad to me that the gold coins could no longer be seen, but in 1914 they disappeared permanently, just after I had bought a silver sovereign purse! I took pleasure from seeing them. After the disgustingly dirty and torn notes of South America I have always felt a note to be a poor substitute for gold, but as the number of staff increased it would have become essential to have envelopes anyway. What an innovation it was, almost as astonishing as my father's discovery that padlocks could have a master key!

Day after day, as I watched the work in hand, I became more knowledgeable and critical. When an old chair needed to be covered in leather I did it myself. I was not taught to do it but I just carried on the primitive, seventeenth-century tradition of stuffing leather chairs from actual observation. I used wood-wool instead of hay, otherwise the work was the same. I remember a visit to Bermondsey to find out more about leather, and the discovery of 'Sudan wrappers', which were native, sun-dried hides, not split, used for wrapping moroccos. They had a beautiful texture and, when not too hard, were just right for my purpose.

Where my father learned to pack things so expertly I have no idea but under his guidance Jim became a good packer. When a large order had to be despatched the whole shop tackled the job. For many years we used Bavarian hop pockets (large sacks) for hessian as these used to come to the Burton breweries in great quantities and were cheap and strong. My father or I packed any glass or china. This was a skilled job which I liked, and I still recall the pleasure with which I read a letter from a customer in Hong Kong who said that of the several gross of hand-made glass he had ordered not a single piece was broken on arrival.

Don left school about a year after I did and was sent for six months to an estate agent in Cheltenham as my father received so many enquiries for properties that he thought of starting a branch office in Broadway. When Don returned home he joined in most of these operations, which enabled both of us to escape from the office. Crates or cases for abroad had to be stencilled and to this day I remember one marked 'SUN-DILE'. I recollect another which contained two cast-iron fire-backs so was flat and not very large. The men kept it till last when loading and then said to George Knight from the railway, a doleful individual who was never known to smile: 'Put the case of pictures on here, George.' George clasped it and every-one watched him as he strained to move it and noted the twisted grin when he slowly realized that his leg was being pulled.

Besides Jim Turner in the shop, there was Savage, who I think may well have been a descendant of a well-known seventeenth-century Broadway family of that name. Then there was Percy Turner, Jim's nephew, and Jim's two sons, Edgar and Clarence, later joined by a third, Sidney. These local men had that deep, simple wisdom—that instinctive knowledge of real values—which often seemed so baffling to inhabitants of the towns. Having secured to themselves a reasonable competence they had no wish to work all the hours that the good Lord sends in order to double it. They wanted to live a full life, to play bowls or billiards, work in their gardens or sit over a pint discussing potatoes, pigs or even less impor-tant subjects. The nitwits who talk of the 'economic man' would have said they wanted to waste time. My father and I did not then fully understand their point of view, God forgive us, but we came later to see how right they were. Jim was reckoned indispensable for such jobs as putting up the supper marquee or polishing the dance floor for the Hunt Ball and other dances at the Lygon, when he was known to drag my small brother round on a mat in a state of ecstasy.

My father took great delight in arranging a visit to London for the men in the shop and the Lygon yard, only one of whom had been there before. I think it was the year of the Franco-British Exhibition, 1911. Before going Jim made terms: 'All as is,' he said, 'I yunt agoin' on the slip-slap'—the flip-flap, whose two giant arms with a cage at the end travelled in a great half circle through the sky and which, from pictures he had seen, struck him as a somewhat 'daddeky' affair. They had breakfast—with, I believe, steaks and beer, a Tudor break-fast—at Kennan's Hotel in the City, with which my father had business connections, and I've no doubt that after starting at break of day it was most welcome. Why, oh why, didn't I go on this expedition? I can't think, but perhaps I was told to hold the fort. After looking at Tower Bridge and the Pool of London they decided that the shipping at Evesham was per-haps on rather a small scale. They went round the Exhibition until their feet gave out. I have an idea that the party, like all really proper works outings, arrived back at some ungodly hour the next morning and the trip was pronounced by all an unqualified success. At any rate, it passed the most searching test for there was a request for its repetition at a date not too far distant.

When my father took over the Lygon he took over the Post Office contract to take the mail into Evesham and back to Broadway. The driver of the mail-cart, which had a lock-up boot and was drawn by one horse, was usually an army pen-sioner, who carried on with precise and commendable regularity until Christmas or a Bank Holiday. At such times he met many and various friends and then a message would come, with awe-inspiring solemnity, saying the mail had not arrived. Such seasons were always busy ones at the Lygon and my father was not in his best form. The thought of a horse with broken knees or a cart with broken shafts enraged him—the possibil-ity of a broken head for the driver responsible for the trouble left him unmoved, apart from the fact that he felt he was personally responsible for His Majesty's mails. And he did not accept responsibility lightly. At last he could stand it no more

D

and gave notice to the Post Office to terminate the contract. The next month he received the usual cheque from them, which he returned politely, and several months later when he got a complaint that the mail was late again he was able to reply that *that* was exactly why he had ceased to be one of His Majesty's Contractors to the Post Office.

All kinds of memories crowd in on me about this time, such as my first journey to London by road, with my uncle Joe, who had taken me to South America and was staying with us at the time having driven from Liverpool in his astonishing car. He was one of those who liked things to go wrong just so that he could put them right. It was much simpler to please him than his passengers! When the car stopped dead he would say: 'Must be that wire I put in broken again. Shan't be a minute.' On the morning fixed for our great expedition we were to start at about six. But it was June, and as in June it isn't noticeably more difficult to get up at four than at five we did so. In the delicious, clear, quiet summer morning Don and I picked a large basket of strawberries. I say we picked one, but as we must have eaten three stawberries to every one that went in the basket we must have gathered the equivalent of at least four basketsful. And then we started off to drive to London, just like that! Ah, well, although in later years I used to drive to London every week I simply can't recall another occasion when it seemed like the road to Samarkand.

By comparison, the journey was indeed a slow and quiet one—it must have taken us most of the day to travel the ninety-odd miles—and the leisurely pace meant that we could enjoy looking about us as we went along.

Cars were few and far between and heavy lorries almost non-existent, which was fortunate as the white road was extremely dusty and the rare car could be seen approaching followed by a dense cloud which settled on the hedges until washed away by a heavy shower of rain. This was a constant nuisance, not least to us in Broadway, where my father had been responsible for raising a fund to spray the main road with a solution which kept the surface moist and so laid some of the dust.

The main country road was much more rural than it is today —there were no petrol stations, granite kerbs or sidewalks of concrete or asphalt, and the grass verges, uncut and un-sprayed, carried in many places a remarkable collection of wild flowers. There were only a few houses on the road between villages. The smaller side roads, startlingly white in the sun, showed clearly how they followed the contours of the hills. Roads might be much safer if we could have them white again, without the dust.

The small towns and villages through which we passed were still largely unspoiled. Woodstock, a charming village nestling beside the walls of Blenheim Park, then had a quarter-mile-long band of brown pebbles laid between the pavement and the road which gave it great individuality and knitted the whole group of buildings together in a delightful way. Alas, this has since disappeared beneath a coating of asphalt. And Slough, then a pleasant small town built of the local red brick and tile and set in some hundreds of acres of the best cornland in Buckingham-shire, has become the Slough of Despond!

Since the early years of the century there has been a well-meaning effort to preserve 'beauty spots' and 'buildings of historical interest' from the blanket of ugliness which passes for progress. One should not underestimate the value of this, but the idea has grown up that if one fine building in a street is preserved all is well. Tears may be shed by a few people when some famous building is destroyed but hardly anyone worries about a whole row of simple, seemly cottages which are an essential part of the character of a street. Indeed, some councils hold the extraordinary view that any cottage over a hundred years old must be a slum. The Frenchman who judges a restaurant more by the quality of the *ordinaire* served than by the most expensive wine on the list has much to teach us. Our architectural *ordinaire* is fast disappearing and there was so much of it for everyone's enjoyment, if they cared to look. It is the small things which are eroded day by day without anyone noticing which show how thin is our veneer of civilization: as Lethaby said, 'A tradition should be a thousand men thick.' We have had in England a wonderful heritage of fine building based on superb hand craftsmanship. We may learn in time to use the machine more imaginatively, but nearly all the buildings which are going up today are commercial efforts to get the maximum floor space at the lowest possible cost. In two wars the enemy destroyed many fine things in England, but the damage they did was insignificant compared with that done by the English to their own country. It seems curious that, largely through the devoted work of our ancestors, we have inherited one of the most beautiful countries in the world yet we have not considered it worth while to learn to look at it.

Again I remember a bicycle excursion with Don. I think we felt a bit like escapists, having been given to understand, in the nicest possible way, that others might have to do our work but when we had gone ten miles we just didn't care. We forgot, totally and completely, about Broadway and all its works and worries. We explored the valley of the Coln, through Fossebridge and Coln St Aldwyn to Bibury. We liked the same things, it was April or May and all the world seemed young, just as if one were seeing a Botticelli for the first time. We chose the narrow country lanes, although many of them were hard going on a bicycle both as to surface and contours, but this merely induced us to make frequent pauses to visit an old church or to examine an inscription or piece of carving, and we always had an insatiable curiosity to discover how things were made. How did one set about building an arch or, more complicated still, a vault? What stress caused such a crack in a wall? Why were the joints in wood sometimes like and sometimes quite different from those in stone? Why did iron have to be a glowing red to weld it? We asked questions when we could, but we observed closely and endlessly and argued about our theories. And then we would sit in the bar of a small pub gossiping to the landlord and drinking beer—very thin beer, I admit, as farming was not then a prosperous industry and tourism had not touched such places. We were gradually absorbing many other things as well which would be put to use later on; among others the ability to detach oneself completely from one's job, to sit around drinking and talking or just to sit, listening to the larks and watching trout in the stream. The pace of life today makes it essential to put up a stiff resistance to constant noise and rush, an atmosphere in which solitude becomes unendurable to many people.

The discovery of Sherlock Holmes at about this time was a memorable one. Not only were these stories first-rate entertainment but they taught me to try to deduce what happened from clues painstakingly observed and tracked down. This has become a source of interest which has grown with the years, of great value to a designer.

Another discovery, perhaps equally important, was Bassett-Lowke's wonderful catalogue of models. This introduced me to Henry Greenly's *Model Locomotive* and Tredgold on the steam engine, which not only taught me exactly how a locomotive worked but held me spellbound by the beauty of early mechanical drawings and engravings. The hatred of all machines so loudly proclaimed by the Arts and Crafts movement was something I could never share, but I hated to see wonderful machines badly directed.

From using the men's workshop at weekends I had fixed up a little shop for myself where I was able to practise various jobs which interested me in such spare time as I could get. I induced the local saddler to make a leather black-jack—a pot, not a cosh—for me. For centuries these grand leather drinking-pots were used in England but not, so far as I know, on the Continent. I made the wooden mould myself and sat with him to supervise the sewing. His workroom had a small window not one pane of which would open—and it was August 1911, one of the hottest within living memory. I've always wondered why cobblers and other leather workers are so terrified of fresh air. Can it be anything to do with their well-known radical tendencies? I pitched the jack inside to make it waterproof and then tried my hand at painting the Lygon coat-of-arms on it. But the results didn't altogether please me, although I had a good deal of advice from Oliver Baker, of whom more anon, so when I had seen enough of how to set about making one I decided to have a shot on my own. Don and I joined in this venture. I made the moulds and got the leather—inner belly sole—and we started. We made several. One had a pattern built up from a series of little brass dies which I made, and a silver mount which I designed and George Hart of the Guild of Handicraft made. We always used one at table for beer, which kept very fresh in it.

It was that remarkable man E. E. Dorling—parson of the Church of England, Herald, Clerk of the Course at Epsom—who led me to take a great interest in heraldry. I can't remember who introduced my father to him but he often stayed with us and he painted a series of coats-of-arms for the big room at the Lygon. He was a beautiful draughtsman, and a great raconteur. He invented a rebus for himself—a little door—doorling—with hinges ending in E.

I used to pay many visits to 'old Kemp's' smithy opposite and have a vivid picture of him on dark evenings in winter outlined in the light of his forge: a small man, thin and with a high-pitched, quavering voice. The music of his anvil brought children returning from school to peep through the open door, lighted up spasmodically as the blast from his bellows raised the fire, and savour the rich smell of burnt hoof and the acrid tang of horse manure which lingered about the forge. Sometimes he would give hammers to several of them and, drawing a red-hot bar from the fire, would urge them to set to. This they did with a will and sparks flew all over the shop but, to my astonishment, none of them was hurt. He would have laughed had he been told he had contributed greatly to their education, as he certainly did to mine. He had a store of knowledge of the old days. One of his early jobs as a boy was to climb into the kitchen-chimney at the Lygon and grease the bearings of the smoke-jack, which turned the spits for roasting meat. I believe he said this was done once a quarter. He remembered walking from Broadway to Moreton-in-Marsh and back (sixteen miles) to deliver a letter before the days of the penny post (1840). I was astonished to hear that he remembered the road to Snowshill, the nearest hill village, being made, as I had thought till then that all roads went back to the eighteenth century at least. But he recalled how, in very hard winters, Snowshill was almost cut off from Broadway and bread had to be taken up in panniers slung over a horse.

His assistant, George, was a steady and ingenious smith. He took an interest in making a hinge to match an old one, fitting a key to a lock and so on. We reached a working partnership in which I made the necessary drawings and talked over the job with him before he carried out the work. I doubt if he ever knew how much I looked forward to visiting him—we don't tell our friends these things as we ought—and the war broke up our relationship for, like so many friends of my youth, he did not return. The virtual disappearance of the village smithy, with its lovely music, is not the least of the heavy charges to be laid against the motor-car.

My father wrote a beautiful and legible round hand and took a great interest in printing. He may perhaps have seen Ashbee's Essex House Press at work in Campden, where at least one of the presses came from the Kelmscott workshop after Morris's death. And I know Cobden-Sanderson of the Doves Press stayed once at the Lygon for I remember his description of how, walking over Waterloo Bridge, he threw one of his typefaces into the Thames after printing a limited edition. Beyond this, the work of the Kelmscott, Ashendene and Doves Presses was dimly known to us. We felt that the printing we were so often offered was ugly and we used to have long arguments with a local printer and to show him the type in old books. When I criticized the appalling type on the cardboard tops for chip baskets I was told they were only for fruit; and when I said I knew that, but why have them so ugly, he replied: 'Well, we print tens of thousands of those every year and you're the very first person who has ever said a single word about them, good or bad!' Apathy is so much more difficult to cope with than downright opposition, as I came to realize more clearly in time.

Later on we came across Cuthbert Wilkinson, who had

started the Arden Press at Letchworth. To him we turned for help in printing a new edition of a little book about the Lygon, a pioneer effort. Till then, as far as I know, no inn or hotel had set out to produce a history of itself, well printed and illustrated, without any advertisements, and to sell it for a shilling. That people should buy and keep something which hitherto had been given to them and thrown away struck other hotel keepers as utterly ridiculous. Our idea was that the ordinary hotel booklet was so dull, ugly and badly printed that usually it was discarded at once, whereas our book, costing much more to produce than its selling price, would be kept as a pleasant record. We decided to call it *The Story of an Old English Hostelry*, at the suggestion of J. J. Hissey, in whose book my father had first read about the Lygon. I spent quite a long and pleasurable time searching out details of the past history of the inn and making pen and ink drawings to illustrate the book. I knew that the Lygon had previously been known as the White Hart, which was the badge of Richard II who died in 1399. This interested me as in a four-foot-thick wall in bedroom number seven my father had discovered an ogival-headed fireplace which appeared to be fourteenth-century work. Nearly all the early fireplaces had been covered by much later grates. The fine doorway on the ground floor with a four-centred arch head and door with strap hinges were of the fifteenth century— and are still to be seen in their original position, although the building has been extended beyond them. Also, in stripping the paint from a mullioned window I discovered a series of dates and initials: Rich Jervis 1586, TT 1623, 1624, 1626 up to 1640 cut in the stone. However, the first mention of the inn then discovered was in the Broadway Parish Register where, under the date of 1532, it is stated that Thomas White of the White Hart was one of forty inhabitants who agreed to build and maintain a six-yard length of the churchyard wall. I have always liked this entry as I have come to be a considerable waller myself! In 1633 the landlord is given as John Trevis (Travis or Travers), whose death is recorded in a delightfully lettered brass in Broadway Old Church—May 27, 1641,

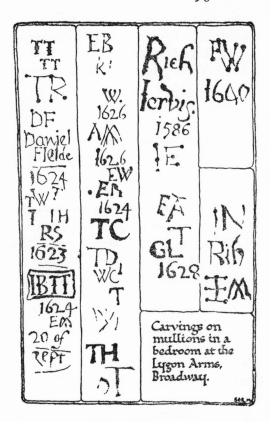

Carvings on mullions in a bedroom at the Lygon Arms, Broadway.

aged 74. It seems likely that the present frontage with its four fine gables was built by him, for his name, with that of his wife Ursula, appears in a panel on the strap-carved doorway. The Travers family held the inn for some 150 years. John's son

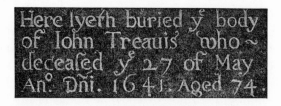

Rubbing from brass in Broadway Old Church

57

Thomas died in 1649 and his widow Ursula in 1654. In 1734 it is described as 'the two burgages of John Trevis being now an inn'. In 1767 Giles Atwood was the landlord and may have welcomed Lord Torrington, who records in his diary[1] on Sunday, August 12, 1787:

'I did not stop at the Unicorn Inn at Bengworth (altho' I knew its goodness), because it was too early for my dinner stop; so kept on to Broadway, in hopes of finding there another inn as good; and did put up at a most comfortable cleanly house, the White Hart, where a delicious loyn of veal was ready to be served, and I was ready for eating it; which I did in ample quantity, and had then a super-abundant temptation by an apricot tart; nor cou'd I determine upon going away, till my manager T.B. call'd upon me, "Why, sir, you will stay here all day!" And why not, T.B., it is a good house? "Aye, so it is, sir, and the hay is so good, and everything so neat, and the dogs so fat!"

'At last off I went, but e're I had rode 40 yards, I said, "T.B., I must return—I am tired—am too full—and can't ride"; so I came back, and hoped I had done well.

'Broadway is a very long village, at the foot of the Broadway Hills, built of stone, and so stoney that it looks like a principal Welsh town.

'. . . after tea I climb'd by a very pleasant foot-path, to the hill-top where Sir John Cotterell has built the most extraordinary gaze-about house in the world, at the summit of an exceeding steep; without a tree about him, and fronting the west;—there it stands looking to Wales—but farther than sight can reach. [This is now the Fish Inn.]

'I seated myself at the brow—straining my eyes at the view;—whilst the distant church bells from the valley, sounded soft'ned and melodious:– and then return'd near the turnpike road, after a pleasant saunter of two hours, and lolling upon every stile.

'At my return to my spacious and clean parlour, I was at a loss for employ, till I borrowed some books of my landlady;

[1] *The Torrington Diaries*, Eyre & Spottiswoode, London, 1936.

which, with writing, supping, and some attempts at thinking, kept me awake till eleven o'clock.'

Monday August 13

'There cannot be a cleanlier, civiller inn than this is; which bears all the marks of old gentility, and of having been a manor house; walls very thick, floors oaken and wide, with a profusion of timber, and the remains of much tapestry, for carpeting, whereon was well told instructive church history.—My bedroom was very large, with black oaken boards, a wrought ceiling, a wide cornice, with a lofty mantle-piece; in short, I appear'd to be in the grand bedchamber of an old family seat [plate 4]. In the kitchen hung a picture, which appear'd to me the work of a great master (perhaps of Rubens), but the landlord, having had a hint of its value, did not seem inclined to part with it, unless some foolish sum had been offer'd him.

'Most inns will do during the summer's heat, but there are not ten endurable in the winter, when you come out of London; from register stoves, and turkey carpets: tho' the inns now mend in their rooms and stabling, as we here begin to enter a fine fox and hare hunting country, to which many gentlemen resort in winter; nor are their charges unreasonable, as you may perceive by the following bill:

White Hart,	Tea	o	9
Broadway	A chicken &c.	2	o
	Tart (apricot)		2
	Liquors	2	3
	Breakfast		9
		5	11	'

In 1793 the inn was run by Christopher Holmes, whose widow sold it in 1807. About 1830 General Lygon, who had served under Wellington at the Battle of Waterloo, bought the Springhill estate near Broadway and it has been suggested that, as so often happened, his retired butler took over the local inn and renamed it after the family whose coat-of-arms—two lions passant with forked tails—now forms its sign.

Our little venture in publishing was a success. Americans often bought a dozen copies of the book and posted them to their friends. After 1920, it was replaced by one of wider scope called *Broadway and the Cotswolds*, edited by my friend Noel Carrington.

In Broadway, Katherine Adams had set up the Eadburgha Bindery—perhaps the best in England at that time—and my interest in leatherwork, in writing and in printing was greatly stimulated by the work I saw there. I cannot remember whether she first mentioned to me Edward Johnston's *Writing and Illuminating and Lettering* but I see my copy is dated 1911 and a very precious possession it still is. It is so clearly written that without any other instruction I learned to cut goose quills, to write on paper and parchment in a formal hand, the use of colour and gold and so on. Beyond these practical matters, I learned how best to space and set out lettering, the use of margins and many other things. I had become aware of the beauty of the old inscriptions on tombstones, some of which I had copied patiently, but hitherto I had failed to analyse why they should seem to me so much better than most modern examples. This book opened a new world to me and I soon had a writing-room in being. I tried my prentice hand on notices, including one which hangs in the Lygon to this day (see plate 5). I have always wanted to relate my efforts to everyday life. As I became more ambitious I completed four books, two on paper and two on vellum, the last one being finished in September 1914, a few days before I joined up. I was much encouraged by Robert Bridges and Sydney Cockerell, who were brought in by Katherine Adams one Sunday morning to look at some of my work. They gave me helpful criticism and advice, and left me with a feeling that it was well worth while to go on.

When Mrs Webb (née Katherine Adams) died in 1952 at the age of 88, I wrote a small piece for *The Times*:

'The absolute integrity which she applied as a matter of

course to every detail of her work, coupled with her fine sense of design and intuitive skill in handling material, have inspired me ever since. The value to the community of such a small workshop where the finest traditions of a craft are upheld is as yet but little appreciated by many people in industry. It is most unfortunate that the conditions of today weight the scales so heavily against such ventures as Katherine Adams started and maintained with conspicuous success, to the great enrichment of the lives of all those with whom she came in contact.'

Shortly afterwards I received a letter from a Miss Hampshire saying: 'You may not remember me but I was a pupil of Katherine Adams in 1914. Since her husband died I have been her companion and now I am her executor. I remember, in 1914, binding a small book of five poems of Keats which she selected and you wrote out for her as a wedding present. As she had no family and as I am sure you can have very few examples of your work of this date I feel she would have felt it would be most appropriate for you to keep it henceforth. If this is agreeable to you I will have it lettered on the spine (which for some reason—perhaps the war—was never done) and then bring it over.' Naturally I felt that this was a most kindly thought and a few weeks later I had the extraordinary experience of meeting once more after forty years both the binder and the book. The former I remembered vaguely as a young woman with a bun of yellow hair, handwoven clothes and sandals. She returned as a white-haired lady, very neatly dressed, bearing the book. Curiously enough, it seemed as if I had never parted from it for, having written out the lovely poems, they had meantime become a great stay and prop to me, at awkward moments in the front line in France, at board meetings, in committee. The book itself is dated August 1914 —a date which few of my generation will forget.

I also joined a small life class in Campden. As far as I recollect, there were about eight or nine of us. There was Paul Woodroffe, who had a stained glass studio, and J. C. M.

Shepard (Shep), who worked in it, Will Hart—woodcarver, George Hart—silversmith, Alec Miller—sculptor. Fred Griggs, the etcher, turned up occasionally. At this time many of the small hill roads, especially towards Snowshill, were gated to prevent sheep straying. There was very little traffic on them and I still recall the pleasure of setting out afterwards in the dark for the walk back over the hill to Broadway. This meeting of workers in so many different crafts was very important to me for it freed my imagination to try my hand at designing various things. Sometimes a customer wanted a single bed to go with old furniture and this I set out in a way of making which was familiar to me. As far as I remember I didn't attempt to make it look either old or new: I was just trying to solve a problem, finding out the snags for myself and endeavouring to resolve them, and it went through all in the day's work. My knowledge of design had grown from looking at good old things, always a sound background. But I looked at them for inspiration, not in order to imitate. Sometimes it was a door, or a fireplace surround, and I can think of small articles in silver and copper, and a few experiments in glass. I was always going off at a tangent and designing the most improbable things, with the complete assurance of youth. By no means all were good, but occasionally I did something in that remote period which I can still face without too great a strain on a queasy stomach. Among such I remember one or two oak beds, a napkin ring in silver, a few letterheadings and some buttons for the head porter at the Lygon (see plate 5). These last were of silver, made by George Hart, with the Lygon coat-of-arms—two lions passant with forked tails—chased upon them. When old Chubb, who had been head porter at the Lygon for years, died, my father, who was fond of him, cut the buttons off his coat and had them sewn on his own dressing jacket, to my great astonishment and delight.

Mr Edward Arnold, the publisher, stayed at the Lygon and, sensing my father's interest in glass and china, gave him a copy of Hartshorne's *English Drinking Glasses*, which encouraged him to add to a small collection, mainly of the seventeenth to the

nineteenth centuries. On special occasions he liked to use the
drinking glasses, always washing them himself. The added
pleasure of drinking wine in lovely goblets greatly appealed to
him. By handling them I gradually acquired a good deal of
knowledge of the subject. This is how I have always learned—
by looking, handling and experimenting rather than by any
formal instruction. Eventually I designed a few pieces and I
shall not forget the experience of visiting Stevens & Williams'
great glasshouse at Stourbridge, with its glowing central stack
of kilns and men working on the red-hot glass in semi-darkness.
I got to know Powell's too and many years later I bought from a
Hampstead dealer as a genuine antique one of my own cut glass
bowls which they had made!

At this time Broadway had become the centre of an artistic
and literary circle, largely American. In the 1880s, J. S.
Sargent, Henry James and Frank Millet had been frequent
visitors. Shortly after that, Mary Anderson, the famous
American actress, and her husband (Mr and Mme de Navarro)
bought a house—or rather two houses, which were combined
—and settled there. Robert Hitchens, Alfred Parsons, J. M.
Barrie, E. A. Abbey, Phil May, Vaughan Williams, Elgar, the
Bancrofts and many others were often seen there. This gave
the village a unique atmosphere and a connection with the
world outside which was not only stimulating in itself but
tended to reduce the all-absorbing interest in petty details
which is normally such a common feature of village life.
Although I was hardly on the fringe of this fascinating group I
realize now that its existence must have played quite an important part in my development by making me more aware of
painting, literature and music.

There was not one of my activities in which my father did
not give me all the help in his power—understandably, perhaps, as they so closely followed his own inclinations.

It would appear that his interest in old buildings and domestic objects of all kinds began to take a practical turn when
he set up house. As I have said, his income just after he married
was a very limited one and when he appeared at home with a

most beautiful eighteenth-century blue and white salt-glazed dish of immense size (I have it now), he received a somewhat frosty welcome from my mother, who could think of other ways of spending ten shillings and did not hesitate to say so. Not at all abashed—at least not permanently—he turned up some months later with a very fine, but extremely derelict, Chippendale chair with a delicately carved back. My mother was invited to inspect this treasure forthwith and with pride he confessed he had begged it for twelve and sixpence. Now my mother never, to my knowledge, looked carefully at the shapes of things, nor indeed appeared to be much affected by her surroundings. But this chair she viewed with great distaste for though it may or may not have been beautiful, it was indubitably filthy . . . like a skilful commander she had chosen her battleground. How difficult it is to press the case for aesthetics when faced with practical considerations of immediate concern! It says much for my father's wily manoeuvring that the despised object was not burnt then and there, but no doubt he pointed out how much more firewood was obtainable for 12s 6d. Anyway, we who still take pleasure in looking at the chair are glad that in this, as in other awkward predicaments, he stuck to his guns! His scope was of course greatly extended when he took over the Lygon. Many people noticed the old furniture, the block-printed curtain materials and the hand-made table glass which he selected for use in the inn, and it was their urgent requests to buy that led to the establishment of a small business in such things, for he was averse to making the Lygon itself into an antique shop.

I wish I could paint a better portrait of the Lygon before 1914. It had a rich aroma about it—I think it still has—which those who stayed there will remember through the years. As my father's idea was not to run an inn, as then understood, but to take the English country house as his model he had all the excitement and disadvantages of breaking with established tradition. Everything had to be done differently. At least, I realize now that it was done differently: at the time none of us had much idea about how the ordinary hotel was run. By blood and sweat we found our own solutions as we went along. So interesting and infinitely varied was the work that it was not nearly as harassing as it sounds. To us it seemed quite the natural way of doing things: that people should come and regard it all as astonishing struck us as very odd.

My father was critical of food and wine, though he ate and drank little. He wanted good English meals—the best material and sound cookery—not the bastard-French hotel tradition. It sounded a simple commonsense idea, like his desire for good printing or good glass, but all the forces of commerce seemed to be marshalled against him and he was made to feel that his requests were odd and unreasonable. Not that he was discouraged by this attitude: it seemed to act as a spur! He had told mother, before coming to Broadway, that she would not have to take any part in the business—if he hadn't done so I doubt whether she would have come and anyway I don't think she viewed this adventure in quite the rosy light he did. He said he had engaged an excellent manageress and all would be well. He spoke too optimistically, however, for the manageress proved a poor organizer—although I must say I can hardly envisage a manageress who could have handled the job. When he took over, all the equipment was so bad, the kitchen was so filthy, the staff were untrained; and there he was, fuming in the background full of new and strange ideas. And just to liven things up a bit, he was apt to pull down a ceiling with very little notice and the whole place would be deep in dust. Through the murk he might be seen with a wet cloth tied over his nose looking for old clay pipes, coins and similar things which had fallen through chinks in the boards. We were quite unable to see why the women made so much fuss about this. My mother was soon drawn into the kitchen, after it had been cleaned up, and it nearly engulfed her, but being a strong-minded woman she made terms with fate. Among other things, I recall that she said she must have half a bottle of champagne every night for dinner, after she had supervised the serving of the guests' dinners. For years she had it and well she deserved it, God

E

bless her. She liked it sweet, and for a long time I thought the *Clicquot riche* must be a special importation, so unlike was it to the usual dry wine shipped to England. Furthermore, knowing my father's marked taste for the exotic, I don't think I should have batted an eyelid if I had found that it was.

Group of 'finds' at The Lygon Arms

My father always liked gadgets, too, and must have had at least twenty or thirty razors of all sorts. He was one of the first subscribers to the telephone when it reached Broadway in 1905, but No. 5 Broadway came under Russell, S. B., in the directory instead of 'The Lygon Arms', which was then much better known than his name—especially to Americans. Later, he was one of the first people in the area to have a crystal wireless set. I think one of the reasons he had so many American friends, with whom he kept in touch over the years—he was a great letter writer—was his interest in all new things, in addition to his archaeological leanings. These two sides of his character were to become most important to me in time.

At the beginning of the century cars were few and far between on the roads and drivers enquired anxiously about possible ways of avoiding Broadway Hill, which is fairly steep and over a mile long. Being on the main road from London to Wales, crossed here by another north-south road, and near the centre of England, most people came to Broadway at one time or another, so the increase in the number of cars was rapid. A long list of visitors' names would be boring, but among others I recall the Prince of Wales, Bernard Shaw and his wife, the Bancrofts, Rudyard Kipling, A. J. Balfour, Henry Ford, Flinders Petrie, Martin Conway, A. C. Benson.

But cars were not the only means of transportation used by notable visitors. In an article for *The Countryman* my father wrote:

'Interesting people have reached the Lygon in coach-and-four, Cape-cart and tandem dog-cart. Early one Sunday morning I was called by the night porter to see a gentleman who could not speak English. I went down to find M. Aumont Théville who explained that he had left Paris on the Gordon-Bennett Balloon Race the previous afternoon and not having seen terra firma for fog when over the Thames valley, had come down on Broadway Hill. After having breakfast, he took me to the spot and I was amazed to find the balloon carefully folded and stored in the basket car, and hidden as far as possible by bushes. Colonel the Master of Sempill was the first guest to arrive by aeroplane.'

Among the host of people who showed interest in my father's venture there were two who gave him valuable support: James John Hissey and Lord Montagu of Beaulieu. Hissey, as a young man, was left by an unknown American uncle 'my piece of land in America', which turned out to be a block in Chicago. So, his future assured, he was able to do what he really liked—to drive a horse and trap about England, exploring its remote towns, villages and old houses in search of vintage port! Such a thing can never happen again. In the 1880s there was hardly any traffic on the roads but coaches were a recent memory. Inns were not yet completely decayed and in their cellars there was port which repaid investigation.

The little market towns of England were as fresh and lovely as a daisy on a summer morning. It was one of Hissey's books which introduced my father to the Lygon; and in another he described their first meeting. He had a coachman who had been with him for years and had been taught to drive a car, but he was never allowed to do so. Hissey always drove. On arrival, he would go up to see his room and then would go down again and drive into the yard. After dinner he went out to see that the washing and polishing had been properly done: there was plenty of brass on cars then! This accomplished, I can see him stumping off to bed with his invariable nightcap of rum and milk. Can anyone think of a better?

For Lord Montagu my father had a great affection. A constant traveller, he was quick to realize the value of this experiment in innkeeping. He wanted to see the motor-car revive the glories of English inns which, stimulated originally by the coach, had been all but destroyed by the railway. He was a well-known authority on transport, interested in food and archaeology, a knowledgeable engineer, a first-rate shot. I doubt whether any other member of the House of Lords was qualified to drive a railway engine, which he did in the general strike. He knew and cared about the social problems of the day. A tremendous worker, he always seemed to have time to put in a word for anyone who was doing a job he thought worth while. My father stayed with him at Beaulieu several times and was always his trusted adviser on furnishing problems. Few men live to read their own obituary notices, but he was one of them for he was in a ship's boat which came in very late from the sinking of the *Persia* during the First World War.

In the last twenty-five years innkeeping has become a recognized pursuit, but at the beginning of the century it was hardly considered a job for a man with any cultural background. I remember that when my father's name was put forward for membership of a London Club he wished to describe himself as innkeeper—a title he always used and liked. But the old friend who was proposing him said as tactfully as he could that 'Director of Public Companies' would perhaps be a more suitable title, just on this occasion.

My father started work at the age of fourteen and worked very hard all his life. He believed in the virtue of work. Indeed, the development of the Lygon was financed largely by his emoluments elsewhere. He was sole Receiver in Lunacy for a large estate, which meant administering a good deal of property in London, including one of the last hotels in the City of London—Kennan's Hotel, Crown Court, Cheapside. He was also managing director of The Headland Hotel at Newquay and others at Bournemouth and Swanage. He had to go to London for a day or so most weeks. Up to 1909 my mother used to drive him into Evesham in the dog-cart with the bay mare to catch a train before seven in the morning and he would arrive back at about dinner-time, very tired. As soon as he got in the house he started an inquest on the affairs of the day, proceeding in a well-known pattern after this manner: 'Well, Gordon, how have things gone today?' 'Oh, pretty well, thank you.' 'Have they finished unloading the truck of coal?' 'Yes.' 'How much was there in it?' 'Six tons, seven hundredweights. Here are the weight-notes.' 'What's Jim Turner been doing?' 'Well, he's nearly finished the court-cupboard repairs, and Savage has started making the cases for Sharpe.' 'Oh . . . any developments on the building? Have you seen Bateman or Bomford?' 'No, I haven't seen either of them. There's been a delay over the lavatory basins, so the plumbers couldn't start.' 'How much did the pigs make at Campden market?' This was the final and most important question so far as I was concerned, for I had omitted to find out about it beforehand. The cross-questioning always proceeded until such a situation emerged and it was no use bluffing. The Guvnor went off the deep end: 'Always the same when I go away. No one does anything. No one cares. That's where the system breaks down.' Years afterwards I wondered what exactly the system was. In fact there was little, for as a general rule my father believed in personal supervision of every detail rather than a carefully thought out plan of delegation. Long hours and devoted work seemed essential to cope with such an infinite variety of jobs, but to me it was wonderful training. Years later the whole family laughed at any mention of the system and my father chortled with enjoyment at his own expense.

By normal standards our efforts must have seemed inefficient: by human standards of richness of life the job was rewarding, if exacting. It couldn't possibly have been anything but a family business, for only a rather odd family would appreciate that it was better to live an interesting life of this kind than to make a lot of money. It does seem to me important that such businesses—small, personal and racy—for which I think English people have a special aptitude should not all be squeezed out by cartels, combines or governments.

CHAPTER 6

Cotswold Architecture and Building

Perhaps one of the most important things as a background to my life was my father's vivid interest in building, of which he became a knowledgeable critic although he did not practise any of the crafts himself. My mother did not share his pleasure in this to any marked extent; she was too conscious of the dirt and disorganization it caused, and she had to pacify the staff. This forced him to think up plausible reasons for doing the work. One year we had a plague of flies which invaded the kitchen at the Lygon and the following year my father said he was determined to prevent another visitation of this sort. He had worked out a theory that the manure heap at the back of the stables on the far side of the yard was the source of the trouble and my mother was delighted when he said it should be moved down the orchard. He added, as an afterthought and in an undertone, that perhaps a garage would go well on the site but the full implications of this statement did not strike her until all the familiar equipment of the builder appeared one day. Hammering and shouting started, dust filled the air as the stables were demolished, men walked in and out of the kitchen asking to borrow brushes, cloths, buckets and what not 'just till our'n come tomorrow'. It was my father's day in London and when he re-appeared in the evening it was with an air of innocence and a gold bracelet which he had happened to notice in a shop window and fancied my mother might like.

But to him and to me building was a taste of heaven, as it was

71

an exhibition of crafts assembled for our delight. First of all there were long discussions between my father, Don and myself, then with our architect, C. E. Bateman, who had an eye for a sound job, and the builder. The most astounding possibilities were evolved, discussed and, as a rule, turned down because of the cost. I was always raising some fresh hare and why I wasn't thrown out on my ear I just can't think. One of the very first things my father did, in 1904, was to have a complete survey made of the property. This was of great value to us when planning alterations over many years. As adjoining properties were acquired they were added. A set of the plans showing the dates of each section hangs in a passage in the Lygon.

My father had never had any illusions about the assembly room which had been built against the east wall of the Lygon in 1869 to make it possible to hold the annual ball of the newly formed North Cotswold Hunt (see plate 3). It was a gigantic brick box and, like most of the office buildings of today, was an embodiment of determination to achieve the greatest possible cubic capacity at the very lowest cost. There was no single thing about it, from the mouldings of the doors to the pitch of the roof, which would make anyone who cared for architectural proprieties want to look at it again. It was not possible to use it as a dining room in the summer for it was eighteen feet high and so forbidding that the first couple shown into it would inevitably feel they had been put into a floored-over swimming bath. My father therefore commissioned Bateman to design a room which could be used as a ballroom in the winter and dining room in the busy summer season. This seemed to present insuperable problems and when we had reached scheme E and were beginning to feel that we weren't getting anywhere, mainly perhaps because we had not thought out our requirements clearly enough, an odd thing happened—as I have noticed it so often does in life—which completely changed our thinking. Sir Aston Webb and his wife turned up at the Lygon one evening and after dinner my father explained our predicament and asked him whether he would be so good as to look at the plans. He said he would do so quite unofficially and the moment he saw them he asked why we proposed to put the new room exactly where the 1869 building was—there was a considerable frontage so why not use it and, by placing the new room parallel to the street, get a quiet garden behind? So that is how the Great Hall came to be built where it is today. It was one of those strokes of genius which seem so obvious when one looks back on them. As a lesson it was of immense value to me later on—always go back to fundamentals before you get tied up with detail. Years later, I thought he might well have applied the same basic thinking to his design for the Victoria and Albert Museum, where floors are at several levels, there is no lift for heavy items and a much simpler background would have enabled interest to be concentrated on the exhibits.

The addition of the Great Hall in 1909 (see plates 3 and 4) considerably increased our dining space, which was particularly useful as the growing motor traffic meant that far more people were coming in for meals. There was, too, a greater demand for overnight accommodation so my father decided, in 1911, to add a wing which would have single bedrooms and bathrooms above and larger and more convenient kitchen premises below to cope with the extra catering. It was built on the site of a redundant nineteenth-century brick stable block— one side facing the yard and the other facing the garden. It proved a success but the basic problem was how to avoid losses from October to March. Occasionally one or two hunting people stayed for a month or more, and they usually had their own sitting room. There was the North Cotswold Hunt Ball and perhaps two or three other balls, for all of which outside caterers were called in. Few people travelled by road in the winter, however, but those who did so usually arrived just before dinner time, cold, stiff and miserable. They expected a meal at once and were not pleased to dine *à la* Crusoe. But my father always had a splendid log fire in the dining-room, a marvellous disperser of grumpiness and one with which no radiator can compete.

I was fascinated by the whole technique of building and delighted to see the work of every trade going on day by day. Large blocks of stone were brought from the quarry on a heavy horse-drawn dray, sawn up by hand on the site and then worked to size for all dressed parts such as doorways and window openings. This was the work of banker masons, i.e. masons who worked at a banker or stone table. Sometimes we had as many as ten of them working in a row, under a rough shelter of corrugated iron. Each banker was formed of two low walls of brick joined by a cross wall, an H on plan, on which was laid a paving slab at about table height. Here, using mallet and chisel, the mason cut the split or sawn stone to shapes indicated by zinc templates, the clean stone chips gradually forming a thick carpet underfoot. These men were bred and born in the Cotswolds, the sons of masons who, like Michelangelo, had sucked in chisels with their mothers' milk. From the time they could crawl they had handled and caressed the lovely stone of the neighbourhood. From a glance at a piece they would say at once from which quarry it was likely to have come. They knew which quarry had a hard bed for steps and paving, a good freestone for working, good walling stone, good stone for dry walls and stone for slates, for in Cotswold building—among the very best in England—stone served every purpose.

The slates varied astonishingly in size. I measured one on a cowshed at Withington and its width was just the full span of my arms—six feet two inches—but this was exceptional. As they came from the quarry in varying sizes they were graduated from large at the eaves to small at the ridge, thus ensuring a good overhang and the strength to take a ladder on occasion. To sort them the slaters used a measuring rod with a pin at one end to go in the eye of the slate and marks to indicate lengths. They would talk of cussomes, wivetts, batchelors and long elevenses and to watch a good workman laying a valley, without any use of lead, was something to remember for many a long day. The slates were hung by wooden pegs, either pitch-pine or oak, on to oak rent laths.

The inside of the roof was then 'tauched' with mortar to prevent driving snow coming in. When properly laid the resulting roof, which had to be steep in pitch, would last for many years. If a slate cracked with frost it could easily be replaced without disturbing more than two or three others. It was cool in summer and said to be warm in winter, but it was heavy and therefore expensive in timber and skilled laying.

Dry walls, that is walls built without mortar, were used instead of hedges in the Cotswolds. Other counties have them too but none has walls of such delicate colour. Observe them before it is too late, for barbed wire, that most loathsome of fencing materials in peace as in war, is a powerful rival. To see them in full perfection I think these walls must be looked at in winter-time, like the trunks of beech trees. They are always built to a batter, that is they are thicker at the base than at the top so that each side slopes inwards. The stone is laid in courses, just as it comes from the quarry with only a corner knocked off with the stone-axe here and there, the thicker stones being used first, at the bottom. Each stone is wedged so as not to move, using small flakes of stone for the purpose. Occasionally a long stone is laid right through the wall as a bonder—this is called a porpin, a word I cannot recall ever seeing in print. It often projects on one side of the wall, so avoiding the labour of cutting it to length, but townsfolk are apt to think that these are steps put in for convenience in climbing over! In laying the wall the tail of one course sits, wherever it is long enough to do so, on the tail of the one below on the opposite face of the wall, which means that it is more than half the thickness of the wall. This gives a useful tie. The wall is completed by a cresting of 'combers'—cocks' combs—which stand on end across the wall. If these are laid with mortar it makes the best job. Where the wall is six feet or more high a mortared course would be built half way, giving a valuable bond. Anyone interested should look carefully at the wall round Blenheim Park, most beautifully built and containing thousands of tons of stone. This work was, in old days, taken on by gangs—sometimes whole families—who were paid by the yard. The farmer carted the stone and laid it out about a yard from the site of the proposed wall.

Often those who visit Gloucestershire talk as if stone walls were all alike. Walk up the street of Broadway, Chipping Campden, Burford or any other Cotswold village or small town and notice how many different types of walling there are. First, there is the dry walling, which is not used for houses but for garden and field divisions. Then, for barns and cottages, rubble walling, using exactly the same sort of stone but laying it in mortar. Then, for farm houses, squared rubble which, as its name implies, is more carefully shaped and finished. Both of these have joints about $\frac{3}{4}$ inch wide. Then, for more elaborate building, 'knotters', i.e. fairly large squared stones with a dressed face left from use of the stone-axe. This has narrower joints, of about $\frac{1}{2}$ inch. Finally, there is ashlar—large stones finely dressed with a chisel and with fine joints not much over $\frac{1}{8}$ inch. Often ashlar is used for chimneys only and sometimes it is finished quite smooth with a drag, that is a piece of an old saw about six inches long. Ashlar is expensive if worked by hand, but the new carborundum and diamond-faced saws used at some quarries reduce the cost of sawing a good deal. Today stone is nearly always sawn and often worked at the quarry. But the surface left by a power-saw is already flat, quite unlike that from a frame-saw which requires dressing with a hand chisel, so in order to achieve quickly an imitation of a hand-chiselled surface the sawn face is gone over with a 'bolster', making wide cuts about two inches apart. I have no use for such bastard effects: either have good handwork or good machine work.

Since the Second World War the shortage of skilled masons has led to the use of reconstructed stone on a considerable scale. There is no reason why this should not be a useful building material but unfortunately it is made with an imitation stone surface in several standard sizes and is not laid in courses with the larger ones at the bottom of the wall but in maddening repeats on one large and several small. This has now been

imitated in plastic sheet which can be nailed to any kind of wall
—even, of course, a genuine stone one!

When left to their own devices the masons knew how to
point a wall properly, that is finish the mortar between the
stones, but superior architects sometimes gave odd instructions. The work done under the guidance of Ernest Gimson,
the Barnsleys, Norman Jewson and F. L. Griggs was remarkably fine in this respect, with joints of lime mortar well flushed
up and rubbed over when nearly dry. This took away the
polish of the trowel and gave the joints a texture nearer that
of the stone. I must say I like to see a rubble wall slurried over
with thin lime mortar, as was done in so many Gothic buildings. It must be admitted that the morals of some wallers had
already been corrupted by engineers and town builders so that
they used cement and sand mortar, which has not the quality
of lime, and 'cut' the joints, a horrid finish which enraged my
father. Today this is almost standard, being both cheaper and
quicker, for walls are often laid by bricklayers, who barely
know the difference between Cotswold and Portland stone.
As sure as there's a God in Gloucestershire this is wickedness.

In looking at what has come to be called 'Cotswold building'
—i.e. good seventeenth-century domestic work—one notes
how admirably it solved the problems of its age. It did not strive
consciously to be picturesque. Stone was plentiful but transport exceedingly difficult as roads were bad and there are no
rivers of any size in this hilly area. The mullioned window
solved the problem of forming openings without any stones of
great length. The leaded lights enabled comparatively small
pieces of glass to be used. The span of the gables was fixed by
the timber available, in this case hardwood—oak or elm—
which does not normally grow straight in very long lengths as
softwood does. The pitch of the roof was fixed: it had to be as
steep as possible to throw off the rain but not so steep as to
drag out the wooden pins from the eyes of the slates, that is
about 52 deg. in practice. Lead was very costly indeed, so wide
overhanging eaves courses had to take the place of guttering
and downspouts. Cast iron had not yet been used for this pur-

pose but, in any case, iron too was scarce and was only used for casements, hinges and such like. In the Cotswolds one seldom sees the massy cast-iron firebacks which were usual in Sussex, though they were used and doubtless some came from the Forest of Dean. Guy Dawber's book, *Old Cottages, Farm-houses, etc., in the Cotswold District*, gives a good account of Cotswold building. I wish someone would write an exhaustive comparison of two regions, say the Cotswold Hills—lime-stone, hardwood and rain, with a valley in the Tyrol—granite, softwood and snow. Way of life, materials and climate affect the forms of building profoundly, and when transport was difficult they gave wonderful regional variety.

For some reason which I cannot explain my father seemed to have an instinctive appreciation of stone although he wasn't brought up in a stone county. When my parents returned from a visit to the United States—I think it was in 1911—he told me how he missed the dry-stone walls. He said his nails had got into a parlous state: he used to stand by a wall and trim them on it as he talked and he regarded a nail file as a poor sub-stitute! I remember, during leaves from France at long in-tervals in 1915–1918, the same nostalgic longing for the sight of the first dry-stone wall. To live away from a stone country would seem like exile to me. And how the mere thought of good building stirred our blood!

Besides the masons there were carpenters, joiners, plasterers, glaziers, smiths, slaters, plumbers, painters and labourers, al-though in country building a skilled man often practised more than one trade. I had friends among them all, watched them at work, asked questions. Gradually I learned how jobs were tackled, what was good work and what bad and the immense importance of texture. More than that, I learned to value men. I saw how degrading was any system which forced a good work-man to do bad work, something which has been at the root of more industrial trouble than most people realize. At this time most skilled men took a pride in the job and I have always found satisfaction in working with people who are keenly interested in what they are doing.

CHAPTER 7

Memories of the Antique Trade

I was given plenty of responsibility and besides being put in charge of the repair shop I was allowed to buy antiques of all sorts. At first I bought by ones and twos but later I spent a good deal of money. I read every book on architecture, furniture and decoration that I could get hold of and the houses illustrated in *Country Life* week by week were a special delight to me. The influence on me of our friend Oliver Baker was very great. He was an artist, the son of an artist, who had recently opened a small shop in Stratford-on-Avon to sell old furniture. I knew him well for over thirty years but I can't remember that he seemed a day older just before he died than when I first met him. He had a wide knowledge of furniture and domestic objects of all sorts, and of ironwork, tapestry and leather vessels. To have heard him reading Shakespeare's sonnets, sitting in a corner of the great open fireplace at the Lygon before a blazing ash fire, was an experience I shall never forget. He walked slowly, for he liked to look at things: he talked slowly and with dry humour. I remember walking up Broadway street with him and saying of a new cottage of red brick and slate: 'It's pretty awful, isn't it?' He stopped and, regarding it steadily for some moments, said in judicial tones: 'No, it's *not* awful,' then with measured and dreadful solemnity, 'IT'S HELLISH.'

Through my father Baker came to know a fellow antique-dealer from Manchester, one Booth Jones, who was his exact opposite—a good-natured hustler to whom solitude was an unknown word, never still for a moment, full of pep and advertising ideas. On one occasion he was carried in a sedan-chair to a race-course to advertise an antique shop he had just opened at Colwyn Bay. Arrayed in eighteenth-century costume, he sat distributing leaflets headed 'Ye Olde Manor' or something of that kind. He ended, as he lived, in the limelight for, with his wife and two children, he went down in the *Lusitania*. Saddened as I was at the time, I could not help feeling it was the end he would have chosen. How he would have relished the headlines: 'Whole family wiped out'.

His show house at Colwyn Bay was full of an astonishing collection, packed to the doors. Old furniture, eighteenth-century clothes and shawls, a human skeleton and a suit of armour, horn lanterns, Japanese masks and a bronze Buddha, all sorts of odds and ends, some good some not so good. After an unsuccessful attempt to rush him round, a somewhat dazed Baker was asked what he thought of it all and replied: 'I haven't seen a stuffed monkey anywhere!'

To see these two making a deal was remarkable. Baker always wore Booth Jones down by his flat refusal to be hurried. It went something like this. 'Now, Baker, let's settle this. You say you could do with the tridarn, ten rushed chairs, two Lancashire settles and large copper pot at Colwyn Bay; the two panelled armchairs, three samplers, two spits and leather-covered stool at Manchester . . .' Quite unruffled, Baker breaks in: 'Just a moment, say that all again please while I write it down. I can't carry things in my head like harum-scarum people from the North.' He writes very slowly, with long comments at short intervals: 'Lancashire settles . . . I wonder you never think of getting the right sort of rope for them. It must be a good hemp rope—the others stretch too much. You know, Booth Jones, I should have thought your family would have a traditional knowledge of hemp rope. But as you haven't I'll give you the name of a man who sells just the very sort. He used to be in a little alley off Cornhill. But, wait a moment, I'm misinforming you—someone—now who was it—perhaps it was Russell—I can't remember—but I'm sure someone said he had died or moved—one or t'other or both —several years ago.' 'You call it a copper pot, do you? It's really an old boiler. When I was a boy and used to paint in Shropshire every farmhouse had a boiler like that for brewing. And that reminds me, did I ever tell you my theory that the barrel-makers and coopers started their apprentices making harvest-barrels? I knew an old man in Ludlow whose uncle was a cooper and who said that . . .' By now Booth Jones was ready to explode. He blurted out: 'Among your stock there's the six-legged table, four cricket tables, fifteen Dutch brass tobacco boxes, three sets of steel fireirons, the large painted chest and the panel of needlework. I'll add ten pounds to these and call it a deal.' But Baker wasn't going to be rushed. He wrote all down as before. Then he looked up what each item had cost him, which meant searching for various books in most unlikely places and separating the prices of things he had bought as a lot. Meantime, he carried on a long and learned dissertation on chests which were not chests but really counters used in shops in Shakespeare's day, with many references to actual examples and so on. And then, at the critical moment, when Booth Jones thought the deal was reaching a climax and he had turned to the fire to light a cigarette, Baker disappeared silently from the room. He returned after ten minutes, munching an ancient bun which he had left to season in the pocket of his overcoat. There were few things he liked new. He had, it seemed, forgotten all about the deal and launched into a long and well-documented disquisition on Shakespeare's visits to the Cotswolds. But Booth Jones' nerves weren't equal to the strain. The original £10 he raised to £20, £30, £40 and at £45 the deal was clinched. Later, he realized he had paid more than he had intended, which never failed to surprise him. He was, he argued, a shrewd businessman from the North and regarded Baker as a 'charming artist'.

The term 'antique dealer' covered a very wide range. Baker was notable because he remained an artist throughout his life. But there were others who were artists in a lesser sense, and many of them fascinated me. Frost was of a heavy build, not very tall, with a coarse, florid face, a loud voice and a large tie-pin. His ample paunch supported a near-gold chain and his fat fingers often jingled the coins in his pockets. He was remarkably honest, but had a large share of native cunning which served him instead of knowledge. His headquarters were in one of the finest Gothic timber houses in a cathedral town. He was a petty capitalist surrounded by satellites called 'knockers', that is, men who went round on foot or with an old cart and knocked at doors where they thought they could either sell or buy. Sometimes they took with them fish, paraffin, firewood or marine stores. Often they had a few illustrations from *The Connoisseur* or *Country Life* and said to the farmer's wife or the cottager: 'I suppose you haven't any old glasses like that, or any dirty old bits of furniture?' Like John Webb Singer of Frome, who employed such methods, they met sometimes with disappointment. Singer showed a cottager a picture of a yard-of-ale glass—a considerable rarity even then—and she said: 'Why, us had'n the very dead spit o' that. But it weren't no use to we, so us smashed 'un and stuffed 'un down rat's hole.' Sometimes, however, they bought quite good things cheaply. But money ran through their fingers and anything of any size had to be referred to the capitalist. If he thought fit, Frost would go and have a look at anything so discovered, do a deal if he could and then stand the original finder a few shillings. One of these men, a very seedy-looking individual, unwashed and with finger-nails in deep mourning, had an ancient brougham and nag. He was reputed to earn the main part of his living by helping absconding bookies off the course at race meetings but between times the brougham served as 'knocker's transport'. Frost used to look at him and, shaking his head sadly, tell me: 'Well eddicated feller—writes quite a clurk's 'and. Wine and wimmin's 'is trouble.'

The knockers used to congregate in a little group at the bottom of Frost's yard. From this parade ground he whistled them up like dogs. He would shout out: 'Jaack, 'ere.' Jack approached at a shuffling semi-double and, standing ill at ease, unshaven, with an ancient cigarette stub in one corner of his mouth, awaited instructions. Frost fixed him with a gimlet eye and said: 'Mr Russell 'ere might do with a dresser. You know that Jaackobeen one you seen at Dudley. You said the drawers was all baulked out. What sort of legs 'ad it got?' I always thought that to Frost Jacobean had some connection with Jack and the Beanstalk: at any rate, it connoted a fairy story. Jack scratched his ear, determined to create a favourable impression. Meanwhile, his shifty eyes looked sideways at me, as if he were weighing up how much I would swallow. 'Well,' he said at last, 'it's the finest dresser as ever I seen in me life—in a little public in Dudley. All oak. Beeutiful. Queen Anne [a gentle correction of his boss's knowledge of periods] legs—oh, they was caberole legs, with carved knees and dawg's feet.' Here he traced with his hands on his own knee imaginary shells and flutings of incredible richness, meantime turning one foot out at an impossible angle. 'And,' he added very slowly and in his most impressive manner, 'there was ten on 'em!' 'What, ten legs,' said Frost, incredulously. 'Put a sock in it, you bloody liar. Clear off!' Frost then turned to me and said: 'You know Jaack ain't a bad bloke when 'es sober, if 'e wasn't such a bleedin' liar. 'E can't 'elp it and sometimes it's useful. The week afore last 'e comes to me and says, "Guvnor," 'e says, "I knows to the best Jaackobeen chest as ever I seen. The drawers is all baulked out and on a stand with twissed legs and twissed rails. And great big bun feet. They been offered thirty quid for it but I reckon it's worth double." "Where is it?" I says. "In a little fried-fish shop in a back street in Kiddy-minster," 'e ses. I thinks for a minute and then I ses, "Look 'ere, Jaack, I got an idea. If it's reely a right 'un we'll buy it. And this is 'ow we'll do it. I'll put on me pea-green overcoat. I reckon I look quite the toff in that, 'specially with me sportin' cap and a seegar. We'll go over there in the motor. You shall buy a steak and take it in to the shop and say, "is Grace the Dook o' Newcastle is outside and 'as sent me in to tell yer to cook this regardless of hexpense." "And onions," he ses. "That'll knock 'em. When I comes in I'll buy it for thirty-five quid afore they've recovered their saveoir feer."'' He said the scheme worked perfectly: if it didn't it was not for lack of impudence. He was full of tales and reminiscences, most of them very plausible.

Then there was Fred West who kept a small antique shop not far from Snow Hill Station in Birmingham. My father discovered him one day and for many years we bought things from him. Unless he liked people he would have no truck with them. I have seen him stand in the door of his shop and say in the blandest way that it was not open. He neither moved nor argued, and when the potential customers had gone away he would come back and say: 'We've got quite enough to do this morning without having customers in the shop, 'specially ones like them. Now, do you think you could do with a drink?' Like himself, his spelling was original. We bought many walnut Queen Anne pedestal tables from him, these being described on the bill as K.O. Table, sometimes Q.A. K.O. Table. Q.A. was Queen Anne but we never knew what K.O. could be until one day he put it in full—Knee 'Ole: A very proper half-brother to O.K. (Orl Krekt) I always thought! His small shop was arranged in the simplest way: a passage was kept clear from front to back, and on either side of this things were piled up nearly to the ceiling. The back row hadn't been moved for years and nothing was ever repaired, cleaned, dusted or marked, yet so remarkable was his memory that he knew the price of everything. On several occasions, to try him out, I asked the price of the same article after an interval of months and the answer was the same. The odd thing was that he did not quote the same price to everyone. He only liked to sell to the trade; private customers gave so much more trouble. As far as I know he never kept any books and there were many thousands of articles, always changing, in his stock. Besides his Birmingham shop he had a large house and outbuildings in Warwick. Sometimes he would say: 'Let me see, last time I asked you thirty quid for the cupboard and I think it's cheap. But I'm tired of seeing it about. Have you got your buying boots on today? If you have, it's twenty-five but I tell you straight I don't know what my old queen will say to me!' His wife was always his old queen. She had a business in second-hand clothes which filled chests, wardrobes and cupboards of every sort and overflowed on to the handrails of the staircase. I must say they added to the frowsty air of a house which suffered little from cleaning or the opening of windows.

I was always shown great kindness by the Wests. He was very entertained when Don and I, both young and green, bore down on him for the first time. We offered him 10s for something for which he asked 12s 6d, and putting half-a-sovereign in his hand, we picked up the article and prepared to go. He said nothing then but he told my father afterwards that he had all but kicked us out of his shop. Instead, he had sat down and laughed till the tears ran down his cheeks. He took the kindest care of my buying reputation. He would say to me when I asked the price of something he had just purchased: 'That, oh, I thought it was a sweet little piece. I gave four pun ten for it and I ought not to have bought it. But my old queen and me went out for half a day last week and we had to buy something, just to pay our expenses. I shan't sell it to you. Your father wouldn't thank me.' Or even: 'That settee, well, I bought it as a right'un but somehow I don't like it. It looked very good in a doctor's 'ouse. I don't know why I don't like it but I don't and that's that. You can have it for ten quid and if it's all right it's dirt cheap. Here's the dirt anyway'—giving the upholstery a ferocious bang—'but I'd much rather you didn't have it, swelpmebob if I wouldn't.'

They were hospitable people and I was always asked to tea. There was a large kitchen with a big kitchen-table in the middle but there was never any room at all on the table as most of the top was always covered with things they had just bought, waiting to be moved elsewhere. There were all sorts of things, from slip-ware dishes—which he well knew I loved —to tea-sets, pewter pots and dishes, iron trivets, samplers, copper kettles and so on. Then, on a cracked Crown Derby dish, there might be a leg of mutton from which slices had been hacked off rather than carved and which looked as if it would be kept on the table until it was finished. There might also be half a loaf of bread and some butter in a piece of paper, several bottles of sauce—very grubby outside, some empty beer bottles and a delicate eighteenth-century silver cruet with cut glass bottles, one of which might have pepper in it and one mustard a month old. The whole collection would be pushed up together to make room for a large teapot. The floor was much the same as the top of the table, at least in the corners of the room; but the amusing conversation of my hosts made up for all deficiencies of this sort.

On one occasion, it must have been about 1912, West told me of a very fine Jacobean six-legged table which he said he had been trying to buy for some years. It belonged to an old north-country farmer in Warwickshire, who had brought it with him from Lancashire. The farmhouse, West said, was a fine specimen of timber-work, but the table was kept in a shed, where the farmer used it as a bench for cleaning lamps and boots, although he refused to take a penny less than £60, I think it was. West said he didn't feel inclined to give this for it himself but he thought we might and if so we could stand him a fiver. It all sounded very interesting to me so it was arranged that West should take me to see it. By great good fortune, as I have always liked walking, we went on foot, I remember. I suppose I must have thought of the expedition as a pleasure more than a business trip or we would have gone by car. West was easy-going by nature and didn't like exercise a lot but he took kindly to the idea of a day off. It turned out a lovely summer day and I remember sitting under a tree outside a pub with pots of bitter in front of us whilst we ate sandwiches and bread and cheese. West told me about himself and how as a youngster he was apprenticed to a printer who specialized in Christmas cards. He had a bent for drawing and in the little circle in which he worked his robins became well known. At the end of four years he felt it was time he ceased to be an apprentice so he decided to run away and get a well-paid job with a competing firm. This he did and all went well till the firm produced its series of Christmas cards, for his old master happened to see them and said at once: 'I'll bet a fiver that's one of Fred's robins!' His enquiries made it necessary for West to change his address at short notice.

He did various odd jobs, and a year or so later was in a pub with only a few shillings in his pocket. He got into conversation with another man, Bateman, who proved to be hard up too but knew a little about antiques. They decided to pool their resources and start as dealers. West said he 'knew to' an old clock—in a marqueterie case, he said it was—kept under a bed in a cottage. There was some story that when the local great house caught fire years before the nearby inhabitants salvaged many things and not all of them were returned. Anyway, the two of them went to make enquiries. The clock was still there, but the price asked was more than they could find, though Bateman thought it really was cheap. So they held a council of war and decided to see a dealer in a town fifteen miles away and offer to introduce it to him on commission. The dealer came along with them and looked at the clock with great distaste, telling them not to waste his time with rubbish like that—just a crude imitation, he said. Though their enterprise was not starting well, they thought they would have another shot and before going to a second dealer they decided to investigate the history of the clock a bit more. So off they went to put some searching questions to the cottager. When they knocked at the door she opened it and said at once: 'You've come for the weights and pendulum, I suppose? Here they are.' They managed to hide their surprise, and went off triumphant. A day or so later they went into the town once again, taking the weights and pendulum with them but leaving them at the railway station. Then they walked by the dealer's shop, hoping to be seen by him. The ruse was successful: he rushed out, telling them to hand over his property at once or he would put the police on to them. They were outraged and disclaimed any knowledge of the whereabouts of the clock or its parts, but at last one of them made the ingenuous suggestion that he 'knew to' a beautiful pair of brass-cased weights and a pendulum and he was willing to go to any amount of trouble to get them to help the dealer out of a hole. He said he didn't suppose they could be bought for less than a fiver but that was much less than it would cost to make new ones! Threats and offers both failed and their working capital was increased by £5.

He told me how, when he took his first little shop, there was often not sixpence in the till on Saturday; all his cash was tied up in stock and sales had been very bad. So, taking a small object of value, a silver snuff-box, he went off to larger dealers in the town. He asked £2 for it but was told they already had more snuff-boxes than they wanted. It was plain that West was hard up so it was no use denying it and he asked for an offer. None was forthcoming. Any offer? Ten shillings, they said. It was far less than he had paid for it but he must have something so said he would take fifteen. The two partners were adamant. They said they didn't want it and were only making an offer at all to help him. One took each of West's arms, kindly but firmly led him outside, put ten shillings in his hand, went back, closed and locked the door. A few weeks later he got a friend to go and enquire the price of the boxes and found there wasn't one at less than £3.

West told of his early struggles simply, without rancour. When he had done a good deal he took a day off and went to the races. When I first knew him he liked to have a cheque at once. Yet above his shop he had a small collection of early Worcester porcelain—blue and white, mostly crescent marked—which he only showed to intimates and never sold. I believe he genuinely liked looking at it.

We came to the farm at last and the farmer proved to be all that West had foretold. He hadn't asked us to come, he said, and we could give him £60 for the table or leave it. Seeing no chance of any lowering of the price West tried to get a side of bacon thrown in. No use. A ham? Still no good. Two dozen eggs? No. No. No. At last he said: 'Well, it's a very hot day, you'll give us a cup of tea apiece?' 'That I won't,' said the farmer, 'but I'll let you have two cups of tea for sixpence! And if you don't want them you can walk six miles to the town, for there's nowhere else!'

Then, too, I remember Jack Hutton—always known to his

companions as Jaack 'Utton—stout, thick-necked, with a greasy look about him. He nearly always wore a reddish neckerchief and a wide leather belt round his middle. He drank a good deal, could not write his name—he signed with a cross—and was honest. When he had any funds at all to invest in stock he went round selling various things from a coster's cart. One afternoon he took me on this to see a Gothic hutch with pierced panels, somewhere near Cleobury Mortimer. I have seldom enjoyed a drive so much. To me it was a holiday, in new country, and as we rolled slowly along Jack answered my eager questions with low-toned grunts. I bought the cupboard, which is now in my house.

And there was Josh Somalvico, whose family had made thermometers and barometers in Hatton Garden for more than a hundred years. A little pinched man who spoke broken English in his little pinched shop. He sold old clocks too and knew how to silver mirror-plates with mercury, a dangerous job which he always did himself. And W. H. Fenton, who had a small shop in New Oxford Street. He specialized in arms and armour and knew well a great many collections both in Europe and America. He lived in a really lovely eighteenth-century house at Heston where I often stayed later on. In one large room there he kept a museum of most interesting things—arms and armour, costumes, leather jacks, bombards and bottles, rushlight-holders, candlesticks, tongs and so on. It was so pleasant to be in a museum where the exhibits could be handled. I remember an old gun which he bought in an odd lot at Christie's. When he took delivery of it he found it had a parchment label of sixty years before with a description in his father's writing. A large garden surrounded the house, with cedars, elms and mulberries in it and a brick dovecote for a thousand pigeons; and in a paddock were his own cows. Jerrybuilt villas surged closer each year and have now engulfed it all in a tidal wave, I believe. It was only a few hundred yards from the Great West Road.

I came to know a great many antique dealers, but few of them were men of taste. Most of them were honest, which was surprising in view of the temptations of the trade. There was a minority of predatory individuals who cared nothing for the things they sold. They were always 'on the make'. I suppose I would never have made a very successful dealer for I was interested in things because of their beauty of shape, their colour or the way they were made, much more than their rarity or cost. Most especially I was enchanted to see things in the places for which they were made. A Welsh dresser in a Welsh farmhouse gives me real pleasure: in a museum or a villa near a big town it becomes another thing altogether. I felt this so strongly that I was known, on occasion, to beg owners not to sell!

In 1913, a Campden man came over to Broadway and asked my father to buy two large open stone fireplaces. It appeared that he had bought a somewhat tumbledown property as a speculation and he offered to show the fireplaces to us. I was sent over to investigate. I found that it had once been an old Campden inn, the Green Dragon. At the back was a large, early seventeenth-century room, with the two fireplaces in it. Below were various rooms and cellars—one known as the cockpit although I cannot believe that it was used for cock-fighting as there was so little room for spectators. But certainly an old bill of Dover's Games early in the nineteenth century says: 'A main of cocks will be fought between the gentlemen of Worcestershire and Warwickshire at the Green Dragon.' The whole place was most romantic to me. I went home and reported that it was not too far gone to repair, that it would be wicked to pull out the fireplaces and that we ought to make an offer for the property—which we did, and bought it! Our idea was to repair it and open it again as an inn, run on the same lines as the Lygon. But following the outbreak of war it was only possible to patch a little here and there to keep out the wet and after the war there seemed no hope that we should be able to find enough money to repair it. My father sold the property to John Fothergill but he too felt it was a bit beyond him, eventually decided not to complete the purchase and bought the Spread Eagle at Thame instead.

This he made a memorable inn, in which it was a great pleasure to stay, as recorded in his *Innkeeper's Diary*.

Any description of the buying of antiques would be incomplete without some reference to sales. No one will deny that attending a big sale is an interesting experience and is full of excitement, but to me it was always a little like peeping through a keyhole. To see a house in which a family has lived for years—perhaps even, as at Wroxton Abbey or Montacute and many other houses, for centuries—thrown open to the crowd seemed to make one a participant in an unwarrantable intrusion on privacy. To witness the vultures assessing everything in cash, utterly unmoved by the higher values involved, was to see human nature at a pretty low level. And when the auction of the furniture and effects was to be followed by the auction of the house in lots for demolition and the land in lots for building then the whole scene was heart-breaking. Yet to these people with their thick necks and fat oily faces, their fur-trimmed coats and gold rings, the raping of England was a joke.

The small country sale came into a somewhat different category. Not so many of the big-town dealers attended and the whole affair was so obviously a day off for the neighbourhood. Old ladies came early, took front seats and remained all day, missing nothing but not making a bid. The room—or perhaps it was a marquee on the lawn—became so congested that sweating porters could hardly force their way in and out with the lots. But whoever else became hot and bothered it was never the auctioneer. The good auctioneer knows everyone in a wide area, he sees a wink as readily as he hears a shouted bid, he is firm in settling some controversial point but always tactful and conciliatory, he is never rattled, has a free flow of banter and chaff and only uses sarcasm in extreme cases. A popular figure himself—as like as not he is a good cricketer or shot—he has a large following and a sale conducted by him will seldom be a flop, even in very adverse weather conditions.

My father was a well-known figure at such sales for miles

around and as he always refused to join any dealers' ring he was a welcome sight to auctioneers. Often Don or I went with him and we returned home with the most astonishing things from time to time. Even he, however, refused to make a bid for a pair of whale's jawbones which tempted a wag at the back of the room to exclaim in a hollow voice: 'Poor old Jonah!' In the village of Mickleton there was quite a lot of excitement in 1909 when my father bought a very fine Elizabethan table for £132 10s 0d in what was just a farmhouse sale. Afterwards people walked round the table, touching it, and it is to be seen in the Lygon to this day. At another small sale my father noticed a box included in an odd lot in a loft and on opening the lid he saw about a couple of dozen bullseye panes of glass packed in sawdust. They must have been there for seventy years. The lot was knocked down to him for 3s 6d. After the hammer had fallen 'Old Jacques'—a very well-known Broadway character—peeped into the box. As he had a standing arrangement with the Guvnor to take any bullseye panes he bought at 1s 6d apiece his face can be imagined and what he said was both picturesque and pithy.

I wish I could remember more of 'Old Jacques'—protégé of Phil May and Frank Millet, who had a house in Broadway and was lost in the *Titanic*. Jacques had an antique shop just opposite the Lygon, always wore a swallowtail coat of a brownish colour with cavernous tail pocket, and had a notable vocabulary. It was, I think, partly for the benefit of his immortal soul that I was asked to write out a notice, 'Curses, like chickens, come home to roost', to hang in the bar at the Lygon! My only regret is that I was not there to hear his mordant wit when he first saw it, for I never shared my father's dislike of bad language although I always felt that it should be used with artistry and in the right place. So used, it may well have saved my life later on, but of that I shall speak again. Anyway, Ben Knight, the prim barman at the Lygon, used to complain of what he called 'flowery language'. And such complaints were often directed against Jacques, whom Ben disliked because of his general air of untidiness. With

Knight neatness was carried to extremes—even his taper had a piece of string tied round it and was hung up on its own special nail. I must admit that I had a soft spot for 'Old Jacques'. Dr Alexander of Broadway told of him, during his last illness, sitting up in bed in his room full of stuff he couldn't sell, undusted for years. With an ancient coat over his shoulders he was sipping a cup of tea, his hand shaking so much that the cup chattered. In reply to the doctor's enquiry as to how he was he broke into a string of oaths, but his voice was so weak that the full savour of them was lost and it seemed that he was drifting imperceptibly into his natural place among his worn-out relics.

My father's liking for out-of-the-way objects was well known. On one occasion a customer of ours followed a porter carrying two enormous glass brandy bottles, empty and unwrapped, the whole length of No. 3 platform at Paddington. When he discovered my father he said: 'Ah, I wanted a word with you and I knew I had only to follow the bottles!'

The interest in old things which developed towards the end of the nineteenth century undoubtedly saved a number of old buildings and much furniture and so on from destruction. The manifesto of William Morris's Society for the Protection of Ancient Buildings ('anti-scrapers') was, in fact, written by him in Broadway Tower, in which he used to stay in the summer with Burne-Jones and Rossetti for several weeks at a time. The Society did most valuable pioneer work and evolved a first-rate technique of repair which is slowly spreading in this and other countries. It was a pity though, that this interest was fanned into a craze for collecting: everyone wanted to 'pick up' old things and pose as a 'collector' or 'connoisseur'. It soon became impossible to see any more good things in most old houses, farmhouses and cottages. The pleasure of walking down a village street and glimpsing a good solid oak dresser through a cottage doorway is now denied us, such things having been replaced by the ghastly productions of competitive industry. But the rot went much further than that. People bought 'antiques' if they could afford them, reproductions of antiques if they could not, and there was to them nothing else. Furniture of their own time simply did not exist for them: they laughed at the bare idea. The works of Morris, Voysey, Lethaby, Heal, Ashbee, Gimson and the Barnsleys was known only to a tiny group. So, ignored by the majority, many such craftsmen withdrew into their shells out of the main stream of life, to the great loss of the community. And, of course, the supply of antiques—'real period pieces' as they came to be called—was not equal to the demand, so that good workmen wasted their time making fakes and the greatest possible amount of encouragement was given to flagrant dishonesty. There was plenty of money to spend in advertising, so that many periodicals were full of articles on 'Apostle's Spoons', 'Monk's Benches', 'Refectory Tables' and what not. And each had its 'Collector's Corner' or 'Connoisseur's Notes'. The destruction wrought in fifty years by untutored fans was much greater than that caused by a century of neglect. And for this I must take my share of blame.

Yet I can at least say this for the antique trade: through it I came to have a workable knowledge of English furniture and a deep appreciation of its many admirable qualities. My family could have made large sums of money by making reproductions, and even more by making fakes, but we always resisted the temptation. Curiously enough, when we later started to make furniture to my designs most people thought we were making fakes: that we should endeavour to make things of our own day was quite beyond their comprehension! It was partly because of my disgust at what I saw going on that I decided to try my hand at designing furniture of and for my own time. I had only the very inadequate training I have described, but I had enthusiasm and a good deal of patience.

CHAPTER 8

War Service 1914–1919

It is odd that the earliest days of both the great wars remind me of remarks by my mother. In 1914 she said: 'Well, I can't think why they want to start a war in August.' August was then the busiest month at the Lygon. In 1939 she said: 'I don't mind what I have to do so long as I'm not forced to eat margarine!'

I don't remember very clearly what my reactions were in August 1914. I was doing a job which I found of great interest, in fact all absorbing. I had fixed up a small workroom in which I was writing a copy of Omar Khayyám on vellum and sometimes I slipped away for an hour or two to draw a piece of furniture, an old building or something else that took my fancy. Occasionally I was lonely, for I was too shy to make friends easily, but I never remember being bored. I seldom played games, not because I didn't like them, for I played football and cricket at school with enjoyment, but because life seemed to have so much to offer that there wasn't time. There was such a lot to find out and I liked learning by personal investigation, as I have said. My short time abroad had given me a taste for travel which l had not been able to indulge. I wanted to go to France and I imagine I thought of war in a romantic way.

I joined a territorial battalion of the Worcesters in September 1914 and for the whole of that fine autumn was billeted in Worcester. We were a motley crew, without either rifles or khaki. After crowded duties at home, I found it hard to believe that it was necessary for pay parade to take up a whole afternoon, at the end of which we had each drawn a few shillings, but it was all part of an extraordinary new way of life, the reality of which was underlined by the fact that I was ordered about by a corporal who, a few weeks before, had been kitchen porter at the Lygon. He was an old regular soldier and I greatly admired the ease with which he accepted his new role and patiently explained to us the ways in which we were expected to cope with the most surprising and un-expected situations. On the whole, however, the army seemed too astonished to be able to deal with recruits who were actually anxious to learn the trade of soldiering as rapidly as they could.

About Christmas time we were sent down to Maldon in Essex as a draft to the 1/8th Worcesters. Khaki and rifles were issued at last and in wet weather, on heavy clay, we embarked on a series of field operations. We marched for miles and on cold wet days were kept standing about for what seemed hours. No one gave us a clue about what we were supposed to be doing and I discovered that if, after a mock battle round a hay-stack, I was captured by our cheerful enemies, the Warwicks (or, indeed, if I captured one or more of them), the prisoners were marched back, and at the singularly modest price of a few pints, spent the rest of the day before a good fire at the Blue Boar having at least acquired a useful knowledge of tactics if little of military strategy! The men, I remember, were greatly incensed at some of the army punishments, especially being tied to a cart-wheel—no doubt a modified survival of the horrible breaking on the wheel—and shortly it was abolished.

In March 1915 we were sent to France. On a brilliant moon-lit night we embarked for Boulogne, landing there in the early hours of the morning. Towards evening we were packed forty in a cattle truck and started a leisurely journey towards the line, arriving at the railhead about midnight. We then marched for several hours, ending up in a barn in time for breakfast. Our farmhouse was substantially built of brick and had a large dog wheel, roofed over, for drawing water from a well. I noticed that the powerful dogs drew little carts as well. There were ditches but no hedges and every inch of the ground was admirably cultivated. There were few signs of war, apart from the men and equipment of our army and notices chalked up in English. From here, Terdeghem, we marched towards the line. Occasionally we saw a tree scarred with shell splinters, or roof tiles broken by shrapnel, but no extensive damage was visible at first. Suddenly, however, I noticed that the garden bed in front of a small house was planted with a wooden cross on a mound and a café had its front blown out, the explosion having thrown one of the bentwood chairs up to the ceiling and forced its top rail through the plaster. Nothing recorded in *Alice in Wonderland* seemed strange any more!

As we neared the war zone we noticed far more damage but people were still living in parts of ruined houses. The immense waste of army rations was also noticeable. Units stayed in such accommodation as was available for only a night or so and anything which could not be carried on had to be abandoned or destroyed—there seemed to be no system of salvaging. Even rifles and full boxes of ammunition were lying in the mud just behind the line, although there was a great shortage of both. In the village of Ploegsteert—Plug Street to every Tommy—there was much more damage and every house had a dugout of sorts. When the shelling, which was not heavy, stopped we were astonished to watch the children trooping eagerly out of the dugouts to search for souvenir splinters of shell, which were usually too hot to hold and were thrown from one hand to the other with squeals of delight.

After a day or so we learned that we were to go into front-line trenches for instruction by the 4th Division and then take over from them. At dusk we started to move up, each platoon having a guide. A rail across a road had a notice on it, 'In daylight Death beyond this point' and soon afterwards a fingerpost pointed to Shaftesbury Avenue. Signs of wreckage increased and unpleasant smells increased too. Greenish flares from Very pistols lit up the scene of desolation from time to time, often followed by a burst of machine gun fire or the

G

whistle and slap of bullets. I felt that we had cut ourselves off from normal life and entered a mad world. From a shattered *estaminet* which, surprisingly, was still carrying on business, a trench led off, not a deep one as in this flat country one soon came to water. The sides were built up with sandbags and there were duckboards in the bottom. With our heavy equipment we sweated in the cold night air as however slowly the first man walked the last one always seemed to be running. A bullet hit the tiles of a ruined building and as the fragments crashed to earth it seemed we must have been spotted, especially as the Very lights gave the impression that the enemy was all round us. The front line itself was primitive, with small dugouts built into the parapet and screened by ground sheets. Another man and myself were allotted one of these to sleep in and keep kit, and when I asked about a curious, wobbly place on the floor into which my hip fitted I was told it was 'some poor sod's belly!' Full of disbelief, I dug a few inches away to investigate and found it was true— buried in his greatcoat less than six inches underground.

We were told that in places the German line was only twenty yards away and that in daylight a lookout was kept by periscope: to put one's head up was very dangerous and many periscopes were hit by snipers. Soon I was standing on the firestep, with my carefully cleaned rifle resting on the parapet before me whilst I gazed intently in the reported direction of the German lines. I was told to keep absolutely still when a flare went up. I was able by degrees to piece together a picture of that bizarre country known as 'No Man's Land'. It was like the most fantastic rubbish dump one can imagine, with old cans, hats, boots and what not, stakes at all angles with shreds of barbed wire round them, shell holes full of water and so on. This had been a fertile countryside! Looking around, I found myself staring into the wide-open, unseeing eyes of a rain-washed face. Corpses were buried everywhere and they explained the sickly, tainted air. I was rather overcome by the horror and squalor of it all and not sorry to get out for the first few days' rest. The prospect of being in and out of the line for years was not a pleasant one, but one had to live for the day and take things as they came.

Almost at once we lost our Adjutant, a popular and efficient young officer. He was buried in Ploegsteert wood, just as night was falling. A great many men attended the funeral but the service was a short one because it was foolish to have large groups together in the open. The intermittent, sinister chattering of machine guns was punctuated by odd 'whizz-bangs' and 'crumps' and when for a moment there was a lull in this chorus one was aware of the gentlest sighing of the wind. In the misty drizzle the flare of Very lights made an odd, greenish pattern of flickering shadows through the mutilated trees and highlighted the silent, muffled forms of the men. The feeling of sorrow was overwhelming for not only was there genuine sympathy but his death brought home to unseasoned soldiers like ourselves that one of us would be the next. It was, I think, perhaps the most moving funeral I have ever attended.

From Ploegsteert we were sent to Loos, just after the battle had started, and then in August 1915 we marched down to Artois and took over from the French in a quiet sector which was to become one of the noisiest of the war—the Somme. We bivouacked in a wood of splendid beech trees, among the best I've ever seen. The weather was beautiful and we were able to enjoy it, as we were sent up the line to dig at night and had the day to ourselves.

I had been in the army about a year now and was beginning to feel quite an old hand. I remember asking my father for a copy of the plans of a small, old house at Snowshill, near Broadway, which he had bought. These I studied with great care as they gave me a valuable link with home. I practised visualizing them in three dimensions, which has never been too difficult to me, and I wrote detailed reports on different aspects of the planning and the carrying out of the repair work. When I look at the piddling little sawn stones that now pass for quoins I remember the urgent stipulation I sent home that quoins must be substantial and properly worked. It was duly noted.

In talking to many of the men I discovered that they regarded their civilian jobs as necessary ways of earning a living but otherwise not of any particular interest. Indeed, when they described them to me they often sounded rather dull, with one day so like another that football or cricket on Saturday afternoon was far and away the most important event of the week. Although all of us hoped the war would soon end I perhaps looked forward more keenly than most to returning to constructive work. The enforced change of job and scene was valuable to me by providing an opportunity to review what I had attempted up to date and think about further lines of development, which I might never have done if I had not left Broadway. All imaginative people must have quiet periods and, I think, solitude and whilst I didn't get much of the latter I was able to detach myself from my surroundings and consider what the position at home might be after the war. The disgusting waste of war in men, countryside, buildings and all the finer things of life made me determined to create something of value to help balance the senseless destruction.

The autumn rains had a disastrous effect on the deep trenches we had dug so carefully and we lived in a sea of mud, but I shall always remember the affection I felt for the trench as I set out on patrol. After a wet spell, parts of our trench system were flooded a foot or more deep and as I heard men ploughing through the water and cursing at the discomfort of it all I felt was 'Lucky devils! How I wish I were in that water!' I was to gain considerable experience of patrolling. One night later on, near Passchendaele, the patrol I was leading was shot at and the man next to me was hit. I imagined we were returning to our own line of shell holes but we might easily have strayed into the enemy's. The situation was saved by my indicating to those firing—in the most lurid and blasphemous English—exactly what I felt about them. Skilled cursing in one's own language is pretty sound evidence of nationality! The firing ceased as suddenly as it had begun and I was greatly relieved to hear a somewhat shaky voice say: 'Gorblimey, Bill, I'm buggered if it ain't our bleeding orficer!' I have seldom appreciated a welcome more. We had four days' duty in the line and four days out, when we were billeted in barns which were full of rats. None the less, we were thankful to be reasonably dry and to have a fire and a roof over our heads even if we weren't much warmer than in the line. Being rather thin, I felt the cold intensely. However, the winter ended at last and in the spring I was given leave.

I remember the excitement of seeing stone walls again, of discovering that hot water actually appeared when I turned a tap, of having a meal served on a table and of escaping from the disgusting mud, which has haunted me ever since, even to the extent of making me extremely unwilling to go through a farm gate in winter.

Back in France, it was obvious that something was going to happen on the Somme. Miles of railway line were laid, stacks as big as houses of ammunition and stores appeared and there was a general feeling of optimism that we should not have another ghastly winter in the line. We were told we should go straight through the German lines and about the middle of June a terrific bombardment started on miles of front. The battle which began on July 1st has been fully described and certainly anyone who saw it at close quarters will never forget it. Our division had a brigade each of Worcesters, Gloucesters and Warwicks, the last-mentioned being detailed to attack, with the other brigades in support. I saw later how they went over the top in exemplary formation, only to be cut down in swathes by enfilading machine guns. Not only would a bullet pass through one man and then hit another but a man who was hit might have half a dozen bullets through or in him before he reached the ground. We were in reserve when we were ordered to take over front-line trenches from a battalion in front which hadn't enough men left to hold them, and so we did. We found about thirty dazed and silent men—the survivors of 800. All around were the others, piled up four feet high in gaps in the wire and covering the ground everywhere in all sorts of sprawling attitudes. It was hot and the smell was indescribable—the whole Somme area stank for

miles. Two of my sentries were posted between two dead
sentries who, with arms folded on the parapet, had died as
they stood and remained more or less upright! Just in front
was a pair of legs, one foot minus its boot. The thin calls of the
wounded came to us in the night and we went out and found
some. We brought in alive one man who had been lying out for
thirteen days, but it was quite impossible to sort them all out
and searchers were fired on if seen. After a few days a division
which had been badly knocked about came to take over from
us after a rest and we were pulled out. Later, my battalion
suffered a good many casualties from gas shells although I myself escaped the worst effects thanks to my height and the fact
that I had been on my feet during most of the attack, keeping
the men together. We looked back on the previous winter as
one of comparative comfort. There was no organized front
line—just a string of shell holes half full of water—and when
we came out, our feet very painful from being in wet gumboots, we were put into bell-tents in a mud swamp.

In January 1917 I was asked again whether I wanted to take a
commission and although I knew I would miss my friends I
felt that I should be interested to see the war from the
officer's end as well as from that of a Private and Non-Commissioned Officer, for by this time I was a Company Quarter-
master Sergeant and also Sergeant instructor of bombing.
When I told my Company Sergeant Major of my decision he
spoke sadly of my 'reverting to the rank of Second Lieutenant'!
But my decision was made and I returned to England to take a
course at the training school for officers at Lichfield, from
which I was able to get home occasionally on an old BSA
motor bike. It seems that I had sorted out my ideas pretty
fully in France, as I find that I described myself in my officer's
record book as 'Designer of Furniture', an expression of hope
rather than a statement of fact!

A few months later I was back in France once again, sent to
join the 1st Worcesters in the Ypres sector. When we arrived
we marched through Ypres past the ruins of the splendid
Cloth Hall, which seemed to me a link with Gloucestershire

for in the middle ages much Cotswold wool found its way to Flanders. I have seen photographs of Ypres taken before 1914. It must have been a delightful mediaeval town, mostly built of thin brick and full of surprising little alleys and courtyards. Considerable lengths of the town wall had survived, surrounded by a moat. Such little towns were the very warp and weft of European civilization, built up by generations of men over the centuries, men who liked to live where they worked and so were proud of the place they lived in. Ypres was only one of many which were reduced to heaps of rubble by a military machine which seemed unaware that not only was it destroying things which architecturally were irreplaceable but a decent way of life too. One of the numerals on the great Gothic clock of the Cloth Hall, picked up in the gutter, finds a place on the distinguished war memorial at Westwell, near Burford, a sad reminder that it must once have been of service to many Cotswold wool merchants.

It took us about six hours of strenuous effort to cover the three or four miles to the front line and it was indeed a stout heart which did not feel chilled by the immensity of the devastation. As far as the eye could see was a flat expanse of country which contained no single tree or building unshelled. No tree stump was higher than perhaps ten feet, though few trees or buildings can have been as much. The grotesque shapes of the shelled and splintered trees were to me most harrowing. Some primeval instinct makes it possible for me to understand the worshipping of splendid trees and great monoliths. There was not a blade of grass to be seen, for almost everywhere great and small shell holes seemed to touch one another and where they were slightly further apart the top soil had been covered with the soil from other shell-holes. All, including the sky, was a dead, leaden, murky colour as if the imbecile behaviour of man had left nature herself both dejected and forbidding. A narrow corduroy-track was our road and at junctions it was shelled at regular intervals and often hit. Then one had to make a detour, up to one's knees, and sometimes waist, in mud, which made progress slow at the points where speed meant safety. It was a superhuman job to get the wounded back and those killed on the track were simply pushed to one side. In many places it was not possible to see the track at all as it was covered with earth and mud thrown up by continuous shelling. Occasionally an effort had been made to indicate its site by wide white tape, but of course this did not stay white for long and was frequently broken. At one corner it was hitched round the neck of a dead German. The mud was like Dickens' London fog—it was everywhere. We walked and slept in it, it covered our hands, our rifles, our clothes and even our food. It got in our hair and eyes. Messages were written with muddy pens on mud-stained paper. It sucked at one's gumboots like an octopus and prevented rapid movement when that was highly desirable. If one stumbled into a shell hole, which of course could not be detected, it surged over the top of the boots and made one's feet cold, clammy, wretched and filthy. If the shell hole was a large one it was the easiest thing in the world to be drowned in mud, for the sides were far too slimy for a man with heavy equipment to be able to get out unless a friendly rifle was handed to him from outside. We lost several men in this way. And the dead were buried in mud.

We spent the autumn and winter of 1917–18 in and out of the line there, in indescribable weather—snow, sleet and bitter rain and wind. The Passchendaele ridge was as bad as anything on the Somme and in addition to casualties we lost a number of men through illness, because so many of the drafts then coming out were not sufficiently fit to stand up to the conditions. Before dawn on February 13th, after some shelling, one of my posts was rushed by a storming party and I organized a counter-attack. The official statement says laconically: 'Casualties 1 killed, 3 wounded, 3 missing. 2 Lt. Russell, who was in charge of the Company, was awarded the Military Cross.' Just after this episode I was ordered by my CO to form and take charge of a battle platoon. This was to be trained as a raiding party and I was told I could pick any men I wanted from any of the companies. I got together a pretty good bunch of rum-drinking, coke-stealing pirates and the Boche looked as if he was in for trouble, which he avoided by taking the initiative in a big way.

We were in reserve, some way back from the line, when the great final German attack started on March 21, 1918. They threw in everything they had and when we were rushed up to the Somme Canal on March 22nd they had broken through on a wide front. Trench warfare had given way to open fighting and when the next morning a scrap started in a churchyard I was shot through the left arm at twenty yards range. I spun round as if I had been kicked by an elephant. At such close range, a bullet makes a nasty hole where it comes out but fortunately the bone was not smashed. My equipment was cut off but the field dressing did not stop the loss of blood so I was sent to the dressing station, where I was treated and then sent to await a train. The disorganization was so great that I spent forty-two hours in a civilian train with a bottle of Burgundy but no food. When I got to the Base the arm was badly swollen and it was indicated that I should be lucky if I kept it, so I was packed off to England forthwith and after some weeks in hospital spent the summer in a convalescent camp at Eastbourne. Here massage and electrical treatment helped to restore strength to the muscles of the arm and as time went on I was able to play tennis most afternoons with Charles Mellersh, a friend I had first met on a bombing course in France, who was now recovering from a nasty wound in the back. We also explored by bicycle the downland country which my father knew so well. But often I went by myself on random excursions: to Lewes, where the main street had some lovely shop fronts and where the White Hart carried on manfully; to Hurstmonceux, where I spent an exquisite afternoon making a drawing of the Castle, and to stay with a dear friend of my father's, Harry Jones, at his house at May-field. It was still beautifully kept up, with a small lake which had been an immense attraction to me as a boy because it had a boat on it. After an evening meal, for which he had managed to get a fine piece of salmon, we sat on the veranda smoking cigars and listening to the nightingales, which were singing lustily against the background rumblings of the guns in France. I felt blissfully at ease but also slightly guilty as I realized that I had no desire to go back to that other world. Why couldn't the guns leave the evening to the nightingales?

When the Armistice was announced on November 11th a few of us decided to go to London and after dining at the United Universities Club we witnessed the frenzied reaction to the pent-up feelings of these awful years. That the whole affair was not a nightmare was proved by my Record Book, in which my Commanding Officer, Lt-Col F. C. Roberts, had written: 'Lt Russell is a capable and fearless officer, with great influence among men.' As Roberts had been awarded the DSO when a Subaltern, which was most unusual, then the MC and finally the VC the night before I was hit, I was naturally proud of his good opinion.

What had I got to show for four and a half years of unpleasant exertion? I think my health, which had always been good, actually improved through the much greater time spent in the open and I could not help feeling I had indeed been lucky in this—and indeed to survive at all when so many of my generation would not return. But the most important result was the stocktaking I have mentioned leading to my decision to do at least something constructive when I returned to civilian life. One of the things which greatly affected this was my horror of senseless destruction and waste. I found, too, that I had achieved an enhanced status at home and this, and the fact that I had learned not only to take command of men but to understand the ordinary man's point of view as I could not have done had I remained at Broadway or if I had not had a long period in the ranks, gave me confidence to tackle a job in a different way. I had spent much time pondering what my future plans might be and had come to see that if one can state one's problem clearly it is already half solved. I also realized that it is seldom that an objective can be reached at one bound: it must be taken in stages and at each stage it is essential to consolidate thoroughly and quickly before the inevitable counter-attack can be launched. This had been made painfully clear on the Somme, where a handful of men with Lewis guns detailed to guard the captured German front-line trenches whilst other units pushed forward could have dealt with the hundreds of the enemy coming up one at a time from the deep dugouts to cut off our forces in the rear. Neglect of this precaution cost us many thousands of casualties. This lesson was of immense importance to me later on in civilian life and it is one which has not yet been fully absorbed by many designers.

Again, in the army I had begun to realize the extraordinary importance of morale: I had seen the ridiculous optimism of 1914—'Berlin by Christmas'—turn to a mood of dogged determination to cope with a very tough job indeed. But the frightful slaughter of the Somme stripped the last vestige of romance from war and men began to wonder whether the General Staff knew what they were about. Was it possible that trenches which were heavily defended in depth by tough troops could be broken by frontal attack? No doubt a lot of the criticism could have been answered but unfortunately there was a lack of communication between the staff and the men in the ranks and our civilian army was no longer prepared to accept the Establishment at its own valuation. I could not help wondering whether much of the friction one read about in industry was not due to a similar situation and I resolved to see if anything could be done, for it was obvious that the men who returned would not be prepared to put up with the inequalities which were apparent before 1914.

On the other hand, the army taught me a great deal about the delegation of responsibility and the *esprit de corps* of a well organized unit. The County Regiments seemed to me pretty good at building up pride in serving in them—and the counties, too, were proud of them—but it was much more difficult to get the same affection for the larger units, the brigades, divisions and army corps. One sees a parallel case in the business world today. Then in the army there are thousands of routine jobs, each reduced to simple terms, clearly explained, and understood by everyone. I, who had never coped with routine work, was impressed by this and began to wonder how far some of our jobs at Broadway could be formulated in such terms and much blood and sweat saved by delegating. But I observed that many 'old sweats' felt there was an answer for everything in King's Regulations and this spared them the trouble of thinking. In the army any signs of imagination were then frowned on. Nevertheless, here again I learned an important lesson—the value of a chain of command which was carefully worked out, with the responsibilities of each officer, warrant officer and non-commissioned officer defined and appreciated. If all of these became casualties the senior private soldier had no doubt that it was his job to carry on. Devotion to the work in hand was paramount. And this spirit was not achieved by giving great financial rewards or unusually comfortable conditions. I came to the conclusion that there were lessons to be learned in the army which could be applied in civilian life—and vice versa.

PART II

A Fresh Start
1919–1940

CHAPTER 9

Making Furniture by Hand

Demobilization—the magic word we had all been waiting for! Early in January 1919 I was told to report somewhere on Salisbury Plain. I wasn't kept waiting there long and was given a warrant to Broadway, but I went to sleep in the train and found myself at Newport (Mon.), in the early hours of the next morning. However, I arrived at Broadway before midday, dirty and perhaps, if the truth were known, slightly apprehensive for I wasn't at all the same person who had left Broadway four and a half years before. My links with the job in that previous existence seemed tenuous and shaky and as I had come to accept a way of life utterly beyond the comprehension of anyone at home I wasn't sure how I could set about re-establishing them. My parents had always shown me great consideration but since I had been in khaki the relationship had changed in a subtle way, as if the difference in age had been bridged. In spite of overwhelming evidence of its improbability, I had never doubted that I should come back, but I couldn't help feeling that it was odd when it really happened. More than a million of my generation, among them most of my school friends and men I had lived with, would remain in the fields of France. There was hardly a family we knew which had not lost someone. I was lonely and uprooted a second time. I found civilians sympathetic, even respectful, but I couldn't explain my vague uneasiness, which may have been partly a kind of delayed shock. I was rather uncertain as to how long it would take me to pick up the threads of any civilian job again, after a lapse of what seemed an age on another planet.

Probably I stayed at my father's home at Snowshill. I know I spent the next day at Broadway and paid a round of visits, including one to the repair shop. Jim Turner was still there, plodding on steadily as ever, but he seemed older—as indeed he was. He gave me the feeling that he was pleased to see me back, although it needed a practised eye to disentangle the trace of emotion behind his gruff greeting. But to me the mere fact that he was still there was infinitely reassuring and I felt grateful to him for existing, a solitary landmark in a chartless sea! His only assistant was his youngest son, Sid, then about fourteen, whom I had vaguely heard about as an infant in my previous incarnation. At lunch time I came across another old friend which raised my morale: a fine Sheffield-plated tankard—always known before the war as 'Mr Gordon's tankard'—had been disinterred by a kindly well-wisher from some safe lurking place. She must have remembered how much I had always loved bread, cheese and beer. But the Lygon had then a goodly store of tankards, both plated and pewter—proper tankards for those who care what they drink from, for tankards, like women, should not have thin lips. The following day I chose a quiet empty room in the wing my parents had occupied before moving to Snowshill. It was cold but I was used to that. I hadn't a clear idea of what work I should do in it, but I wandered round, a bit like Crusoe, collecting various things which might turn out useful: a drawing board, a table, a chair and so on. That the drawing board which I had used before the war for my writing was the first thing I searched for was a portent. I remember sitting on the chair and wondering what on earth I was going to do next. It was all most perplexing. I had had no real training for any particular job except soldiering and I was nearly twenty-seven. Looking back now over a number of widely different jobs at which I have tried my hand soldiering remains the only one for which I have had formal training.

I had had no statement of policy from my father, who seemed relieved and pleased to have me back, but suggested that I should take things easy for a bit although he himself was in a highly nervous condition and had been overdoing war-work for some time. Lately, he had been acting as a kind of temporary locum in Snowshill to Dr Alexander of Broadway—during the influenza epidemic in which whole families were incapacitated. Alexander had a sound theory that a glass of port was the best preventive so they solemnly had a glass together before going on their rounds. A lady in Broadway said to the doctor: 'I hear you've discovered a wonderful gargle against influenza.' 'Yes,' he said, 'Dow's 1900, but I rather think you might be more likely to get it at the Lygon than at Foss's' (the chemist's). Anyway, things seemed in somewhat of a state of suspended animation at home.

However, a few days later a telegram arrived from Don, saying that he was to be demobilized and was coming back almost at once. He was a 2nd Lieutenant in the 3rd Worcesters and had been wounded in August 1918, fortunately not seriously, when advancing near the village of Locon in the Lys Valley. I was mightily pleased to see him. The next day, over a glass of port at eleven, my father said that if we would like to join him he would take us in as partners, altering the name from S. B. Russell to Russell & Sons. The partnership would consist of my father, my mother, Don and myself—Dick being still at school in Cheltenham. He felt that Don was more especially interested in the running of the Lygon and I had always shown aptitude for the business in antiques, but there was to be no very clear line of division: Don, who had a sound knowledge of antiques, would buy any he happened to see which were suitable and I would be responsible for building and repair work at the Lygon. Here, at any rate, was an outline plan and I think it was a stroke of genius on my father's part to put the idea forward at once. Certainly I found any chart of this strange, new world most helpful and I think Don did too.

My father had been brought up in Victorian England, which was permeated with a feeling of security and superiority utterly incomprehensible to us today. It was perhaps inevitable that, like most of his generation, he was somewhat disturbed by the fact that the war had been on such a different scale from nineteenth-century skirmishes. But having won it, as he had no doubt whatever we should, he naturally assumed that the country would take up once more a way of living which had become almost a fixed law of nature. My brother and I, thrown into such very different surroundings for a considerable period, sensed that a fundamental change had occurred and that there could be no going back. I am sure, however, that none of us fully realized that the pre-1914 age was already almost as remote as the days before Waterloo. It was clear, too, that in a business which depended on selling a service to the public there were bound to be differences of opinion as to what the public would be likely to want and how we could best supply it.

First of all we tried to define what we meant by 'the public'. To the Guvnor it meant that section of the public which was well-educated, had an ample income, was used to good service, dressed for dinner each night and often had wide interests. For them he had attempted to base the running of the Lygon on a country house, but Don and myself had become used to judging men as men in a much starker way, and by that standard we found that no class or group could claim superiority. The bar had been closed during the war owing to shortage of labour and my father was not anxious to re-open it, but we argued that a country inn should aim to give a service to all well behaved travellers, even those who had only travelled a hundred yards! We knew, too, that many visitors would like to meet local people there.

As was only to be expected, the war had caught us with much work half finished and when it ended we were no longer quite so certain that all our development was on the right lines. For instance, the lock-up garages demanded when a marvellous car was entirely in the care of a skilled and trusted chauffeur were of less importance when the owner drove his own car and was not interested in spending half the day cleaning it. On the other hand, there was a great increase in cars hired for short periods, mainly by Americans, and my father quickly sensed the importance of seeing that the drivers, who had had a long and tiring day, were given a comfortable, if small, room with running water, that there were bathrooms near and that good food was available in pleasant quarters. Anyone who drove a hired car in the early 1920s will corroborate that this attitude was unusual. Before the war my father had built some quite good quarters for his own staff. After it, we tore up the plans for further lock-up garages and built a large garage with chauffeur's quarters over—a plan which was possible because a site had been acquired before the war.

We also went ahead with a new and much larger powerhouse, as we were unable to get any positive information as to when electric supply would reach Broadway and our pre-war plant was hopelessly overloaded. Only those who have run an hotel will realize the full implications of a breakdown in electricity, water or gas. When my father took over the Lygon there was a small and thoroughly inefficient gasworks in Broadway. It was by no means unusual for a man to be sent round in the evening to warn everyone that gas would be cut off at nine. Every dry year water ran short owing to lack of storage and had to be rationed, but as a result of my father's persistent efforts, the local council built a smaller tank for emergency use—still referred to by old inhabitants as 'Mr Russell's little tank'. The introduction of central heating immediately after 1918 was not at all easy in a house like the Lygon with so many different levels but, efficiency apart, it was no longer practicable to have coal taken up several flights of stairs to bedrooms. The fire risk, too, was considerable in rooms which were unoccupied between dinner and bedtime.

The addition of bathrooms and lavatories also created problems but went on steadily. Our partnership meetings were not occasions we looked forward to, and I remember a particular one just after 1930, when things generally looked a bit gloomy, at which we were discussing the installation of lavatory basins in the old bedrooms. Don was well aware of the difficulties and mess that would be caused but he felt it was an

essential thing to do. I agreed with him and thought the partnership was fortunate to have someone who was prepared to
see the operation through. My father pointed out how short
of money we were—not for the first time—but Don and I felt
that if we waited for a favourable time it would then be too
late, because rooms which were now fairly often empty would
no longer be available or, if available, it would be because they
were not lettable without running water. So we held our
ground and at last the Guvnor got up and went out. 'What do
we do now?' said Don. 'Go ahead,' I suggested, 'I'm sure it's
the right thing to do.' Anyway, it was on the strength of this
or some similar skirmish that Don went off and bought a horse!
The pleasure he got from riding and hunting was good to see.
It took him away from business cares, brought him many
friends and gave him an entirely new slant on life. I don't think
my father was ever quite fair to Don. There are times in life
when it is important to have a blind eye but the Guvnor had the
habit, when several things had already gone wrong in a morning, of pointing out one more and Don couldn't take it. Later
on he could see there was an amusing side to it, for basically
he likes to look at life in a whimsical way, and he used to come
and tell me about it with much picturesque detail.

Don had been impressed by the way the army took trouble
to train recruits, in the same way that many trades took
apprentices. But the hotel trade was so scattered and its units
often so small that there was as a rule little organized training.
Don argued that friendly recognition of the customer, study
of his or her wishes and an obvious desire to carry them out
efficiently were the very life-blood of an inn. However, they
were not always easy to achieve. One night there was a fire in a
builder's yard in the village, causing quite a commotion, and
an American lady tackled Don the next morning saying that
she had specified a quiet room when she booked weeks before
but had been put in a room facing a fire! Notwithstanding such
accidents, efficient and friendly service should be the aim, but
Don recognised that it could not be achieved without training
and enthusiasm. Here he had the Guvnor's support for he had

always wanted to provide decent working conditions and realized that without these a high standard of service could not be expected. For example, he had noticed how much wait-resses suffered from tired feet and had paid for regular visits to a chiropodist. Whilst Don was fully alive to the value of a fine building with fine things in it he felt it was not by any means enough, and his interest in staff training has had wide repercus-sions in the hotel trade, as I shall explain later. My father was never a reactionary, he liked experiments and was willing to listen to arguments, and when something that he disagreed with had been put in hand and was seen to have been right, his praise was usually generous. A working compromise was reached and I have no doubt at all that the new approach which Don established was of great and lasting value to our business.

On my side of the partnership I also had some ideas of my own, about furniture design, and had decided in the army that I wanted to experiment in getting some pieces made at Broadway. To deal in things didn't seem a real job to me. I felt very strongly that my generation, which had destroyed so much lovely work, had a constructive duty to perform; some-how or other we had to hand on to those coming after us good things of our own creation. I was aware that a venture of this sort, in which we would learn as we went along, would cost money, but there was money about and there was a great pent-up demand for goods of all kinds. My working knowledge of old furniture gave me a respect for tradition, which I believe to be most important if one wants to try to see today's work in perspective. To me it was a poor age which could make no con-tribution of its own. I argued that if the eighteenth century had been content to imitate the seventeenth, then the finest age of English cabinet making would never have been born. Further, it was my great love for old things which made me wish to design new ones: I had far too much respect for the past not to be revolted by the regurgitations I saw on all sides. I had no qualifications beyond a burning belief that my own age might recover its self-respect, a sound knowledge of old furniture and construction and an interest in the possibilities of the machine, and—by no means least—an indulgent family who were willing to back with hard cash an idea in which they believed.

Obviously the first thing to do was to get our business in antiques on its feet again, for this might provide the capital for my projected experiments. With considerable energy, I therefore started to organize the repair of such old pieces of furniture as we had in stock—and we had a great many, several sheds full, in fact, bought before the war. One or two men, including Jim Turner's sons Edgar and Clarence, gradually came back, but it was impossible to repair things quickly enough; no sooner was anything put on show than it was sold. It was a hectic life, with no time to think much about making new things, and it seemed odd that but a few months before I had been wondering how to employ myself. I was buyer, manager, salesman, packer, book-keeper, transport man, workshop manager—all, of course, on a diminutive scale. In some ways it was a job that suited me for I would never have been able to carry on, day in day out, doing one thing. And from time to time I was able to do a little drawing as ideas were gradually crystallizing in my mind.

About this time we bought an old farmhouse about a hundred yards from the Lygon (see plate 10), with a great barn at the back. We repaired the house for use as showrooms, Miss Bailey was installed as housekeeper, and Ben Knight, one time barman at the Lygon, as general factotum. Ben came of a family of sixteen, one of the results being an anti-social complex. He always wore a little black beret and for some unexplained reason found it more convenient to cut six inches off the sleeves of his shirts, possibly so as not to have dirty cuffs. Many barmen have a firmly rooted idea that visiting pals in other bars is a good way of spending off-time but Ben never went into a bar. His beard, his steel-rimmed glasses and his beret gave him a somewhat prim air and he had that rare quality—all but destroyed by the press and the cinema—a sense of the beauty of words. He spoke slowly, and chose his speech carefully. I never remember seeing him reading anything other than the Bible, Shakespeare or Milton. These characteristics were so impressive yet so natural to him that the other men always referred to him as Mr Knight.

Ben was joined later in 1919 by a man of an entirely different type, Herbert Dolby, who had been with my aunt in Buenos Aires and whose brother had just come to the Lygon yard as head mechanic. Herbert was small, hard-bitten, with a pretty sense of humour. He seemed to have wandered all over the world and done most things: there wasn't a job he was not prepared to tackle. He had come to the right place! He looked after a building squad, opened up a quarry, drove a rickety four-ton army lorry, got an ancient steam engine going and, by wiring down the safety valve, managed to cut quite a lot of firewood! He was quite imperturbable and taking risks was meat and drink to him. I was told by a friend who was sitting at the foot of Campden Hole, a very steep and short hill, that he heard a shattering explosion at the top and our old BSA with sidecar came hurtling down, driven by Herbert. He failed to take the corner at the bottom and shot up the bank into a bush, but he got up, put the conveyance back on the road and came over to my friend. 'Funny thing,' he said, 'that's the second time I've done that just there. Must look at the brakes.' Without another word but with a charming goodbye smile he drove straight down Broadway Hill home, relying on his boots to slow him up.

One day I was discussing with him the price to be charged to the Guvnor for a small lot of stone slates sent to Snowshill for repairs. At length I suggested ten shillings to close the matter. 'What,' said Herbert, 'ten shillings! Why there must have been at least a hundred, and only t'other day the Guvnor pointed out to me two that should have been on the heap. "Herbert," he says, "these're worth sixpence each, so take care of 'em." Why, I shouldn't be surprised if the thousands that Henry Ford has just bought from Eyford quarry and had shipped to Detroit in barrels for Edsel's house won't cost half-a-crown each, time they're fixed. Struth! Ten shillings. Oh no, you can't do that, Mr Gordon. The old man'll think you've gone off your onion!'

At about this time my youngest brother Dick left school and it was decided that he should start on my side of the business. From the first he took the greatest interest in the making of new furniture but he carried on first with small jobs in the office and then with other work, much as I had done.

In 1920 my father decided that I needed more help so we advertised, on our famous 'engineer—lace maker—draughts-man—jam bottler' principles. One of the replies was from a young woman who said she was very interested in the adver-tisement because it seemed an unusual job. She explained that she was trained in secretarial work and was the daughter of an Irish doctor. Poor wretch! She little dreamed of the depths of unusualness to which the job might sink. She was young, attractive, intelligent and quite unmoved by conventional snob advertising. She really appreciated an odd job and did not blush if her friends saw her riding on a lorry with a queer assortment of goods—our old Sunbeam which had had a lorry body put on it during the war. She wanted to get out of London for she liked living in the country, and it was obvious from the first that Toni Denning was an essential part of this fas-cinating jig-saw puzzle. Even the coincidence that she came down to see us in Broadway on my birthday and started work on hers seemed to confirm it!

So the delicious summer of 1920 slipped by with a good deal of work and then walks or jaunts in the side-car or the lorry or the old Scout two-seater which I had collected from their works in Salisbury in 1912. Thoughts of the Somme, Passchendaele or Ypres faded and Toni, Dick and I talked often of the days when we might be able to start making things in earnest. We were already making a few stools and other small things which were solid if somewhat rough. Some of them, I remember, had up-holstered tops which I covered in leather just as, before the war, I had covered Cromwellian chairs. A man who had just bought a house near Snowshill asked my father to do some

With my brother Don, 1917

My wife, Toni

7   Bedroom furniture of oak with laburnum handles, of which the octagonal pillars are an interesting constructional feature, 1920

Post-1919 development of furniture-making at Broadway
Designer: Gordon Russell

Walnut cabinet inlaid with ebony, box, yew and laburnum, in the manner of Ernest Gimson, awarded Gold Medal at the Paris Exhibition, 1925

Cupboard with flush doors veneered fiddle-back mahogany with handles of brass and ebony, 1925

8 A bookcase with narrow doors of stainless steel and engraved plate glass, enabling all titles to be read easily, 1928

Experimental dining room for series production, 1929

Designer: Gordon Russell

The first cabinet (1929) and a later one (1936) for Murphy Radio Ltd

Designer: R. D. Russell

9   Early unit furniture in English oak, 1934. Designer: R. D. Russell

Living room in the British Pavilion, Paris Exhibition, 1937. Designer: W. H. Russell

fitted furniture for him and I was delighted about this as I felt I could cope with joinery for an old house.

In November Toni and I became engaged and after a cheery Christmas party she went off to a domestic economy school. Then my efforts as a furniture designer were carried a stage further by an attempt to produce a fitting double bed! This worthy object was the recipient of much solicitude, both on my part and on that of Edgar Turner, who was charged with the duty of making it. At one time the horrid possibility that it might not be finished in time was envisaged, but Edgar, who was about to be married himself and for whom I had had an affectionate regard since I had known him as a boy and later we had gone to France together, was obviously the right man for the job. I was also doing some work to put Spencer Cottage, next to the Lygon, in order as a temporary home. We were married on August 8, 1921, one of the luckiest dates in my calendar. As Don had been married about six weeks earlier everything seemed to be in the melting pot that summer.

I was stimulated rather than dashed by this exercise in design. I made drawings of a chest of drawers, a dressing table and a sideboard. It is significant, I think, that it never occurred to me to design a bedroom or dining-room 'suite': I had been brought up on old furniture and I thought in terms of in-dividual pieces, knowing nothing at all of the customs of the furniture trade. The men in the workshop were really joiners, used to repairing seventeenth-century oak furniture—solid, honestly-made pieces with none of the cabinet maker's deli-cate skill which developed in the eighteenth century. There was no doubt that the idea of making things interested them, but they had little idea of how to set about such a job or of how long the work ought to take. They were not cabinet makers, and Broadway was not a cabinet making centre. Our problem began to take shape. What sort of things should be designed? Should we attempt to train or import cabinet makers? It seemed unlikely that this new development could take place in the same workshop as that repairing old furniture, and housing would present a problem if we imported men. We should have to learn to buy timber in quite a different way and it would mean tying up a great deal of money in stocks while seasoning. How should we sell the resulting products, as the furnishing trade was quite separate from the antique trade? These were tough problems and as we looked at the evidence which the furniture trade provided and as we talked to its members it was obvious that they felt they had convincing proof that we should be attempting to make something for which there was absolutely no demand whatever. Contemporary furniture indeed!

When the first few pieces were made, including the necessary hinges, handles, lock-plates and so on, which were produced by an outside smith, my father photographed them. One of the most charming memories of this birth of furniture making in Broadway is the touching belief in, and genuine liking for, the new designs on the part of my father. He had seen some of C. R. Ashbee's work at Chipping Campden and had been to Ernest Gimson's workshop at Sapperton before 1914, and perhaps one or two other shops of a like nature, but apart from any knowledge obtained in these fleeting excursions he had none of modern furniture design, any more than I had. On the other hand, he had a good eye for an old piece of furniture, he liked a good job and he loved seeing things made—any things, horseshoes, drinking glasses, wagons, trugs, hedgers' gloves, cloth, ladders, thermometers—and when he gave encouragement he gave it wholeheartedly. Mother also liked the pieces—more, I suspected, because I had been responsible for them than for any other reason. Don wasn't quite so certain but was most anxious to be helpful. He felt there would be difficulty in selling high-priced, modern things, as well he might! After all, almost everyone bought antiques if they could afford them, reproductions if they could not. What else was there or could there be? And, looking at the furniture trade at that time, one could not help wondering. He did not share this point of view, but there was no denying that it was the normal one; and he proved to be right, for it was difficult to sell them, and it was still more difficult not to lose money doing so in the early stages. We had to educate our public, and that's a long job, but we were fortunate in that the Lygon brought well-to-do people to our doors and we were able to explain what we were trying to do. If our venture was to be successful I realized I would have to spend a great deal of time explaining my ideas, by writing articles and talking to groups when asked to do so, or even taking the initiative—aggressive advertising as the Americans have it! In 1923 I wrote a pamphlet called *Honesty and the Crafts* and several articles, but talking to an audience was a new experience. Here again my army training was useful, for drilling a platoon had proved a fine antidote for shyness. Toni and Dick believed in the experiment with deep-seated fervour and I too possessed great enthusiasm without sufficient experience to see all possible snags, a powerful combination.

In this frame of mind, and from this strange and unlikely background, I set out for London armed with the photographs. I went to see John Gloag, the architectural historian, who was then assistant editor of *The Cabinet Maker* and whose name was familiar to me through the Design and Industries Association. I had come across this body only recently and I cannot say how much I owe to its early members, men like Harold Stabler, Crofton Gane, Ben Fletcher, Frank Pick, Charles Holden, Ambrose Heal, Noel Carrington, Harry Peach, Hamilton Smith, Herbert Simon, Harold Curwen, Alfred Read and Leslie Mansfield, all of whom were willing to share their experience with a greenhorn. Gloag was a keen protagonist of better design. He was interested in the photographs and asked if he might print them. The interview started a friendship which has grown with the years. Then I saw Percy Wells, head of the cabinet making section of the LCC Shoreditch Technical Institute, whom I had met before the war when he was walking in the Cotswolds. He was charming to me and from that time on for many years his great practical experience was always freely available to us and his interest never flagged. He offered to come down and discuss the whole problem on the spot, an offer which I accepted gladly. We came to the conclusion, as we sat in a Lyons' teashop somewhere off Old Street in the City, that it would be necessary to repair antiques in one shop and make furniture in another, which would enable us to get or train a good cabinet-making foreman and to raise the whole standard of finish to somewhere near that of the best hand shops. As a family we mostly choose the difficult way of tackling a problem, so we decided to offer to train Edgar Turner instead of importing a ready-trained man. Edgar was rooted in the shop and had its interests much at heart. Moreover, as his army record—Military Medal and Bar—proved, he was good at handling men. He jumped at the chance and Wells fixed him up in a 'small master's' shop in Shoreditch.

In 1922 we were invited to send some exhibits to a small show in the Art Gallery at Cheltenham, arranged by its able and hardworking director, W. H. Herdman, who had visited our showroom. This was our first exhibition, and it was a fortunate one for Major A. A. Longden of the Department of Overseas Trade went to it, then came to Broadway and asked us to exhibit in 1923 at a show he was preparing in the North Court of the Victoria and Albert Museum in London. We did a café, which caused much fluttering in the dovecotes. It wasn't a bad little job, though a bit rustic and unfinished, and we learned a great deal from it. My father and I got quite a lot of amusement from going up to help arrange it; and it was responsible later on for an order for panelling and furnishing a complete room in Rochdale, including carpets, curtains, electric fittings and so on, which made our organization creak in the joints! In the exhibition there were only two furnished cubicles—one by Heal's and ours, which seemed to me a curious blend of an old-established firm with a great reputation and pretty green newcomers. The friendly intercourse between Heal's and ourselves which started there has persisted. Sir Ambrose Heal often came to see us. Hamilton Smith and Harry Trethowan, two of their directors, came down and talked to our staff and I talked to theirs. A few years later Anthony Heal came to us as a pupil. Like many young men, he was passionately interested in motor cars and bicycles. His masterpiece was a chest of drawers, finished with great care and deliberation, but by a mischance it was put overnight in a damp shed. In the morning the storeman asked him to come and look at it as the drawers, being well fitted, had swelled and stuck. Coming back to the shop after the examination he announced in despair that it had 'seized solid'!

We were beginning to produce cabinet-work of high quality and our status as furniture makers was confirmed by an invitation to send some exhibits to the Palace of Arts at the British Empire Exhibition at Wembley the next year, 1924. Our principal exhibit there, a walnut cabinet on an ebony base, was made by Edgar Turner whilst he was at Shoreditch. Lord Dunsany bought it at the exhibition for £200 and in doing so gave us most powerful help at a critical juncture—not that we made any profit out of it, for we cut up half a ton of ebony to make the base, but his gesture proved that there were people who would pay prices for good modern work which compared with those paid for antiques. This greatly impressed my family, in addition to getting us a good deal of useful publicity outside. My ambition was to produce furniture of the highest possible standard of workmanship in which the best material would speak for itself, so that in my designs I tried to make the most of these qualities. But it was not easy to achieve these aims. Few cabinet-makers from outside were used to such accurate work and if we trained local boys it was bound to be several years before their standards were really high, and then they were inclined to think that the time taken to produce things was of no importance. I made a practice of going round each bench in the shop with the foreman every morning, in the same way that my uncle had carried out an inspection in his ship every day. I had often accompanied him and had noticed both how his gimlet eye spotted any irregularities and the electric effect this inspection had on members of the crew. In the army I had hoped that my daily inspection of my platoon also had these galvanizing qualities!

My experience had taught me the importance of keeping the men in the ranks informed about the work in hand and there is no doubt that the improving standard of our shop was partly due to the evening classes in cabinet-work which I started. These proved popular and were attended by staff from the showroom and office as well as the workshops. Not only did these men and boys gain valuable experience of what was involved in furniture making but the classes did much to break down the white-collar mentality. As an extension of this scheme I managed to persuade all kinds of people to come down and stay with us, giving a talk while at Broadway. This happened every two or three weeks in the winter, and I know that most of those who attended these classes will remember them all their lives. Indeed, several of the young men became teachers themselves and later held responsible posts at such Colleges of Art as Birmingham, Loughborough and Derby. They were entirely informal, a cheerful and friendly atmosphere was noticeable and questions were asked. Often my father or Harry Dolby would work the lantern, and as a rule the comparatively small room in which they were held would be full. I remember George Hart talking on silversmithing, John Adams on pottery, Harry Trethowan on display, Paul Woodroffe on stained glass, Hamilton Smith and Percy Wells on cabinet-making, my father on tombstones and old houses in Sussex, Harold Stabler on metal-working, and I myself acted as stop-gap whenever our programme broke down. One of our scoops was C. F. A. Voysey, then over seventy but very lively if somewhat wan. He talked to us on architecture and said that even then he was building, but only one house: 'It's a house for a lunatic,' he said, 'such a nice man and his doctor thought he might take an interest in the building of it. But I find it difficult. None of my friends can tell me how to deal with a client who, when the contract should be signed, gets under the table and refuses to come out!' These gatherings led to amateur theatricals, in which I generally seemed to be cast for the part of down-at-heel waiter or distressed damsel, and I must say we got a lot of fun out of them. A. V. Freeman and Ted Darley, with their wives, were prime movers in these. I don't know whether the audience got as much enjoyment as we did, but there were always demands for another show so perhaps they did. Anyway, even if we did it badly we did it ourselves instead of just paying to be entertained. Then there were the works outings in the summer, run by a committee whose one ambition, it seemed, was to go further than they went in the previous year!

From the British Empire Exhibition at Wembley it was not a difficult step to the British Pavilion of the Paris Exhibition of 1925, where we were awarded a Gold and two Silver Medals. The cabinet we sent there (see plate 7) took William Marks, a superb craftsman, three or four months to make. It is still in Broadway in a small historical section we have got together in the showrooms which are now open to the public several times a week. I suppose the fortuitous launching of our enterprise by a well-marked sequence of exhibitions—1922, 1923, 1924, 1925—must have made us 'exhibition-minded'. We showed each year at the Red Rose Guild at Manchester, run by Margaret Pilkington, at the Arts and Crafts Society at Burlington House and at the Royal Academy Interior Design Exhibition 1934. We went to Stuttgart, Dunedin and Glasgow, and again to Paris in 1937. We even took part in an exhibition in the Town Hall at Oxford, as to whose purpose a certain lady must have been somewhat misinformed for she adjusted her lorgnettes with care and, leaning over, said to me in a stage whisper: 'And do you mean to tell me that all these things have been made by mental defectives? How very remarkable!' But it was tiring work, much dust and chatter to few informed questions, and it took several pints at the Roebuck to wash it away. This was before the Roebuck, one of the nicest small pubs in Oxford, had itself been washed away by a chain store, doubtless to be regurgitated elsewhere by a chain-brewer.

It is a fortunate thing that at the time we take any action we don't realize its full implications for otherwise I doubt if I should have started making furniture and in some ways that would have been a pity. I wanted to design furniture but I was forced to learn to run a business. I set up a small drawing office in part of the new showrooms and for a brief two or three years I was able to spend quite a lot of time either there or in the workshop, for I liked the close link between designing something and supervising its actual making. This was the sort of job I had dreamed about and I worked at a great pace, but perhaps work is not the right word, for when one enjoys a job it ceases to be work! There are times when, like the tramp, 'I 'ates work'. But this was sheer delight—like visiting an enchanting woman on a May afternoon, or eating the first oysters of the season, or being given a few days to carve stone, or going abroad for a holiday, or . . . but you can fill in your own ideas. Drawings poured out, something like five hundred of them, and a wonderful air of enthusiasm and expectancy pervaded the whole place. Nothing was fixed and experiments of all sorts were the order of the day. After my time in the army I greatly appreciated having a house of my own, quite close to my place of work so that I was spared the misery of commuting, and fortunately my wife and I had much the same ideas on how we wished to live.

There was no doubt at all that people found our showrooms an interesting place to visit, although many seemed to think we were crazy. They simply could not understand, for instance, why we refused to stain our furniture, as at that time almost all furniture was finished a 'rich Jacobean colour' or, in the trade, 'Jaco' for short. We followed the example set by Gimson and other designers of showing the natural wood, just because it was a lovely material, but the bare idea of any departure from established conventions seemed ridiculous to some people. Quite a number, indeed, were horrified at the mere idea of making new things in an ancient village and they didn't hesitate to say so. But, fortunately for us, it was a revelation to many others, who became staunch supporters.

'Nothing is always', and problems of one sort and another began to pile up. I hung on grimly but it was obvious that in time I would be dislodged from my designer's stool. Work was increasing rapidly and there must soon come a time when I could not get through it. Many of the things we produced—indeed most of them—were made to individual requirements so that a very great strain was placed on the designer. The number of men in the shop was increasing steadily, too. Wells had sent down to us some of the likeliest lads from the Shoreditch Technical Institute and we had also trained a number of local boys. What was the best way to deal with the situation? It was further complicated by the fact that we had also started a small metal-working shop as we had been quite unable to obtain special fittings of the required standard in small quantities to our own designs. Harry Gardiner, who took charge of it, had been in Gimson's Sapperton smithy and then in Birmingham. He was, and is, an excellent workman and a most amusing raconteur: there is a catch in his voice when he says that he looks so like a policeman off duty that he can never get a drink out of hours!

I thought about the whole problem pretty thoroughly. I saw that one could not be interested in furniture design and leave it at that. Design affects the whole pattern of life and good design was an essential part of the good life. A manufacturer who became conscious of good design would set a standard which became higher year by year, not only for the things he sold but for his factory buildings, his note headings, his office layout and lighting fittings. And even one such manufacturer could affect a whole trade, as Frank Pick in London Transport has affected transport design everywhere in greater or lesser degree. I began to consider the training of designers. It seemed to me that one could either start with a young artist or architect who had a knowledge of design and teach him the manufacturing end, or one could take exceptional men from the bench and teach them the design end. The essential thing was to have both ends closely integrated. It must be remembered that in the 1920s no school of art, so far as I am aware, had accepted the principle that designing for the machine needed a very different training from designing for hand production. Most of the schools were in charge of painters, who, cradled in Arts and Crafts Society theories, were antagonistic to industry and did not hesitate to say so. Industry naturally reacted by ignoring their existence. There were cases, such as printing, where the whole of the practical work—composing, making ready and

I

printing—were dealt with in the Technical School whilst book illustration, layout, type design and so on were dealt with in the Art School, which was quite separate. In few towns did the Principals co-operate—in some they had never met. The pioneering work of co-ordinating the two, which was carried out by Professor Walter Gropius at the Bauhaus in Weimar, was little known or appreciated.

Looking back at the men who had done interesting furniture under the inspiration of William Morris's teaching—men such as Lethaby, Voysey, Mackintosh, Ashbee, Heal, Gimson and Sidney and Ernest Barnsley—I noticed that all but Heal were architects. This could hardly be a coincidence. But they had all made a special study of the subject and several had worked at the bench. I was well aware that others without specialized knowledge had produced some execrable furniture. There appeared to have been no comparable group of experimenters within the trade itself: if there had been they were unknown outside, which wasn't likely. So Dick and I decided that he ought to become an architect and he took to the idea with great enthusiasm—but we still had to sell it to my father, who would undoubtedly point out that we should lose Dick's services for several years, at the end of which he might well decide that he wanted to set up his own practice and so would be lost to us for good. It seemed that the architect's background training and the fact that he had always to think in three dimensions was as important in designing furniture as houses. The notion which was common then and unfortunately still persists in places that professional advice is only necessary for special and costly buildings was so obviously wrong: it is more than ever necessary to have this for large-scale housing, if only because there is so much more of it and it is essential that it should be well planned. The placing of houses on the site is vitally important. So, just as architects were reaching out to layout, streets, town planning and so on, it was not unreasonable that they should reach into the rooms and the details of a house. This did not mean that they necessarily designed individual items for each house; it meant that they strove to ensure that well designed articles were available from stock. How simple and utterly commonsensical this seems, yet forty years of struggle have not achieved it.

Anyway, I persuaded the Guvnor to send Dick to the Architectural Association's School for four years. None of us regretted this step, although it threw a good deal of his work back on me. Not only did it widen his outlook by taking him out of a village to London but it gave us all a link with architecture and taught us to think in terms of rooms rather than individual pieces. Later on, it brought many other young architects into our drawing office for long or short periods— Eden Minns, R. Y. Goodden, Marian Pepler, David Booth, Sandro Girard, Jimmie Wilson, all of whom became well-known industrial designers. Marian Pepler, who later became Dick's wife, did especially useful work with the textiles we sold and the colour harmonies of rooms, as before her time we had little accurate knowledge of the use of colour. She designed, also, some excellent rugs.

Training at the AA was a long-term project but how should we deal with the short-term problem, especially in view of the fact that Dick had been taking a good deal of weight in various sides of the venture? I knew I should feel his loss greatly, so I looked round the shop to see if anyone with a sound knowledge of furniture construction had an aptitude for drawing. I picked on W. H. (Curly) Russell, who was Shoreditch trained, and I have every reason to feel it was a good choice for he became an excellent designer, responsible for some of the best work done at Broadway. No one could have shown more devotion to the job and through the years I have gained a friend.

Dick took over the drawing office from me when he returned from the AA and his outlook was of the greatest importance in our development. We established a valuable precedent in mixing theory and practice—architectural students and cabinet-makers. Even today art and technical education have not achieved anything like such close integration in many cases. Meantime I was being called on more and more outside, which was perhaps a good thing.

CHAPTER 10

Machine Production

I had already begun to see that there might be other ways than ours of running a business. Here again the army, with its rigid definition of responsibility, taught me quite a bit. I realized that we had a growing business and that cracks would appear in all directions unless I found ways of delegating. Our pre-war methods were only suitable for a very small concern. I even grasped the possibility of planning my life to some extent —at least I realized that to do this I must have a fairly clear picture of what I wanted to do. I was nearly thirty and had a great many interests but little specialized knowledge. I knew I wanted to design furniture of my own time and I had realized that this meant starting from scratch, not only at the drawing board but in the workshop, for there was never any doubt in my mind that designing and making ought to be closely inte-grated. Whilst I had a great respect for the work of many of the Arts and Crafts Society members, I had no wish to acquire their somewhat 'precious' outlook, which I felt cut them off from the main stream of life. I wanted to make some impact on my generation and to alter, in however small a degree, the thinking of the furniture trade. This meant going out to sell things—ideas first, goods second—instead of waiting for an exclusive clientele to insist on buying. I saw that to carry out my ideas would probably involve a considerably larger work-shop, that it might eventually mean the use of machinery and that this would call for a knowledge of management and distri-bution. At least I had not the distaste for any kind of machinery which the arts and crafts movement had fostered: it seemed to me just a more complex tool and it was the way in which it was used that mattered. If this was merely so as to get the maximum profit by the quickest possible methods one could not expect to achieve worthwhile results. After all, the simplest tool such as a knife could be used to cut a slice of bread or cut a throat, it all depended on who was using it and how! Looking at the chaos created by the misdirection of the machine William Morris came to the conclusion that a return to handwork was the only hope yet, curiously enough, as Peter Floud has pointed out, many of his finest designs for wallpapers and textiles were in repeating patterns which were eminently suitable for machine production. The Arts and Crafts Society which he founded had a considerable effect, not only in Britain but in Europe and even in America. But it did not deal with the fundamental problem, which was to use the machine in the best way for the work for which it was suitable, and to maintain a fine standard of handwork, showing qualities which a machine could not give. It does not seem to have been clear to Morris that the machine had come to stay, because it alone made possible the production of ordinary things in sufficient quantity for everyone to be able to use them. He was annoyed, too, to find that his beautiful handmade things were expensive and could only be bought by people whose incomes came from the use of machinery.

It is almost impossible today to realize how great and how passionate was the opposition to modern architecture or furnishings in the early 1920s. The interesting thing was that the most virulent attacks, as well as the strongest support, came from architects. Many people stood in front of our earliest efforts and laughed. It was obvious that what I was attempting to do needed explanation, and it was equally obvious that I should have to give this myself for, after all, I was the prime mover in this odd enterprise. Yet I was acutely aware that I was myself a learner in promoting ideas as in other directions.

As a start, in 1923, I wrote a leaflet which set out some of my ideas, as follows:

"'Wonderful, isn't it? Only an expert would ever guess it

wasn't old!'' How often has one heard this remark made in a tone which leaves no doubt that the speaker considers it a vast achievement, like the drawing which is ''just as good as a photograph''. But how many people who make similar exclamations ever pause to consider what they mean? Is there indeed so great a gulf fixed between the faking of houses and furniture and the faking of £5 notes? Are we to admire things because they are beautiful, or because they are old? The doctrine that nothing is beautiful unless it is old has created an army of swindlers, whose artful work may in time even bring discredit on the lovely craftsmanship which they attempt to imitate. It is therefore high time that we paid some attention to the question of reproductions, which seem to be the present fashionable craze.

'To begin with, the mere reproducing of so-called ''period designs'' is useful only in so far as it gives the craftsman a truer insight into the proportion, the lines and the method of making old work of every kind. We use the term ''method of making'' advisedly, for it is all-important. It is possible to make furniture by mass production, it is even possible to make good furniture in this way, but it must be designed with all due regard to its method of manufacture. For instance, a copy of a seventeenth-century dresser so made is a mere caricature of its original, a soul-less sham.'

Years later I was astonished and flattered to find an extract from this pamphlet, *Honesty and the Crafts*, quoted next to a piece of prose by Osbert Sitwell in an English handbook for schools.

It became part of my job to see committees which had expressed interest in our work. I remember one morning when Professor Ferguson and his wife, bicycling in the Cotswolds, called at the showrooms and after they had looked round asked to see me. As librarian of King's College, Aberdeen, he was much concerned to get the library refurnished in a way which made it possible for students to use it, and he asked me to go up and look at the problem on the site. It appeared to be absolutely essential that the scheme should be backed by Professor Macdonald, the GOM of the University, so Ferguson had arranged a luncheon party at which I was put next to Macdonald. Some years afterwards Mrs Ferguson told my wife how relieved they were to see us engaged in deep and earnest conversation. Things appeared to be going well. She listened intently and had she not been a devoted gardener, admitted she would have been astonished to hear that the subject of such intense interest to us was . . . muck! The re-planning of the library was assured.

One of the really pleasant features of this time was the encouragement and support given by some of those who used to visit the Lygon Arms regularly. Charles Laughton and his wife, Elsa Lanchester, were among the few discriminating people who at this time collected modern things—pictures, furniture, pottery, textiles and so on—many from our shop in Wigmore Street. After a lunch-time discussion in an astonishing little house they had in the middle of a large wood somewhere in Surrey, I designed a large wall fitment for them. The moral support of such enthusiasts was of great importance to me at this stage, and I valued especially being able to call on certain well-known businessmen for advice on our problems, among whom I always recollect with gratitude William Cadbury and Cecil Pilkington. They were never too busy to help a project they regarded as worth while. On one occasion I went to see Pilkington at Boar's Hill at a very awkward juncture: we had a considerable bank overdraft, owing to rapid development, and a very important account had not been paid on the due date. 'How much do you need to carry on?' he asked. I told him £12,000. He pondered a minute or two, asked several more questions and then, going to his desk, started writing what I imagined were brief notes. Coming back, he handed me a cheque for the amount—to my utter astonishment. 'What kind of receipt shall I give you?' I said, after a brief word of thanks. 'None,' he said, 'pay it back when you are over the hump. Worthwhile concerns are built up by your kind of drive.' Such generous and understanding support made up for months of apathy on the part of others.

There was a never-ending series of problems of workshop space, equipment, showroom space, finance, timber buying and so on. On the retail side there was the buying of table glass, textiles, carpets, pottery, and so on, in which my wife took her full share. She used to visit all important exhibitions of craftwork and acquired a very sound knowledge of what was going on, buying the work of the best makers for the showrooms and laying the foundation of some sort of organized buying system. Also to be undertaken was the buying of antiques, which remained a valuable part of the business until well into the 1930s, and took much time and care. From time to time we also tackled quite a bit of building work.

We had an immense variety of jobs to do at one time and another. Henry Ford came to the Lygon a number of times (see Plate II). My father got on very well with him and sold him things for his museum at Detroit, including a blacksmith's shop with all its tools and equipment just as the last blacksmith had left it twenty years before. It was fast becoming derelict and it seemed the only way to preserve it. I went to see it at Dearborn and although it was closed for the winter the director kindly had it opened for me when its origin was explained to him. And I was told that, just after it was finished, Ford used to like to have a brazier lighted in it so as to have genuine smoke on the roof and walls. He would then take picnic sandwiches along. Such are the simple pleasures of millionaires! He also wanted a great deal of ironwork made for a house for Edsel Ford which was then being built in the Cotswold manner near Detroit. When the blue-prints were sent to us we were asked not to let them go out of our hands: they were afraid of kidnapping, and apparently it was not a groundless fear.

When my father went to the States a few months later Henry Ford asked him to go and look at a piece of walling which was put up by an old Scots mason as a sample for the house. When the Guvnor got to Detroit he rang up Ford's private secretary who said: 'Although Mr Ford had hoped to come out to look at the wall with you he's had to go to a conference in the

West. But he left a message asking me to look after you and if you will say a convenient time his own Lincoln shall be sent to pick you up and take you to see it. And if there's anything else you want to see, in the works or elsewhere, the chauffeur has instructions to do as you wish.' So that was that and a time was fixed. After looking at the wall the Guvnor said he wanted to see the spraying shop, which he believed was at Highland Park, but he told the driver he wanted to gain a better impression of the works by walking towards them for a little distance. So he got out and left the car at the top of the road. Eventually he came to a large entrance and joined a number of men who were going in but he had not gone many steps when a burly giant laid his hand roughly on his shoulder and asked him unceremoniously what he wanted. He was annoyed and said he wanted the office, to which the other replied that this wasn't the office entrance. Thoroughly nettled at the lack of courtesy, my father said: 'I have come here in Mr Ford's own Lincoln, which I've left at the top of the road, and I shall report the way I have been received here.' An incredulous smile broke out on the oaf's face and, muttering, 'That's a bloody likely story, out you go!', he hustled my father into the road. When he got to the office eventually, breathless and indignant, he was received most kindly and they were full of apologies, explaining that each works entrance had a chucker-out to deal with gatecrashers.

Another interesting American customer was Mrs Pope Riddle who, having been trained as an architect and left a large fortune by her father, decided to build and endow a school at Avon, Connecticut, grouping the buildings round a green in the manner of an old English village. Everything was to be handmade and by her express orders no lines, levels or plumb-lines were to be used. She said she went out before breakfast one morning and found several men with plumb-bobs, so she confiscated them. All the roofs were framed up to look as if they had sagged between the principals. They must have had fun. She wanted various things for the school, the first being pewter plates: could they be obtained? She would want

137

several hundred. Yes, I said, they could as I knew a firm who had the original eighteenth-century moulds. But later she suggested that acid fruits might attack pewter and it seemed that was so. Then there were turned wooden candlesticks for the tables; pewter spoons and horn-handled knives and forks by hundreds; a ton of distemper and half a ton of paint; table glass, pewter peppers and salts, handwoven linen for cloths, a hundredweight of handmade nails and so on. Then I mentioned to her one day that I had been reading Sturt's *The Wheelwright's Shop* and thought it one of the very best descriptions of hand-work I had come across. I lent it to her and nothing would then do but she must have a wagon for the school. So I wrote asking Sturt who could still make a good wagon and he gave me the name of a wheelwright at Cropredy. The wagon was made and shipped and later she wrote for a set of harness and a farm-cart. Later still, a large and rattling case was received from America and on unpacking it we found over one hundred pewter spoons, all damaged. It seems the boys had discovered that if the spoon-handles were held in the candle flame for a few moments the pewter melted, leaving the reinforcing steel wire exposed. When I last saw Mrs Riddle she said they had got a military man as headmaster and things were going better!

Then there was the box of bricks of unusual woods, all lettered by my father, made specially for Queen Mary as a gift for the then Princess Elizabeth, and the chest-of-drawers made for Lloyd George from a holly tree that had blown down in his garden at Churt, which was a tricky job as the timber wasn't seasoned and he wanted it at once. What made the business so interesting was its variety. But this was also the source of most of our troubles and no one would claim that I was a born administrator. I was hard pressed, but not sub-merged by it all. I have always stood out for time to do certain things that interest me apart from business affairs. I liked gardening. I liked walking, and solitude seemed more neces-sary to me than to most people. I liked good food and drink. I liked looking at buildings and pictures, and I liked to keep in touch with my friends, and to go abroad once a year. One finds time to do the things one really likes, except during a war or near-war period—which have in fact taken such a large slice of my life. I was very clear-minded that I would not do what I saw so many businessmen do, whilst priding themselves on their efficiency, that is to concentrate on business to the exclusion of everything else, and then find themselves at the age of sixty-five dead on their feet, with plenty of money perhaps but no idea what to do next. And I count myself one of the most fortunate of men in that my most staunch and loyal supporter has always been my wife, not merely from a sense of duty but because she also has a real and live interest in things of importance, in what makes people tick, in pictures, in the art of garden design and the practice of horticulture, in cooking and red wine, in early stained glass and tapestry, in love-making. But she draws the line at locomotives and armour, which I have to go and look at by myself! On the other hand, she likes riding and languages, especially French, in which my interest has always been somewhat spasmodic. We both like walking in an unhurried way and looking at buildings and scenery.

In 1926, it seemed a wise thing to form a small private company to deal with the furniture side of the business and so separate the accounts from those of the Lygon Arms. Owing to this development, R. H. Bee, who was later to become chief executive, joined the company as secretary. In addition to a flair for accountancy he had sound organizing ability. He had not then any specialized knowledge of furniture but he was not one to sit down and let it go at that: he came to the evening classes and made several things himself. Later on, his mechanical aptitude—he had served in tanks during the 1914 War—gave him a great advantage in studying the problems of mass production. Under his direction it was not long before the office was perhaps the most efficient department of the company. The original title of The Russell Workshops Ltd. was altered shortly afterwards to Gordon Russell Ltd., because the former title was felt to have a somewhat exclusive, handmade air whereas the latter tied up with the writing and lecturing I was doing as well as the fact that we had started to develop well-made and well-designed things—things of quality—which were produced by machine to a considerable extent.

I think this point needs elaborating. Our earliest efforts were made entirely by hand and were directly inspired by the work of Ernest Gimson, many aspects of which I had greatly admired. I feel very strongly that handwork of the best kind is essential in any civilization: in fact, I would go so far as to say that, in the long run, I do not believe that fine quality machine work can exist without it. Handwork enables the worker to get to grips with his material and collaborate with it in a way that is infinitely more difficult if he is operating a machine. There has never been a time when I have not felt the necessity of working with my hands, but early in the 1920s I realized that the most urgent job of all was to teach the machine manners. The civilization that had been built up was based on the machine, without which goods that were considered essential could not be produced for the masses. The kind of goods produced and the effect on the people producing them seemed to me most important. As we had a number of enquiries for furniture for schools, public houses, hotels, hospitals and municipal buildings I determined to see what could be done about it.

In taking this line I landed myself in trouble, not for the first time. On the one hand, many handworkers regarded me as a traitor to the cause, although we continued to produce a good deal of fine handwork, and on the other, many manufacturers in the furniture trade regarded me as a crazy crank full of strange and unworkable ideas and said, 'You can't do it: it's never been done!' Still, in spite of the complacency of many firms in a prosperous trade, there was a fair sprinkling of people who were unhappy about the way things were going, feeling that much furniture was bad and that it was getting worse. This was due to a number of causes but I think that the introduction of hire purchase and the short-sighted way in which it was run was one of the chief of them. Hire purchase, which might well have offered considerable advantages to the customer, became in many cases a money-lending racket of the most blatant kind. Both customer and retailer almost forgot about the furniture; the length of credit and the amount of weekly payments took all the limelight and genuine value for money was overlooked. Pretentious furniture which is flashily attractive in a carefully lighted shop window, offered on hire purchase terms which seem acceptable, is not necessarily a reasonable background for living. Many hire purchase firms spent their time battering down manufacturers' prices to a level at which it was impossible to make an honest job, at the same time offering the customer terms of credit which gave ridiculously high rates of profit. Of course by no means all of them acted in this way, but the drift of the whole trade made it more and more difficult for the honest ones to carry on. This state of affairs had repercussions outside the hire purchase side of the trade. Many of the large stores also used their considerable buying power to force down prices unreasonably. The machine, which might well have been used to produce a decent job of work, was often used purely to obtain cheapness at any cost.

Can anyone imagine that such conditions offered a healthy seed bed in which good designs might grow? For good quality —quality of design, of material and of workmanship—is the outward and visible sign of good health. It is not something which can be assumed at short notice, like the sham styles so beloved by the furniture trade, but something by which our whole standard of civilization can be tested: either you believe that the physical background of life ought to be pleasant, seemly and satisfying or you think it doesn't matter. I simply cannot see the point of view of people who think that the only way to interest businessmen in good industrial design is to tell them it will earn them larger profits. An American super-stylist stated some time ago that he was surprised to find in England that people talked of aesthetics in connection with industrial design: aesthetics, he said, had nothing to do with it, the only test was a beautiful sales curve shooting upwards. I know there are some knaves and morons in industry, but such nonsense presupposes that there is no one else. If an appeal to low cunning and cupidity induces one of that kidney to try to improve his standard of design, he will drop the whole idea like a hot brick if it does not at once do all that is claimed for it, whereas there are many firms who want to do a decent job and to keep abreast of their times. It is quite safe to tell them that good design, like democracy, is not the easy road but that in the long run it is abundantly worth while. And there are also numerous instances where it has paid dividends. After all, good design must be nourished by sales and reasonable profit is essential. I suppose I was optimistic but I imagined at one time that good design would grow rapidly once it became known. My own outlook on life made such a thing seem possible and desirable. The nineteenth century felt the same way about a liberal outlook. But the problem is a social one, as William Morris saw. Good design is one aspect of a good pattern of life and unless the foundations are sound the super-structure will not last.

I think it must have been in 1926 that Powell's of the Whitefriars Glassworks invited me to give a one-man show of furniture in their Wigmore Street showrooms. I had met Barnaby and Marriott Powell at several exhibitions and had liked their general outlook and the things they made. They had a large and somewhat rambling room on the first floor at Wigmore Street and into this we put a collection of things which had a slightly rural air in the sophisticated atmosphere of the West End of London. Our customers, many of whom took a very friendly, even paternal, interest in our strange venture, rallied round us valiantly and the whole affair was a success in a human, unpremeditated way. Our good relations with Powell's were cemented and as they were interested in my outlook generally they asked me to design a few pieces of glass for them.

Glass is a material which has always delighted me. I spent many happy hours poring over the illustrations in Hartshorne. Who can look at the tavern glasses of the early eighteenth century unmoved? Their baluster-stemmed prototypes of the seventeenth century are fine things indeed, but for sheer mastery of line in making, for the way stem melts into foot in a graceful curve, for brilliance of metal and adequacy of scale, for the joyous 'ring', due to the lead in the glass, these are marvels. In 1911 Rees Price, who had a remarkable collection of English glass, took me to see the lovely set of Jacobite decanters and glasses which were then at Chastleton House, near Moreton-in-Marsh, but have since been sold. What a setting it was for them! I have been to Chastleton many times, before and since, in fair weather and foul, in rain and snow, by sun and moon, and have never failed to experience a feeling of eager anticipation as the great house came in view.

The next year we had another small exhibition at Powell's and Lady Maud Bowes-Lyon, who lived in Broadway, was kind enough to write to her niece, the Queen Mother (then Duchess of York), about it. The Duchess came in one day, unannounced, no one recognized her, and when she asked a young salesman if I was there he replied no, but would it be convenient for her to call some other time and he would let me know so that I might be sure to be there? She received this droll suggestion with charming good humour, and even acted on it, for a few years later she visited our Broadway show-rooms (see plate 11). She had an affection for Broadway, where as a girl she had spent holidays with her aunt.

Again in the next year, 1928, we had a one-man show, this time at the Arlington Gallery in Bond Street. This was quite an event and the Press were tickled at the idea of furniture in a Bond Street Gallery. I worked overtime on the new designs to be shown. There was no doubt about it, our standards of workmanship were getting pretty good, and I can still look at some of the designs with a certain amount of satisfaction, although I must admit there were several pieces whose ghostly presence still haunts me in the small hours. Perhaps the only good thing I ever heard about the London blitz is that, to my certain knowledge, it destroyed more than one of them.

Then in 1929 we decided to open a small shop of our own in Wigmore Street. Ted Ould (later to become managing director), who had been with us for some time in Broadway and was an ardent supporter of modern design, was put in charge of it and the opening took place on October 1st. Within a few weeks the Wall Street crash had created panic in America and within a year had destroyed our considerable American market in antiques, handmade glass, textiles and so on. The repercussions over here were so violent that the market for high-priced furniture, for which we had opened the shop, almost disappeared. The gale swept our little ship from stem to stern. Not only our furnishing business suffered, for the Lygon Arms had a very considerable circle of American visitors, many of whom came year after year, and they just stopped coming. This caused much heart searching.

I was very interested later on in two stories the well-known designer Gilbert Rhode told me of America at this time. He designed an excellent range of furniture of the unit type, the first good modern design I had seen from America, for a large store, who pushed it by advertising that it was so well thought out that two pieces gave as much accommodation as three of the old type. This was true and they did very well with it. But directly the slump lifted their sales manager said: 'This is no good. People have money in their pockets and we can sell the three pieces again now. No more economy talk.' So the good designs were swept off the floor and imitation Colonial, Hepplewhite, Louis XV and what not became once more the order of the day. He said also that there was an American radio company which considered itself the last word in efficiency and had an answer for everything. They prided themselves on having worked out the most efficient way of designing cabinets. When the new season's sets were being considered, drawings were asked for from cabinet-makers and the Board selected those they thought 'good sellers', from which samples were made. These were all put on the Board Room table and the president's wife, a lady of culture who had travelled widely in Europe, was called in. She sorted out all she thought of good design and from the remainder they made the new season's models! This, they said, saved them thousands of dollars. I didn't believe this cynical story, which he swore was true, but the American cabinets of the time seem to make it plausible. Since that time America has seen the establishment of many first-rate designers and, perhaps even more important, large firms prepared to employ them.

Still, we weren't the only people in a mess in the slump. We gritted our teeth and lost money with as much pleasure as we could conjure up, but I think I was born under a lucky star. Little ships, it is said, should keep close to shore but safety first has never appealed to me much as a motto. I like exploring, and I suppose unless you've nearly been lost you can't get the full savour of a return to port. Nor are you likely to grasp the opportunity which a desperate situation so often presents. Such an opportunity later came my way and took us into mass production, and into further and greater storms. For the present, it was enough that we were 'shipwrecked into health again'.

CHAPTER 11

Mass Production

It was quite obvious that if we were to survive the blizzard we should have to concentrate on lower-priced furniture, which meant altering our type of design and using machines to produce series of six or twelve rooms rather than making individual pieces almost entirely by hand. We found a considerable demand, but our Wigmore Street shop was so small that it was almost impossible to sell enough of such furniture there —it could not be shown—and many people who looked in the window and liked it thought it was much more expensive than was actually the case, Wigmore Street having an expensive reputation, so they didn't come in to enquire. We were to find how difficult it is to manufacture for two retail outlets only: either we made a large enough series to achieve economical manufacturing costs, in which case our retail stocks were too high and we were faced with high interest charges on stock, damage in store, etc., or we made small series and so achieved a reasonable retail turnover but our manufacturing costs were too high. Unless we increased our retail outlets, either by having more shops of our own, which meant losing a good deal of money to get them going, or by retailing through the trade, which did not believe in the possibility of selling contemporary design, it was not easy to solve the problem. But certainly the situation would be greatly helped by building up a much bigger business in things we did not make, such as woven materials, carpets, glass, etc., to compensate for the profitable antique and luxury business with America which had then almost ceased.

Whilst we were concentrating on this job the telephone

rang one day and when I took the call a level-toned voice said:
'My name is Frank Murphy. You won't know me, I'm an
engineer and I've just started making radio sets but I have a
low opinion of the cabinets I am offered by the cabinet-makers.
I've been to see the editor of *The Cabinet-Maker* and the L C C
Technical Institute at Shoreditch and at both these places
your name was mentioned as being especially interested in
good design. What about it?' 'Well,' I said, somewhat taken
aback, 'it sounds a very interesting problem but I know
nothing about making radio cabinets!' 'That doesn't matter at
all,' he said, 'if you're interested we'll come down tomorrow
afternoon.'

So down to Broadway they came—'they' being Frank
Murphy and his partner, Ted Power, wearing old mackin-
toshes and cloth caps and looking as if they worked round the
clock. Dick and I met them but no time was spent on formali-
ties. Murphy launched into a description of his project in a
spate of words. It seemed he had been in the Post Office before
1914 and when he came back from the war he went into
advertising with a friend of his, C. R. Casson. Then one day
Murphy went to the office and announced to Casson that he had
been enthralled by Ford's *Life and Work*, and had decided to
throw up advertising and start making wireless sets, so giving
employment and paying high wages. He felt that radio was too
complicated: he wanted simpler, better built cabinets which
were as good as the sets. 'Look at this,' he said to us, producing
a portable cabinet, 'it's just a box. No ideas. Ted and I have
spent many hours trying to find out how we can keep these
ugly knobs out of sight without making them inaccessible but
we haven't got anywhere. We're at a dead end. What's the
next move? The matter is desperately urgent. We've been
working on the set for a year, we're starting to tool up and
sets must be in dealers' shops well ahead of Christmas. The
portable will have to go as it is, there's no help for it, but the
next model just must have a better cabinet, the problem is
how?' He stopped talking and they both looked at Dick and
me.

I realized how deadly earnest he was: the whole future of both of them seemed, in their eyes, to hang in the balance. I felt that the only thing to do was to put all my cards on the table, so I said: 'I'm not an engineer and I'm not a wireless fan. I haven't got a set—I listen in only occasionally at my father's house—and I must admit I've never studied the design of such cabinets, although I have occasionally looked at them. And I'll tell you what I think is the trouble. The whole approach to the problem is wrong. This is what I imagine happens. The set-maker sends a blue-print to a cabinet-maker and asks for a few sketches. The cabinet-maker does no real research into requirements. His draughtsman—who is not a designer—knocks off a few sketches, then some samples are made and sent in and one is chosen. The set-maker or the cabinet-maker buys some cloth for the loud-speaker opening, asks a printer to set out the names for the stations and buys some plastic knobs from a catalogue, or perhaps he first sends the size to the manufacturer and leaves the choice to him. No one competent designer has been responsible for all the visible parts of the set and has welded them into a complete whole and until some pretty fundamental research is done and the whole business is approached in a new way I can't see that you can expect much advance. Now is that a true picture of what happens?' 'Where did you get your information?' said one of them. 'That's just about what does happen.' 'From the set,' we said. 'Consider the problem of the knobs, which are not for pulling out a drawer—although by their shape you might think they were. By a careful study of the requirements you could make them much more pleasant to handle and to look at without costing any more. They should be designed as an essential part of the whole job. If they are good to look at and well placed they will enhance the cabinet and it will never again occur to you that it would be desirable to hide them. The design of the cabinet ought to start when you design the set, not as an after-thought.'

They sat back in their chairs and looked at us in astonishment. That such simple facts should have escaped highly

148

intelligent men shows how low design had fallen. They said they hadn't felt so hopeful for months and Dick and I promised to go down to their works and discuss the matter further on the spot. They had all the engineer's confidence that a thing could be made once a specification was laid down, but to me cabinet production presented a considerable problem. We went down to Welwyn Garden City, where they had a small factory, and it was obvious that they had given the same concentrated attention to every side of their job. I loved the way they took nothing for granted. They wanted to know the why and the how. Frequently C. R. Casson, their advertising agent, was present at these discussions. He had a humorous face and liked to pretend he was just an ordinary member of the public, testing their odd theories. At a pause in the spate of words he would sit back in his chair and say: 'I'm Billie Muggins, so you must explain what the hell this new idea is! There's no doubt I'm dull-witted, so make it simple.' 'Making wireless simple' was Murphy's slogan, printed on every carton. To my surprise, the question of public acceptability never entered the discussion at this stage: they wanted to find the best possible solution, to tell the public about it and then they felt the public would accept it. They were pioneers, with a zest for the job, and that link held us together through several very tricky years. I never remember them saying 'Oh you can't do that—it won't sell', like so many people in the furniture trade. I think that to intelligent, hardboiled engineers there seemed something a bit odd about wrapping an imitation Queen Anne case around such a precise and complicated piece of machinery. This was an advantage. The furniture maker was not brought quite so suddenly against his own age: he sold his wardrobes neat whereas people bought a radio set on its performance and put up with the cabinet.

We began to state the problem on paper, always a useful initial stage to finding a solution. The engineers, accustomed to working in thousandths of an inch, laughed at our idea of a tolerance: a sixteenth of an inch was a crevasse to them! They said we must learn to be accurate, wood or no wood. All measurements had to be from the inside, whereas we were accustomed to working to external ones, and were tied by a number of points where the set had to register. There were problems of supply, of sound, of handling on their benches, of talking to dealers, of packing, and so on. I noticed that they were just as thorough over the last item: they worked out their own cardboard carton with special loose lining and then sent several complete sets all round the British Isles to see what happened.

Never a day went by without their having some criticism to hurl at us. It might be a minor detail, such as a small alteration in the fixing of the silk, or it might be a bolt out of the blue. I remember one evening at home when, just as I was about to sit down to a delectable omelette, the telephone rang and on taking up the instrument I heard Murphy's monotonous voice —he never said 'good morning', 'good evening' or even 'blast you'—'I've been thinking about this cabinet problem and I want to ask you this: why do we need a cabinet at all? Aren't we just accepting an out-of-date solution? I think we've got to get right down to first principles on this job. Perhaps it isn't sense to ask a cabinet-maker whether we need a cabinet, but I trust you to ponder this carefully. This isn't just a stunt . . .' and so on, like water pouring over a mill-dam, for more than a quarter of an hour. I thought wistfully of my omelette and at the first sign of a pause I said: 'Well, Murphy, my first reaction is that no woman will dust all your bits and pieces when she can put a duster over our cabinet in a twentieth of the time. There may be other points. Certainly I'll think about it. Good night.' And as I put the receiver back I said a little prayer for all poor souls who are subjected to the third degree. On another occasion, he propounded the theory that nothing should cost more per pound than beefsteak. He said a Ford car didn't, but our cabinet did. 'Well,' said I, 'do you suppose people would accept beefsteak in lieu of cabinets?' I forget how the argument ended.

Intensive research into the problem led to a tentative solution finding its way on to paper and when this was approved a sample cabinet was made (see plate 8). It was unlike any former radio cabinet so far as I know. The carcass was of solid walnut with two veneered plywood panels and there was a loud-speaker opening with a grid in front of the grey silk. The control knobs were not good but they were much better than in the first model; and owing to the engineers' layout they were in positions which made it somewhat difficult to harmonise them with the cabinet. This demonstrated clearly that to attain a really good design one would have to work in collaboration with the engineers at the earliest stage, that is before tooling up, when such points were often to some extent fluid. Once again, may I repeat that good industrial design goes down to the roots—it is never something added at the end. I remember Lethaby's saying: 'Art is not a sauce added to ordinary cooking. It is the cooking itself, if it is good.' Both Murphy and Power were pleased with the experiment and the time came to show it to the dealers as the new season's model.

I think Murphy and I went to this jamboree. There was, if I remember rightly, a lunch beforehand of the kind that jaded hotel keepers imagine that still more jaded businessmen are bound to like. After this ordeal by mastication the cabinet was produced. The dealers stood up and gazed at it in rapt astonishment and alarm. Then some wit, noticing the grid, christened it the Pentonville and the rest roared with laughter. Murphy was magnificent. He knew nothing of design himself, but he had made up his mind that Dick and I did and that he was going to back us. The reception didn't rattle him a jot. He stuffed his pipe in his mouth and dealt with various questions with perfect good humour. Then someone said: 'It's a good set, but no one will buy it in a cabinet like that. Why don't you get some bloke who knows the job to design it. There must be plenty about. Why, this bright-eyed guy you've picked on doesn't even know the right colour for the silk and in my opinion its wasting time to have people like that.' A murmur of approval ran round the room. Murphy asked me to deal with this, so, in my most ingenuous manner, I asked: 'Could you tell me the right colour for the silk?' 'Why,' said the dealer, now quite certain that he was dealing with a fool, 'it's a kind of coppery colour.' 'What makes you say that?' I said. Hardly believing his ears and astonished that such greenhorns should roam about unattended, he replied testily: 'Why, you've only got to look in the window of any radio shop and you'll see that all the sets have a copper-coloured silk.' 'Yes,' I said, 'that's true, but it does not prove that the colour is right. Anyone who knows anything about colour knows that a hot coppery colour does not go at all well with walnut, which is used for these cabinets. A cool contrasting colour such as grey is much more suitable and that's why we've used it. It will never be Murphy Radio's policy to go through the gate just because it's been opened for the sheep. They have original ideas on a good many sides of their business, as you know, so you may as well realize there's going to be a Murphy Style in cabinets. The only reason for the coppery coloured silks is that a set which sold exceptionally well three years ago had it for the first time. Isn't that true?' A few of the dealers approved the suggestion, and the brickbats slowed up a bit.

I attended meetings of this sort over several years with Frank Murphy and I learned many valuable lessons at them. Perhaps the most important was the one every politician has to take to heart: never, under any conditions, let the hecklers rattle you. So long as you bear this in mind and know clearly what you want to do yourself, you have most of the cards, for few hecklers have a constructive policy. Some meetings were pretty noisy, but the dealers were not slow to see that we meant what we said and gradually the supporters of our cabinets increased. The astonishing thing was that in a few years time the dealers, when shown the new models, often said: 'Nothing like as good as last year's A.3: that was a cabinet that was'—blissfully unconscious of the fact that they hadn't a good word for the A.3 when it was introduced! But for Murphy's personal interest and championship the whole idea could hardly have survived the teething stage. Power was just as interested and perhaps a more able critic but he was tied up on production.

The variety of models to be made increased each year both in number and, many of them, in size. Production became a very big job—40,000 of one model would have seemed fantastic to us but a few years before. We built a small factory in Broadway but it didn't prove large enough and in 1934 we moved this part of our work to a new factory at Park Royal, near Willesden, where we also did a good deal of work for other firms such as Pye, Ultra, Ekco, etc. Looking back, there can be no doubt whatever that this experiment of Murphy's powerfully affected the design of all radio cabinets made in England and I would say that the standard of the best in this country between 1930 and 1939 was as high as anywhere in the world. Such were the spectacular results that were possible in a country where it was exceptional to find any object whose form, colour, texture and so on had been the subject of careful research by a skilled industrial designer, in this case my brother Dick who designed practically the entire range. We were able to prove that a very high standard of design, material and workmanship could be obtained in wood by mass-production methods, and that when such large numbers were involved the cost of employing first-rate industrial designers added hardly anything to the price: in fact, it often reduced it by a better planned approach to the problem.

Perhaps two of the most astonishing things about the last hundred years have been the incredible quantities and varieties of things made and the utter and complete lack of interest in what they looked like. It took from three to six months from the time we started on a cabinet until it was ready to go into production. The immense care that was lavished on the smallest details was often brought home to me when I saw the cabinets in use. Quite often I had to investigate important complaints and I tried to see the actual customers as well as the dealer. I remember it was a shock to me to see, in a house in Kettering, a Murphy set opposite a gas cooker in a little kitchen. It was standing on a round table covered with American cloth, once white, and on the cabinet stood a bowl of bananas! This was the object on which we had spent months of hard work and for which we had also given weeks of consideration to a special stand. I learned a very valuable lesson. As these cabinets had to go into such an immense variety of rooms it seemed important that they should not stress their virtue as pieces of furniture but merge into the background in a discreet way, like a well-cut suit of clothes.

This whole development was hard work all right, but Murphy's point of view was refreshingly new and downright and if we taught them something most certainly they taught us. By blood and sweat we worked out a handling technique which I have found successful on many jobs since. Whilst the design and execution of handwork might be carried out entirely by one man—although few imaginative designers are also expert craftsmen—I felt that designing anything for mass production must of necessity be a team job. In the case of our radio cabinets the designer had to consult the engineers, the press tool foreman, the weavers, the plastic people, the cabinet mill and assembly foremen—to say nothing of advertising agents, sales managers and business consultants. Yet despite increasing subdivision of responsibility, there was in many firms hardly any co-ordination at all, and under these circumstances it was inevitable that the finished product should be merely a variation on old models—stale, hackneyed and lifeless. It seemed to me that the designer might be able to assess all the problems and evolve a satisfying solution if he learned to be the co-ordinating technician and that, provided he had the backing of the Board, he could inspire the whole working group and breathe fresh life and enthusiasm into the factory. Thus it was that I became what was, in effect, an informal chairman of our team, because my knowledge of trading enabled me to interpret the business side for designers and the design side for all the others involved.

Design has long been considered to be something added at the end, some ornament or decoration, and its fundamental character has been lost to sight. Many businessmen realize the necessity for scientific research and know it is often a long-term project; but few appreciate the importance of thorough design research embracing not only the materials to be used, the method of making and the efficiency of the product but also appearance and convenience in use, which in an age of severe competition are often the determining factors in commercial success. Some manufacturers feel that half a dozen sketches should be put on the table without any initial research and that personal likes or dislikes should decide the issue. Some admit that they look around to see which firm in their trade is doing the most business and copy his designs, perhaps with futile variations which, even if the original designs were good, destroy their value. Eskil Sundahl, the architect who did so much for the Swedish Co-operative, told me that when they had a visit from the English Co-operative, percentages were about the only things discussed—understandably, perhaps, as designers were never sent. Again, some permit the whole thought behind a drawing to be entirely altered in production without any consultation with the original designer. This is quite wrong: the designer must have control of the detailing, in collaboration, of course, with the production department, for a good design may be wrecked entirely by unsympathetic detailing. Many small points, some of them fundamental, are bound to occur at this stage and a draughtsman who has not a trained aesthetic sense but is concerned purely with construction may not realize that such points affect design at all. In previous ages craftsmen had the great advantage of working within the limits of a tradition which was well understood by all concerned, whereas in these days a great part of every designer's efforts is spent in attempting to build up a tradition which is suited to our own times and methods of living, to the materials we now have available in such bewildering variety and to the methods of machine or hand production. It must be obvious that the shapes of things which were suitable in the eighteenth century will not often provide the answer! We must have experiment and adventure to deal with a radically different situation.

The board of most companies has members who speak with authority on accountancy, finance, sales, production, transport and costing, but how many have a director of design? A sound working knowledge of design is still rare among businessmen and its importance is not widely recognized, partly due to the ease with which British goods could be sold in the past and partly to the one-sidedness of our educational system. Visual education is a timid newcomer to an over-crowded curriculum in almost every school, so that the essential point of contact is missing and many people go through life without looking at things at all. How can they grasp the designer's point of view without an interpreter?

Lack of perception at management level has, however, been by no means the only cause of failure to achieve a fundamental approach to this problem. There was in England virtually no school where a boy or girl could learn to be an industrial designer of, say, textiles, pottery or furniture. There were art schools where they could learn the theory of design and where they could make things by hand, but the essential practical side of learning the functions of the machine in a mass-production factory was, for some incredible reason, left until they went into industry. When the Royal College of Art was reorganized after the Second World War an effort was made to close this gap. Is it any wonder that the average businessman had little confidence in a system which did not send him fully-trained people? Partly because of this, designers never had adequate pay or status and few indeed developed sufficiently to have their opinions heard with respect at Board level. These conditions made it difficult for them to have a strong and trusted professional body to lay down codes of practice and remuneration and to ensure a standard of professional efficiency by qualification, as in the case of the Royal Institute of British Architects. However, I am glad to say that the Society of Industrial Artists and Designers (SIA) is rapidly growing into such a body. Founded in the late 1930s, it is supported by most well-known designers and great credit is due to the small group who, in spite of extremely discouraging conditions, carried on through the Second World War. Especially, I feel, the thanks of all designers should go to Milner Gray, who was mainly responsible for keeping the Society alive in the early stages. This was no mean achievement, as having been pushed into the background by our civilization, the artist, designer and craftsman has often become somewhat peevish and prickly to deal with. Whilst his improving status is giving him a more balanced point of view it is none the less uncommon to find designers with well-developed political sense. But a good job by itself is not enough: one must know how to steer it past the Scylla and Charybdis of production and sales. To do this one must know when to compromise and when to dig one's toes in, be prepared to learn from anyone and, as design and art are often considered highbrow subjects, never be a superior person.

These attributes are, of course, vital also to the co-ordinator of a production team, for he must have the confidence of all. Each must be encouraged to think not of 'my' work but of 'our' work, then each will give of his best. He must have infinite patience, tact and capacity for dealing with men and women, encouraging all to express their views freely. As a designer is inclined to make his problem a very personal one, few can work well in an unsympathetic atmosphere and I must say that I have known a sticky problem take on an altogether more promising outlook after three or four of those concerned have swapped yarns over some pots of bitter in a bar. And that's as it should be. The necessity of order should be apparent to the intelligence but to get *good* design, which has the imaginative quality of the artist, you must touch men's hearts. Discouraging delays may occur or, after months of work, a design may be scrapped for reasons quite outside the control of the designers or the firm; and whilst it is quite common for a businessman to think that if anyone is paid for his work all is well, a conscientious man has a feeling of frustration if his designs do not get beyond the drawing board stage, however well he is paid. At such times the co-ordinator will try to maintain the morale of his team. At other times he may have to tell them bluntly that, for special reasons, a promising line of approach is not available, or he may have to be fairly terse in other directions. But he will always hold a nice balance between the various technicians, indicating on the one hand that whilst the easiest production answer is not necessarily the right one the designer must not for ever try to make production tread a thorny path. He must, of course, never forget that good industrial design must be nourished by sales. In fact, there must be give and take, which means that goodwill is the one element which cannot be dispensed with; and everyone must strive to get the best answer, taking everything into consideration, not just the best answer for one department.

Whilst all this had been happening on one side of our business a great deal had been going on in other directions. We had been climbing painfully out of the depression, and we had been doing an increasing amount of work for schools, hotels and public buildings. We also increased our range of domestic furniture but it was not the expensive kind of the 'twenties: writing cabinets at more than £100 apiece were rare but we still made a few to special order. Our selection of interesting fabrics and carpets became well known, but we simply had not room to show them. In 1936 we decided to take a larger shop a few doors away in Wigmore Street, next to 'The Times' bookshop. We commissioned Geoffrey Jellicoe to design this and certainly it proved an interesting, if small, example of contemporary architecture, stocked with furniture, carpets, textiles and other things all informed by the same spirit.

It was at about this time that I got in touch with Nikolaus Pevsner, who had left a job in the Art Gallery at Dresden in 1934 because of the growth of Nazism and had come to England. Professor Sargant Florence had persuaded Birmingham University to give him a research job for a year, to find out how goods were designed in England. Never was money better spent. He visited hundreds of firms, ours among them, and collected invaluable information. He lectured to the Design and Industries Association in 1935 about the whole problem and he showed such a comprehensive grasp of the subject that I went over to Birmingham the next day and asked him if he would like to buy textiles, rugs, glass and so on for us. Although he had never been in business he said he would like to consider it and finally he came to us for several years. Under his care, the selection and display of things in our two shops reached a standard which could be compared with the best abroad. I take some credit for the fact that otherwise one of our best art historians might well have found his way to Australia. When he left us, in 1939, he became Assistant Editor of *The Architectural Review* and then Editor of *King Penguins*, of the Pelican *History of Art* and of *The Buildings of England*. His lucid writing and criticism have also done much to improve the standard of industrial design. It was a particular pleasure to me that he and his daughter were staying at Broadway and dined with us at home on the day in 1967 when the award to him of the Royal Gold Medal by the Royal Institute of British Architects was announced, a notable recognition of his remarkable work as an architectural historian. I had already told Allen Lane, who wished to give a party for Pevsner on his sixty-fifth birthday, that Broadway was the proper location, and Broadway it was.

Just before the Second World War quite a trickle of people from overseas who were interested in designing and making things began to come to see us. It helped a good deal in the solution of our problems to talk to others about theirs. Among such people I remember Shoji Hamada—one of Bernard Leach's pupils from Japan; Gilbert Rhode, Sandro Girard, Walter Dorwin Teague, Hollis Baker and many others from the USA; Gregor and Ester Paulsson, Ake Huldt and Ake Stavenow from Sweden; Kaj Dessau, Steen Eiler Rasmussen and Soren Hansen from Denmark; Walter Gropius, Marcel Breuer and von Weech from Germany. Of course many of those who were doing really good handwork in England came to Broadway from time to time. I must mention especially the pleasure and profit I have had over many years in talks with Bernard Leach, Michael Cardew, Harold Stabler, Ethel Mairet, George and Will Hart, Katherine Adams, Peter Waals, Edward Barnsley and many more

On January 26, 1938, my mother's birthday and the anniversary of his taking over the Lygon, my father died. He had

159

had a slight stroke two years before but had recovered and had carried on enthusiastically with his work for discharged prisoners and men in Gloucester Gaol, in which he had taken a great interest for some years. He was also a lay reader and often took part in the service in Campden and other churches. He had not been concerned actively in the business for five or six years, but he came in on most days and also attended meetings. He was an odd mixture—most acquisitive yet unaware of many material things which the world rates so highly. In moments of annoyance he blurted out that all he needed was 'a pound a week and the *Daily Mail*'. All who knew him were mystified, and his family never succeeded in penetrating his thoughts for, either in material or spiritual needs, this fare seemed inadequate! Eric Kennington, who painted his portrait in 1934—it was the first portrait he had painted for years —said he had 'achieved a harmony'. It was indeed true that the anxious fretting of earlier years had gone and I had got to know him much better. He was so much the founder of things that we could never fill the gap he left.

He had expressed a wish to be buried at Campden. We laid him in a coffin of English oak with dovetails that he would have approved and wrought iron handles made by Harry Gardiner. It had straight sides tapering to the foot, without the ugly return at the head, and on the lid was carved, in simple incised letters, 'Sydney Bolton Russell March 28, 1866, January 26, 1938'. I wrote a copy of the Psalm he most loved, 'The Lord is my Shepherd, I shall not want', and put it with him. He preferred it, as I do, in the earlier version. We took him from Snowshill to Campden on the bed of a farm wagon strewn with daffodils—a wagon such as always delighted him and which was swiftly passing out of country life (see plate 13). About a dozen of us, including his three sons, two of his grandsons and people he had known in both the family firms, walked behind it the five miles of lonely road from Snowshill to Campden. The little cortège wound its way down the lovely high street just as dusk was falling and we laid him overnight in the splendid church which had been largely built by another Cotswold pioneer—William Grevel, 'the flower of the wool merchants of all England', as his fine brass, dated 1401, describes him. The next day the church was full of people from many widely different walks of life and for months my mother received letters from remote places. It seemed to me in very truth the end of an age, as indeed it proved to be.

CHAPTER 12

Kingcombe

It is not possible to write any description of the different enterprises in which I have been engaged from time to time without dealing at some length with Kingcombe, our home, our stay for more than forty years in troublous times and still our anchor. (See plate 19.)

We started our married life in Spencer Cottage, adjoining the Lygon Arms. The back part of this small house must have been built in the sixteenth or seventeenth century and early in the nineteenth century it had had an extension built in the front garden. This made the centre of the house dark, but it had a strange and wayward charm of its own which we found a pleasant background. It had no garden but we could, if we wished, use the one at the back of the Lygon and as we were both busy and fond of walking we did not miss this amenity greatly. In 1922 our first child was born and was christened Michael—because a Michael Russell, no relation so far as we knew, had lived in the house and we had found one of his copper tokens there. These were struck for local use by people of standing in order to mitigate the shortage of coins caused by hoarding before the era of banking. It is the only token issued from Broadway: 'Michael Russell, Broadway, 1677'. From then on we began to think of more sun, light and air and a garden for the children, which became a pressing problem after the birth of our second boy, Robert, in 1924.

We had already looked at a number of houses. We did not want to be too far away but we wanted to be on the hills and not in the horticultural district of the Vale of Evesham, and we had a clear choice as the two areas meet at Broadway. As it seemed almost impossible to find a house which met our requirements on a site we liked we decided we would have to build. Under normal practice the building of a house and making of a garden is something which, once decided on, is handled by contractors, who let loose squads of men and after some months of dirt, noise and disorder a more or less finished project emerges. It is not necessarily exactly what the client, and more particularly the client's wife, expected. It is almost certain that it will have cost more than was anticipated and there will still be arguments about patterns and colours in the house and the planting of shrubs and trees in the garden. There may even be last-minute alterations of a more or less minor sort to cope with, things which have been overlooked, forgotten or avoided. But the following year a brand new lawn-mower will purr over a velvet lawn and not a dandelion or daisy will dare to raise its head. Anyone who has been persistent enough to read so far may hazard a guess that our approach might be somewhat different and they will not be far wrong.

For some time we had looked at sites in a detached way but now the pace quickened. In the summer of 1924 a house agent in Chipping Campden mentioned to my wife a field of about one and a half acres lying above the town, near Dover's Hill—the site of the Cotswold Games started by Robert Dover early in the seventeenth century, continued annually till 1851 and revived in Festival of Britain year, 1951. Toni went to look at it, was enthusiastic and insisted on my going over at once. We found a small pond in one corner which appeared to be fed by a spring, an important matter as the site was seven hundred feet above sea level, only fifty feet below the highest point of the hill, and a very long way from any water main. The existence of a spring was confirmed later by my father, who was interested in water divining. I was inclined to be sceptical, but when we took him up and asked if there was any water near he walked along the road with a hazel twig and said there was a spring under the road just above the point where the water came out lower down. As he had not seen the pond owing to an overgrown hedge we were convinced. We bought the field for £60, which seemed very little even then. We were to learn later how much it costs to live on an isolated site, but I don't think we have ever felt it wasn't worth while. The field was rect-angular, the top long side, nearly level, being bounded by Kingcombe Lane and one short side by Dyer's Lane, leading down the hill to Chipping Campden less than a mile away. From the ridge the ground fell away fairly steeply to the south and south-east, giving a lovely view towards Banbury. In the hedge adjoining the field on the lower side were some old elms and an ash, and next to the field was a small orchard of plum trees which we were later able to buy.

I commissioned Leslie Mansfield to make plans of a house. We did not realize how greatly the cost of the accommodation we specified was likely to be increased by putting it on the sloping, isolated site with which we had already fallen in love and had acquired. So, like thousands before us, we tried to adapt our requirements to our purse. We felt that the building must be a solid one of local stone with internal fittings of hard-wood. This meant planning the house in accordance with our immediate requirements and reducing the size of the rooms. But I am rather a large person and have come to value space increasingly. People who talk of passages and staircases as 'waste space' seem to me to show a poor sense of values, so it was not long before we had to add a small, separate block to serve as a workshop/studio for me, with laundry and storage space below.

On Boxing Day 1924 I went up and cut the first sod, for even then I knew how precious topsoil was, especially on hill land. It was good loam, very uneven in depth, with brashy stone below, then fine yellow sand—tricky stuff—and heavy clay several feet down. Early in 1925 we started building, by direct labour. The foreman was a master mason of the old school, Charles Keitley of Campden, and two of his sons worked on the job. If there was some query he met me with: 'We've got a bit of an obstacle race this morning, sir.' He took the greatest interest in everything about the house and had a real feeling for a good job. He loved stone and worked a good deal of it himself on a banker on the site.

In about May 1926 we moved in and when, at the end of the year, our third son Oliver was born in the house it acquired a new status, later enhanced by the arrival of a daughter, Kate. Few young women find themselves in a *Times* leader when only a few days old but this happened to Kate as there were twelve announcements of births that day, every single one of them a girl!

We were delighted by the light everywhere and the singing of birds, but there were mounds of soil and rubbish round the house for we had not thought of the garden and the house together, which seems very odd to me now. Mansfield was not especially interested in or knowledgeable about gardens and I had no experience of gardening, but somehow—in the way things so often happen in life—the garden grew quite unselfconsciously. As the ground was flat in one direction and sloped in another it was natural to terrace it and gradually some sort of order appeared, at least in parts. I began to learn a little about growing things, much encouraged by my mother, not only by sound advice but by gifts of plants. I had one man, Victor Hands, a rubicund Shakespearian character, who reported one day that he had found some 'mice's nesses'! I worked with him when I could and did much of the navvying. George and Tommy Diston, both of Snowshill, came over and built dry stone retaining walls for the terraces. Fortunately, stone was then relatively cheap and most of it came from Westington (Campden), Broadway or Snowshill quarries, involving only a short haul. I also got some hard stone paving locally and more from the Forest of Dean and Street in Somerset and the area round the house was more or less completed. I planted yews for clipped hedges, which are now very good and about eight feet high. They were passable in ten years though only eighteen inches high when planted. I began to get really interested in garden design and gardening: my furniture designing activities had a serious rival!

Meanwhile, I had been devouring garden books, starting

with those to which I constantly return—by Gertrude Jekyll and William Robinson. Then I came across Edith Wharton's *Italian Villas and Gardens* and I saw what gardening had been and might be again, of course on a quite different scale and in another climate. To link house, garden and landscape into one harmonious whole and to plan the garden as a series of outdoor rooms was a new idea which appealed to me. To note the infinite varieties of green and the beauty of texture in leafage, to use water in its every mood from solemn tree-shaded pool to sparkling sun-kissed fountain, to watch the garden under all sorts of conditions, under snow, by the light of a full moon, its intense stillness by starlight, in mist, in brilliant sunlight when the shadow of leaves dappled the paths and lawns and the quick transition to the deepest shade under dense trees such as chestnut, this was a series of new experiences.

Just then, too, I read Shepherd and Jellicoe's *Gardens and Design* and *Italian Gardens of the Renaissance* with its beautifully drawn plans of beautiful gardens—the two do not always go together, as anyone who has studied Percier & Fontaine will see. I got in touch with Jellicoe, whom I had met once at a boat-race party at the Stablers. In September 1931 he came down to look at the garden, on a lovely day when, I remember, we had tea on the lawn. He tentatively approved the general layout so far and made some valuable suggestions, especially about the scale of steps. He pointed out how the very word in Italian for steps—scala—gave us scale. And that, since steps must of necessity be related to human scale, they form an essential link with the occasionally more sublime scale of nature. Later he submitted a plan and a scheme of planting prepared in collaboration with his partner, Russell Page, who has since written *The Education of a Gardener*, which is full of sound horse-sense. These discussions were the beginning of a valued friendship and of many visits by Geoffrey Jellicoe both to Kingcombe and Broadway, for which he later prepared a development plan. As a result of long talks and much strolling in the garden at all hours the final plan emerged. I see that it is dated 1936, and it has annotations by Page. It was not carried out completely owing to the outbreak of war, but on the whole I think the resulting simplification has proved an advantage. It was, of course, carefully related to the site, a particularly interesting one of a kind where, as a Chinese poet said centuries ago, 'one should borrow one's neighbour's view'—although not, of course, from every point: nothing is more boring than a view, however good, from which there is no escape. Jellicoe and Page urged me to get permanent planting of trees done as quickly as possible—an obvious point but one I had tended to put off through not having levels sorted out on paper. When one is young time does not seem to matter so much. Trees were desirable, both for privacy and as a wind-break, for the site on an open ridge meant that we were exposed not only to the south-west wind, which comes in at times with great force from the Atlantic, but also to bitter easterly winds in winter. The only existing trees were the half-dozen old elms, which proved immensely valuable as the backbone of the eventual planting plan. For some odd reason, their significance is not apparent on the original sketch.

We already had a lawn adjacent to the house with an area enclosed by yew hedges beyond. Above was a terrace nearly level with the road which would have a row of purple-leaved sycamores planted behind it so that one would look up at the coloured undersides of the leaves, changing in every breeze. From this upper walk a wonderful view was spread out over the yew hedges, framed by the old elms both on left and right. Below the yew hedges there was to be a small bosco of flowering cherries—we searched Hillier's remarkable catalogue for the most horizontal growing ones so as not to obstruct the view. Below this again would be a few specimen trees such as *Pawlonia*, *Davidia*, tulip, *Ailanthus*, Indian chestnut, Italian cypress, etc., framed by the coppice of elms on the left and some chestnuts, ash and beech to be planted on the right. A stairway divided the more formal planting near the house from the small woodlands beyond, which were to be underplanted with snowdrops, primroses, daffodils and bluebells. (See endpapers.)

For the first time I began to see house, garden and landscape as a whole, but the house seemed to shrink when the boys came back from school and we were considering possible ways of extending it. In 1935 Jock Shepherd—at one time Geoffrey's partner—who had been working on the rebuilding of the Shakespeare Theatre at Stratford-on-Avon, designed a possible addition. It gave us a larger sitting-room with bedroom over and certain other accommodation. It linked the house to the separate block and so made possible a new entrance in a small pool garden protected from the south-west wind, of whose violence at times the original plan had not taken account. We have found that the broadly cruciform plan which resulted gives sun, light and space. It also isolates sound but is not so compact to service or heat. Still, one cannot have everything. The new drawing-room was good for sound and our friends Basil and Elizabeth Fairclough brought chamber music into the house. Although we were not able to screw up our courage to carry out all the work envisaged—including the projected dining-room—owing to the growing European tension, we at least had a background which made it possible to live in a temporary way the kind of life we liked. But it was too good to last. In little more than a year my father's death, followed by the outbreak of war, disrupted all our careful planning.

CHAPTER 13

Walking

It is so much easier to get to know a country if one walks, rides or even bicycles through it than if one goes by car, train or 'plane. As I always like to stop and look at all sorts of buildings, trees, countryside and workmanship I naturally enjoy walking, which leaves me free to do as I please. One savours the atmosphere of the place. One goes into little pubs with a healthy thirst and appetite and one listens with delight to a group arguing about pigs, potatoes, oranges or olives according to the latitude. But put people into glass boxes on wheels and frequently they speed about from one palace hotel to another, looking at the inhabitants as if they were gazing into—or out of—an aquarium. Put a man on a tractor-seat and often he loses that reverence for the soil as a living organism which was inherent in nearly all old farm labourers: instead of something in whose presence mankind must needs be humble, it becomes just another raw material to be processed. Often he sees nothing wicked in littering the earth—the universal mother of us all, as a seventeenth-century gardener called her—with worn-out tyres, old cars and such filthy refuse of industrialism.

Before 1914 I walked over the hills quite a bit by myself. All the marching of the war didn't cure me, and when I came back I sometimes went for longish walks with my mother, who used to plod over the hills with a dog most mornings, rain or shine. But I started covering longer distances on holiday, sometimes with my wife, sometimes with one of my brothers or a friend. Toni and I tried to get away for a week or two each year, usually abroad, and walking was a good change from the considerable job of making a field into a garden.

I remember starting somewhere near East Hendred with Charles Mellersh and following the Ridgeway through the glorious Vale of White Horse, where you could walk for half a day and see no one but an odd shepherd and hear little but the larks—no aeroplanes or tractors then! We walked on green roads for mile after mile, then along the full length of the Quantocks across Sedgemoor into Bridgwater and so into Devonshire.

Again, I recall exploring the Yorkshire moors one January with Noel Carrington. Not many people start a holiday on Boxing Day but we found it quite delightful and when he went back to London I carried on and ended in a nice little hotel in Ripon. It rained for three days but I had discovered *Handley Cross* and I just didn't care a hoot.

I shall always remember a solitary walk from Lake Vrnwy to Bala, over the hills. I had been walking with Dick in Shropshire and had gone on into Wales alone. It was a very wet day, but there seemed no help for it: I must take a road marked on a gate 'Not safe for motor cars' and hope to reach Bala—ten miles away. It was about five and would be dark in an hour. The rain poured down, but once I had got really wet I enjoyed it—it is the intermediate period which is trying. My boots squelched. Everywhere I could hear little torrents rushing down the hill side. My, how dark it became—I never remember being out in such a pitch-black night. Walls of rough stone bordered the road and horned Welsh sheep put their heads over them and baa-ed in a very sinister and disconcerting way. Eventually the road, now deep in water, went into a tunnel of larch trees and the blackness of a few moments back seemed high noon! I nearly walked into a signpost but was quite unable to read it and my matches were soaked. However, I kept on and after what seemed hours I saw the lights of what I took to be Bala over the lake. I found a small hotel, where I was kindly lent some clothes while mine were dried, and after half a tumbler of rum in hot milk with an egg beaten up in it, I recovered rapidly and was ready for any food I could get. I slept like a log, and fell into a train in the morning. But discovering in my

Times that there was a loan exhibition of Van Gogh's paintings at Manchester Art Gallery, I got out at the next station and went back to look at them. Thus are the virtuous rewarded!

One December, Dick and I went to Italy. It was cold and there was snow in the north but after exploring Florence we decided to walk to Rome. We spent some time in Siena—as Mussolini had done on his notorious march a few weeks before —and were absolutely bewitched by the beauty of the Tuscan countryside. Then on through Orbetello and Civita Vecchia, staying in little inns where we paid about a shilling a night. The cooking was excellent, the beds of lovely handwoven linen, snow white, and everything else dirty! There were also the most exciting buildings in the most unlikely places. How sad I felt to read of war damage in Italy and especially of the Campo Santo at Pisa, one of the loveliest burial grounds I have ever seen. We walked nearly two hundred miles but took a train when we got to flat, rather uninteresting country and arrived in Rome just before Christmas.

Toni and I walked in the West of Ireland, to her old home in Sligo. I remember that Kate was expected some six months later, so we came to an arrangement that I carried the luggage if she carried the baby! We went from Dublin by train, having come over on the night boat. We were told there was a breakfast car, but found the guard sorting the mail in a most primitive way by throwing it to the four quarters of the van and so making it almost impossible to pass. 'You'll have to jump over the mail,' he said. Having arrived in the restaurant car, we found it had an air of faded splendour, as if it had been built for the Habsburgs. The panels were inlaid with rare woods and the solitary steward was very dishevelled. He showed us to a seat. In the rack above was a pair of boots. I queried whether this was the local way of indicating that it was reserved but, glancing at the boots, he said: 'Och, that's me.'

We were so very fortunate as to walk to the little village of Cong on Lough Corrib. We were told there were two 'foine hotels' there. One was very dirty outside and the other somewhat less so. Going inside the latter, we found it very dirty so we tried the other, which was much better. We found there an Irishman, who had been educated at Cheltenham, with his sister. He asked us if we had heard of the remarkable event that was happening that night when, it appeared, an Irish American who had left the village with his parents twenty-six years before was returning with his wife and daughter. It was to be his first visit since he left. We walked round the village and found it small and derelict. Where the roof of a cottage in a row in the street had collapsed the people on either side just threw their tins and rubbish through the windows—and this had been going on for years. There was a small Celtic cross— modern, as far as I remember—about four or five feet high at one end of the village. And there was a charming little cell on the lake, built at the same time as Cong Abbey. Next to it was a narrow sluice, at one end of which had been a fish-net so arranged that the weight of several fish in it would cause a bell to ring. The studious brother reading in the cell could then go back to the abbey with the lunch. Excited groups were talking in the village and a tense air of expectancy pervaded the place.

Next morning we got down to breakfast early. The door opened and a very dapper American entered, wearing octagonal spectacles. He was quite willing to talk and told us how he remembered leaving the village as a small, barefooted boy. He had taken with him memories of the blue lake with the mountains behind, of the village and the Celtic cross—all, of course, many times life size and grown larger with telling through the years. The actual size of the cross was a shock to him, and he said he just stood in front of it and laughed and laughed. The village struck him as unhygienic and untidy. It had no sidewalks, or refuse collections. There was a great shortage of cars, which seemed to us an immense advantage, and it struck him as a waste of time for people to take a donkey-cart and spend all day cutting peat by hand instead of having a Ford truck and peat-cutting machinery. His idea was that Ireland would be made a great country for tourists and he wanted to build asphalt roads everywhere, especially to Killarney, so that people could see the 'beauty spots' without leaving their automobiles. He saw nothing odd in this and when we said we were walking he obviously thought we must be very hard-up, which was indeed true, though I suppose we could have raked up enough to ride had we chosen to do so. But it was quite incomprehensible to him that anyone could have the necessary cash and not ride. He did not mention the glorious clear water of the lake and the trout, the royal fern and spotted orchis growing wild in great drifts by the roadside, the astonishing vitality of the madonna lilies and hellebores in some cottage gardens, the mournful beauty of the hills, the peacefulness, the lack of noise or hurry. Truly, a high standard of living can be made to mean many things, but to swallow the American way of life whole takes a wide gullet.

This was only too obvious to us a few days later in Galway. Here there was a primitive fishermen's quarter called the Claddagh, where we were told that Gaelic was commonly spoken. Most of the houses had one room with whitewashed walls and thatched roofs, which seemed to drain the rainwater into the walls as there was hardly any overhang. The lanes between the houses were just wide enough for a pack-donkey —about six feet. It was quite charming, but must have been unhealthy. A seeing eye would have noted the real beauty and coped with the deficiencies. But no, to deal with the situation a concrete road forty feet wide with pavements had been planned in a straight line. However, the cost had not been calculated beforehand and after building a quarter of a mile the constructors had given up and it ended in heaps of ashes and cans. On one side concrete houses of the most repellent type had been erected, half the Claddagh had been torn down and then apparently everyone had got tired and left the whole job.

On another occasion my wife and I walked from Rouen to Les Andelys to look at the marvellous castle and try to discover at the same time some evidence of the existence of the pasque flower, which William Robinson says grows there. (It grows wild in one place I know in Gloucestershire, too.) We saw many little inns with, hanging in front, the traditional 'bush' which good wine is said not to need. We went on to Chartres, which we approached in the only proper way—across the plain on foot, so that one has time to take in the grandeur of the cathedral gradually. I remember seeing the funeral of some local notable there. The great west doors were flung open and a procession rich with gold and colour streamed in, vividly framed in the light of the doorway against the dark, jewelled interior. It was a really grand spectacle. Our age has become so conditioned to dreariness that the faintest hint of a show with any splendour brings loud protests about waste of money and nuisance to traffic. Damn the traffic! In Campden, when we have a torchlight procession the cars have to wait, and then the occupants are able to see something worth while.

And we walked—or tried to walk—in Provence in January. The withering mistral made it all but impossible. We made a pilgrimage to Avignon to look at the Roman glass there, but the museum was unheated and its coldness was beyond belief. I remember that my wife and I glued our noses to showcases and marvelled at the magical handles of bottles and cinerary urns—such handles that, for sheer rightness, might almost have been a natural product—until our teeth chattered. When we could stand it no longer we rushed out into the blistering mistral, drank Cognac and then returned for another gaze. Sip and peep! This was repeated so many times that the ancient concierge was filled with forebodings of impending disaster. His frozen blood was so stirred that he even made the supreme gesture of leaving his minute cubby-hole with its tiny brazier in order to stalk through the echoing and deserted galleries to watch us narrowly. The British Museum, too, has some lovely examples of Roman glass which can be seen generally under conditions less likely to lead to one's being shrammed— though it is infinitely more difficult to supply a similar remedy.

From Avignon we took a little tram-like train to Les Saintes Maries on the Mediterranean. Across the salty marshes of the Camargues, where it seems that only sheep and a tough breed of cattle can live, we reached at last the village and the church there to which many of the gypsies of Southern Europe make a yearly pilgrimage. The sea was as grey and cold as our own North Sea. We went to Nîmes to look at the wonderful public gardens, to Arles to see St Trophime and the Roman work and to Les Baux. This derelict and haunted little town perched on its hill-top is no doubt full of tourists later in the year, but at this time it was empty except for the handful of people who live in the caves in the rocks. It is strange to find smoke coming from a hole in the turf and to discover an inhabited den below. Will above and below ground count as one when some logically-minded French planning committee starts to work out the density per hectare?

We were told, however, that it was certain to be warm in Corsica, so we went across on a most antiquated packet-boat from Marseilles. The deck was crowded with cattle and a storm blew up in the night so that we heard the dull thuds of the poor beasts falling about. We were all glad to reach Ajaccio in time for breakfast. We walked the length of the island, noticing the little mortuary chapels which lined the roads in places, interspersed with great clumps of prickly pear. This must have been a survival of the Roman tradition of burying outside the towns. Near Corte we came across snow—the first, we were told, for twenty-five years. The orange trees, thickly laden with fruit, looked quite magically beautiful in their white background. I'm ashamed to say that I ate two blackbirds, my wife refusing hers, followed by delicious cream cheese with sugar on it. Later in the year I'm told that the scent of flowers covers the island, the Maquis blooms with thousands of Cystus, which are used for fuel in bread ovens. I do indeed hope the inhabitants have not been seduced by tasteless mass-produced bread. I remember seeing a wheel-wright building a cart by the side of the road, making a wheel entirely by hand. I never expect to see the like again—yet I remember seeing pit-sawyers at work by the side of the road in Essex in about 1923. We reached Bastia at last, and still hope to return there.

One year just before the war, in July, we walked down the Loire, visiting Amboise, Azay-le-Rideau, Chenonceaux,

Chinon, Saumur. I was delighted to find Catalpas of great size in the fields, in full bloom, almost as common as horse-chestnuts in England. Toasting Rabelais, we drank the good red wines of Chinon and Bourgeille and the white of Vouvray and Saumur and saw the great cellars cut in the soft stone, also the remarkable Museum of the Vine at Saumur, where every known vine was grown in carefully-tended plots. It was as unusual in its way as the open-air museum at Skansen, near Stockholm, where old wooden houses have been re-erected, furnished with things of the same age and are looked after by people in clothes of the period, as also at Williamsburg in the United States. I recently opened the first house of a similar group at Stoke Prior, near Bromsgrove.

Another year, in June or July, we went to look at the flowers in the Tyrol. We walked up the Oetz valley from Innsbruck, taking our time about it. We found good, clean *Gasthaus* accommodation with excellent cooking everywhere; and different flowers out at different heights until, at about 10,000 feet, there were whole fields of sulphur anemones. These 'flowery meads' were astonishing—gentians, martagon lilies, campanulas and so on growing thickly in hay fields. We discovered that many a small *Gasthaus* had two separate sides: one for the tourists, often with ugly furniture of pitch pine, a sickly yellow; and one for the peasants, with scrubbed pine interior, a delicate grey. So we insisted on having our meals in the latter. In the evening a large group of peasants would come in from mowing. They were more expert with a scythe than anywhere else I know. In the grilling heat of the valley, with troops of horse-flies about, they would mow the steepest slopes all day with admirable grace and economy of effort. Grouped at a large table lighted by a few candles they would have, first, large bowls of soup and then an immense pie would come in. What a gay, vivacious party they always seemed to be, and how it would make one's day to see one of their bronzed, laughing faces among the harassed, sad crowd endlessly searching for bargains in Oxford Street. We came home through Munich, and were there on the Tuesday following the week-

176

end of Hitler's purge in 1934. What a change! In restaurants nervous people glanced apprehensively over their shoulders but no one spoke. We saw several funerals but no one followed them. We were completely mystified and quite un-aware, until we reached England, of what had been happening so close to us.

I haven't done much walking in Sweden as distances are rather considerable between villages, especially in the north. But I remember going to see Hald at Orrefors and arriving in time for an immense 'works breakfast', a great oval dish, the whole rim covered in eggs, being its main feature. And I was astonished that they had 5,000 acres of land, as they grew their own timber for the glass furnaces. There were disused iron-works too with great water hammers like those used at one time in Sussex. Hald told us that the men used to sleep in the works from Monday to Friday and were brought their meals by their wives from the village. Whether this was because it was such a dirty job that the women wouldn't have them in the house he didn't know, but he claimed that it was from Sweden that the English took and popularized the weekend habit! I remember, too, being astonished at the large stores of hand-woven linen in the chests in the workers' houses, where looms were still quite common.

Once in Stockholm two architect friends were taking Dick and myself to see various things of interest. We asked about the possibility of seeing the interior of one of the new blocks of flats and the driver of the taxi, who overheard our conversa-tion, said he would like to show us his home. We were delighted. He drove us there and escorted us up the green marble staircase to a door on which was his name in neat, well-designed metal lettering, introduced us to his wife, showed us the balcony overlooking the lake on which he had his breakfast in the summer, and both of them pointed out how well the flat was planned, how trees had been left around it and so on. They even knew the name of the architect. We shook hands and came away musing that certainly there was no doubt we were abroad—an impression confirmed by *Schnapps* and forty

M

different and admirable kinds of *smorgasbord* at lunch. We went to see Professor Gregor Paulsson and his dear wife Ester, a competent weaver, at Uppsala, where we drank mead from a horn. I am fond of Sweden and have many recollections of the hospitality of the Swedes, in their homes, in the old Town Cellars or Den Gulden Freyden. It is with respect that I have studied the growth of good design in all the many sides of *Kooperativa* since I first knew it in 1929. Here the Swedes have blazed a trail. The English, Scottish and Swiss Co-operatives have only recently become aware that they have any social responsibility in the quality—using the word in its widest and proper sense—of the things they sell.

This chapter started at a walking pace and so it shall end. During the last war I came down from London one evening and arrived at Oxford at about ten. There was no train on from there, I knew. But it was a glorious starlight night and I had no luggage, so why not walk home? I walked through Woodstock and past Blenheim Park, looking marvellous in the moonlight and with owls—one of my favourite birds—hooting in the trees. Without stopping, I walked steadily through the night and caught the 7.30 train from Moreton-in-Marsh to Campden, arriving home for breakfast. It was 28 miles in one stretch—and I admit I wasn't sorry to find a train so nicely timed, and how memorable the breakfast was!

CHAPTER 14

Shattered Hopes

When war was declared in 1939, Don, Dick and I talked over various matters, the most pressing of which was what to do about my mother, who was still living at Tower Close, Snowshill. In an isolated house, with no shopping facilities near, it would be impossible for an elderly lady to carry on if stranded without any help, to say nothing of the fear of bombing. So we suggested that she came down to the Lygon at once and the house was let to some friends who wanted to get out of London. Then Dick, who was about to go into the Navy, proposed to find a home in the country for his wife Marian and their daughter Sarah, who was about three months old, so they came to us at Kingcombe. Dick had been building up a considerable practice as an industrial designer in London since he left Broadway a few years earlier and had just fixed up a new office. In spite of alarms, things had gone well up to 1938, but then the prevailing uncertainty discouraged enterprise and research into new designs and, like the rest of us, he was to see his efforts crumble.

In these early months of the phony war we at Kingcombe became acutely aware, for the first time, of our isolated site. Shortage of petrol made travelling so difficult that one could only go on urgent errands; even friends quite near were cut off, not only for this reason but through sheer pressure of jobs which had not been thought about before—jobs like stoking the boiler, feeding the fowls, pumping the water and so on. When I had to go anywhere I tried to do a little shopping, an occupation in which I cannot claim to excel. I found that fish— one of the few unrationed items—rapidly disappeared unless one was on the spot when it was delivered. I sympathized with the local fishmonger, Mrs Ellis, whose premises were somewhat primitive, when an inspector called one day and asked her where she kept her fish. 'Young man,' she snapped, 'I don't keep it, I sell it!' I got into the habit of ringing up to find out what was available. Posing this question to the Evesham fishmonger, I heard the girl who answered the telephone shout across the shop: 'Mr Russell wants to know what fish there is.' 'Which Mr Russell?' came the faint reply. ''im as comes in with a bucket for fishes' 'eads!' was the readily recognizable description of myself as shopper-poultryman. We were left with no outside help and in the house only Mary Jelfs, our devoted cook, who valiantly saw the war through and is still with us. Although she is lame, she did a great deal of outside work. Indeed, she carries on magnificently our Broadway tradition, for not only is she a jolly good cook but she is also an expert catcher of moles, bonfire builder and grower of plants from cuttings. She is inclined, however, to be somewhat disconcerted by my fondness for fungi and on one occasion, having been persuaded to cook some succulent blewitts, she was greatly alarmed to note a lull in our talk and came in expecting the worst.

It was obvious that food was going to be scarce and I started at once to dig up turf and plant potatoes. This was a slogging job but it was the beginning of a process of turning the place into a smallholding which went on throughout the war. Gradually we increased our fowls and geese, we added ducks, rabbits, bees, and later pigs and goats. And, of course, we found that this addition of livestock gave us a much greater supply of manure than we had had before the war and so increased the productivity of the soil for vegetables and fruit. Fortunately straw, which makes such excellent compost, was one of the very few things which became more abundant and cheaper during the war. We saw that such things as lawns and most flowers would have to go, but I made a determined effort to look after the yew hedges and trees, as they could not well be replaced. On the whole, we were pretty successful in our efforts to become self-supporting—which was indeed fortunate, for at the height of the bombing we had eighteen people in the house. It seemed most odd to me to smell once more the acrid tang of high explosive from an occasional bomb quite near Kingcombe, and what I thought of the Germans for starting this madness three times within living memory would be quite unprintable.

C. H. James and his wife Margaret often came to see us and in 1939 we had found the whole family excellent holiday accommodation with the Badgers at their farmhouse on Westington Hill. They planned to come in August for a month and ended by staying four years. He had been in Lutyens' office and during the war was working on camouflage at Leamington, having lost a leg in the First World War. James brought over his artist friends from Leamington: James Gardner, who was later to become one of the most lively of exhibition and display designers, and Tom Monnington (later President of the Royal Academy) and his talented wife, Jane— both of them Prix de Rome scholars—who stayed with us at Kingcombe for more than a year. And one morning James appeared with Robin Darwin, who was later to be appointed Principal of the Royal College of Art. He seemed somewhat taken aback to find me digging with only a pair of pants on and later on he often twitted me about Cotswold serfs! One of the very few consolations in this dreadful upheaval is that these and others whom we then met have remained our dear friends through the years, and I was closely associated with several of them in post-war work.

Nineteen-forty will go down to history as one of the decisive years, the year of the fall of France, the evacuation from Dunkirk, the beginning of Churchill's leadership and the Battle of Britain. But I remember it too for other things, for the Second World War had an equally disrupting, but entirely different, effect on my life as the First. We had serious illness at home, and our factories were losing money at an alarming rate. Owing to the national shortage of timber the amount which could be used was restricted, so that furniture such as we produced could no longer be made. We had no hope, therefore, of making both ends meet in the showrooms, either in London or Broadway. On October 19, 1940, I resigned from the managing directorship, which was taken over by R. H. Bee, our secretary, whose skill and ability in administration saved the business from disaster and put it on its feet again by reorganizing for war work. With Ted Ould as his right-hand man he was successful in obtaining contracts for, first of all, such simple things as ammunition boxes and later for the much more complicated sections of Mosquito aircraft. Then he produced prototypes of various parts, such as under-carriages, for which forgings had hitherto been necessary. These were built up by gluing metal and wood together, a method which saved several precious weeks. There was also a wonderful model of a new 'plane for testing in an air tunnel. In a separate shop some 700 models of aircraft for recognition were produced each week by about forty married women who had no children under ten and had not worked in a factory before. They were drafted to put in four hours a day. A single skilled machinist was responsible for setting up. This was quite an achievement as the models were less than 1 foot long and had no flat planes or right-angles. Often a telegram would halt production of a model of, say, a new Mitsubishi as a photograph from another angle had shown a discrepancy in the detail made from an earlier shot. Bee was an ingenious man, with a great interest in engineering and so was able in due course to relate the experiments of wartime to the needs of peacetime production.

At the end of October 1940 a German raider on his way to Birmingham was attacked by one of our fighters over Broadway and jettisoned his load of some hundreds of incendiary bombs. Although most fell in the fields we had seven on our premises. Six were dealt with but the seventh landed near the ridge of the great thatched roof of the barn and from the first it was seen to be hopeless. I had a call at Kingcombe saying what had happened and when I went outside the whole sky was lighted up over the hill. The great blaze would have spread had there been any wind, but by morning there was only a vast heap of ashes. The lovely barn, of which I had made a drawing in 1907, had gone, with an immense amount of furniture and some 20,000 yards of fine textiles brought down from London for safe storage. Our world was indeed disintegrating.

Thanks to Don's back-breaking work it proved possible to keep the Lygon going in wartime and in this he was stoutly supported by his wife, Effie. At one stage there was a distinct possibility that it might be commandeered but it is in fact quite unsuitable for office accommodation. He made it his particular care and pleasure to look after servicemen on short leave from overseas, especially those from Australia and New Zealand. During the war over 300 were entertained in this way, without any charge being made, but many of them voluntarily took turns at doing all kinds of jobs as there was, of course, a great shortage of staff. A fortunate result of Don's idea was that one of these service visitors, Douglas Barrington from Perth, decided he would like to stay in England and he was invited to join our firm. He has proved a great success and is now managing director of the Lygon Arms.

When war seemed imminent in 1939 I rejoined the Special Police, for which I had first volunteered during the coal strike in 1911. I was interested in the routine of a country police station. On my tour of duty in the evening I was detailed to look after the telephone, an instrument which I have always regarded with some distaste. The narrow fixed bench was designed for discomfort in a masterly way, but there was a fire and I could read sometimes between calls.

I had no idea how multitudinous were the duties of the police. The sergeant, one of those humane people whose great ambition it is to help others to keep the law rather than running them in for breaking it, used to come in between rounds and sit down to an ancient and dusty typewriter. After strumming away for a while he would pause and say: 'How many f's in roofs? Ah, I thought so. Did you hear . . .' and then I would have a racy account of local happenings. 'The trouble about this job,' he'd say, 'is that you can't get away from it. And often, if you're wanted at all, you're wanted desperately urgent. Why, t'other day a friend of mine, old Joe Hands, asked me and the missus to come to tea and I said: "Why, nothing 'ud suit me better, Joe, if somebody's pig don't die." I reckon pigs know I be going out to tea: twice I've had to put it off and see whether it was likely to be a case of swine fever. And then what with billeting, and accidents, and people having no lights or too strong lights, or losing their watches or bags, and keeping my eyes skinned for likely criminals and escaped prisoners, why it's hard to find time for tea parties. And you see some queer sights too. Why one night, in a thick mist, I was on the top road, going to meet the Blockley man. All of a sudden I saw a small hill coming towards me without a sound. Not a sound. I reckon if I hadn't been in the Force I'd have bolted. No, I never touch a drop of anything on duty. It was an elephant from a circus. And do you know it's an offence to have an elephant on a road unattended? Or a tiger. . . .' He used to come in and scan the book in which all telephone calls were entered. One night he noticed one entry —a woman who had rung up to ask the time, or something like that—which seemed to need no comment. 'Who's Miss Moody?' he said. 'Don't know,' I replied. 'Nor do I. Where is she staying?' I said I hadn't enquired. 'Always take the address. We might want to find her and then it would be serious.' 'Wait a minute,' said I, 'we should find her at Mrs Bennett Clark's: I heard her parrot in the background.' He looked at me as if he thought I'd make Scotland Yard in time! I asked to take duty for the three or four hours up to midnight, which few people wanted. It didn't interfere with other work and I liked walking home through Campden when all was still. I remember the first winter of the war, when trees were covered with frozen rain to such an extent that great limbs crashed as I walked back.

But when France fell and there was a call for Local Defence Volunteers I asked permission to join, as I felt that an unfit man could answer a telephone as well as I could and in the other

The showrooms of Gordon Russell Ltd on Broadway Green

Garage for furniture vans, *c* 1932. Architect: Geoffrey Jellicoe

11 The Duchess of York (now the Que
Mother), the Lady Maud Bowes-Ly
and Lady-in-Waiting in the garden
the showrooms, *c* 1929
Photograph by S. B. Russell

My father (left) and Henry Ford at
front door of The Lygon Arms, *c* 1

Decorations in Broadway planned by Gordon Russell for the Coronation of King George VI, 1937. The tall white posts with large flags placed at regular intervals each side of the long street provided a framework into which the efforts of individual householders could be fitted

13   The wagon bearing my father's coffin leaving his home,
      Tower Close, Snowshill, January 1938

At work on his tombstone

job my army experience would be useful. At first any transfer
was refused, but later, when factory units of the Local
Defence Volunteers were started, I applied again and was
transferred. I expect our unit of the Home Guard—as the
LDVs were later renamed—went through much the same
teething troubles as others. As I had some experience of
lecturing I was sent on a week's course and, armed with this
information, was made Training Officer of the Company,
whose Commander was Major Lees-Milne of Wickhamford.
It was a widely scattered Company—the Broadway Company
of the 4th Worcesters—comprising a number of villages in the
Vale of Evesham. Its boundary must have been a good deal over
twenty miles, so it was impossible to get NCOs together in
one place except on rare occasions, and in spring, summer and
autumn most of the men were desperately busy on the land.
So for many months I turned out on three, four and sometimes
five nights a week and on Sunday mornings. But the spirit was
so good that it was not nearly so irksome as it sounds, and I was
proud of the general standard: we had a number of younger
men who were not called up because they were working on the
land, so this was perhaps easier to achieve than in other units.

Our weekend camps under canvas or in cow-sheds and outbuildings were occasionally amusing. I remember one which
included a general knowledge oral examination. The Battalion
Training Officer, Major Carter, was putting questions. He
was a man of immense girth, very keen and efficient—no one
put more into the Home Guard than he did and many old hands
will remember his excellent broadcasts. A market gardener
came in and sat down opposite him. 'Good evening, George,'
says Carter. 'Good evening, surr!' 'Now, George, suppose
I give you a letter to the CO, where would you take it?' 'To
Wick 'ouse, surr.' 'Yes, quite right: that's Battalion HQ.
Now, how would you get there?' 'Well, surr, I'd go to the
Sandys Arms and turn right on the main A'sum (Evesham)
Road. At Bengeworth I'd turn left down Waterside for Parshur (Pershore) and just afore you comes to the river this side
of Parshur I'd turn right for Wick.' 'Quite right,' says Carter.

'It's evident you know the way. But the Boche is in Evesham. Is there another way?' A pause and then: 'Well, surr, I'd go by the Combertons, if so be as the Jerries aren't there too.' 'Yes, you've got the idea all right. Now, the letter is addressed to the CO. Who would you give it to?' (Our CO was a very popular Master of Foxhounds who had been a gunner in the First World War. He was tall and well-built and was known to have a powerful vocabulary.) 'Col. Taylor, surr'—said with great emphasis. 'Well, what sort of man is he—little man, who squints?' 'No, surr!' 'Why, you speak as if you knew him,' says Carter. George looked at him keenly and said with relish: 'Called me all the buggers in 'ell for 'eading a fox!'

Petrol was short and I often rode a bicycle when the distance was not great. My headquarters was the Fleece Inn at Bretforton, a beautiful little inn kept by an extremely nice family— the Taplins. Mrs Taplin was a distinguished old lady who looked much like portraits of Queen Elizabeth I, and had the same forthright ways. Her son Harold had been a prisoner in the First World War and most of the work was done by her daughter Lola. Here I could leave messages, or my bicycle, or borrow anything needful. On one occasion I met Ted Carter driving an Austin 7. I was quite as astonished to see him ooze his enormous bulk out of the tiny car as he was to see me on a bicycle!

As a relief to the tension of these tremendous times I felt I must do some creative work with my hands, besides the chore of growing food and what not, so I turned my attention to experiments in simple carving. It happened like this. My old friend F. L. Griggs, the artist, had died in 1938 and it looked as if Nina, his widow, would have to sell the house. This had been some years abuilding, and was a remarkable essay in Cotswold stonework, of great textural beauty. Dear Nina, few houses had a more generous hostess. She felt that the house should have some record of the fact that Fred had designed and built it and, knowing I was interested in lettering, she asked me to design an inscription which she had written out. This was a great responsibility as not only had every smallest detail of the house received Fred's careful and knowledgeable consideration but he was also an authority on typography and had designed founts of type for the Monotype Corporation. So I asked for time to think about the matter. Having done so, I went back to Nina and told her that she was asking me to do the job in the normal way, with which I entirely disagreed. I explained that what generally happened was this. The client (who was often a committee) decided that an inscription was wanted and drafted it. The draft was then sent to the architect, who thought where it might go and then got an assistant to set it out. The assistant—who was most unlikely ever to have carved stone or to have any feeling for the special form given to letters by a chisel—turned to a book of lettering. The design was sent to the builder, who decided it was a specialist's job and so sought a price from a firm of monumental masons, who often were not even told how high it would be above ground or what point of the compass it would face. Nor, as a rule, had they any sensitive feeling for lettering, so it was no wonder that the results were bad. I told her that I didn't think such jobs should be designed on paper at all: they should be set out on the stone and carved direct, like the Roman inscriptions. Whilst we were hardly likely to achieve the majesty of an inscription such as that from the Forum at Wroxeter at least we could study it humbly. Although I understood a goose-quill as a tool I had done no lettering with a chisel but I'd like to try. I would get a few chisels and if she didn't like the results she knew me well enough to say so.

On my next journey to London I invested 5s 8d in chisels and a mallet at Tiranti's and seldom was money better spent. When I got home I cut a foundation stone inscription for King-combe. It was near the ground and so rather awkward and the stone wasn't sufficiently large to carry the big letters which would have been more appropriate to the coarse-grained material. Unfortunately we hadn't thought of such matters when my wife laid the stone as the clock smote noon in August 1936, with her family around her urging her to make a speech. I don't know why: just carelessness, I suppose. But I liked carving the letters and Nina liked them too, so I was asked to go ahead. The inscription for her ran: 'Dover's House was designed and built by Frederick Landseer Maur Griggs R.A. A.D. 1926–1934'. I asked her to let me cut the old form 'builded' instead of built as I felt it expressed more exactly the leisurely and painstaking way in which it arose. Built has a clipped sound—and, incidentally, the T came exactly over a vertical joint! I cut it in biggish letters—about four inches high—in one line about sixteen feet long on a course of stone beneath a drip moulding. This I did one weekend—I believe it was in the fevered summer of 1939—and it was an extraordinary experience. The chisel mesmerized me. It took possession of the job, so I worked on regardless of time, and refusing to come in for meals, was handed pots of bitter and cups of tea through a nearby window.

My next carving job—in 1940—was a tombstone (see plate 13). It happened like this. Eric Kennington, when painting my father's portrait in 1934, talked to him of tombstones, in which both of them were interested. I think it was then that Eric had been carving one for T. E. Lawrence. Anyway, he said he would like to carve one for my father, so a stone—from the hardest bed in Westington Quarry, Campden—was got out and sent over to his studio in Oxfordshire. Odd, isn't it, that two hundred years ago there wasn't a village or small town where you could not get a tombstone made locally with good lusty carving and excellent lettering whereas now we have advanced to such a degree that either you put up with the dreadful products of monumental masons or you have to search out a sculptor such as Gill or Kennington? Seldom indeed do you see a good stone carved locally. I went over to Homer—the Kenningtons' beautiful old house—and it was decided that I should do the lettering on the stone and he should carve the head. But he was caught up in his war artist's job and, in order to get it fixed to please my mother, I had to do the whole of it. I didn't dare to show it to Eric; but I think he would have approved my way of setting about it, and I loved working in his studio, in which his effigy of T. E. Lawrence, now at Wareham, was lying. He was always against listening too much to professionals: he liked to have a go and he liked other people to do the same. Yet I don't hold with tombstones really, although I must admit I've spent many happy hours in quiet churchyards looking at old ones. The thought of the acres of good pasture covered each year with beastly monuments of a purely commercial kind is abhorrent to me. I wish to be burned and sprinkled on the top of the Cotswolds!

My next spare time job was carving a date-stone for which a space had been left when we built Kingcombe (see plate 14). I shall never forget the pleasure with which I carved this stone, which I propped up on a wheelbarrow under a tree in the orchard, in glorious weather, while I listened to the music of the bees in a nearby hive, drowned at intervals by the roaring of planes overhead. After that I did other things around the house, and I also did a memorial panel for my friend Robertson Scott of *The Countryman* to go in his garden wall at Idbury to commemorate a young airman who had died in the war. He put a photograph in his magazine, which led someone to write and ask me to do a headstone for a dog!

I must have been a great nuisance to my dear, long-suffering wife for stone dust penetrates and my hair and clothes were full of it. But the main problem with any craft of this sort, as far as I am concerned, is to be strong-minded enough to take the time off to do it. However, one must have some defence against the pressures of life.

Perhaps some of my happiest hours during the war were spent looking after my bees. My father had taken to keeping bees and proved rather good at it. He liked to give little jars of his own delicious wild white clover honey to his friends. These pots were made for him by Michael Cardew at the Winchcombe Pottery and he used to go over and spend a morning there with great pleasure writing, with a steel pen, 'Snowshill Honey' or 'Tower Close Honey' on the soft clay before firing. I still have several of them and very good the writing is. On one occasion a sister-in-law of mine—unused to rural pursuits— rushed into Tower Close and said: 'Mr Russell, your bees are escaping!' At Board meetings at Broadway on hot days in May or June my father used to appear with an expectant air saying that he might get a call. Each time the 'phone rang he perked up and when at last he was told, 'Your bees have swarmed', he fairly leapt from his chair and rushed from the room with every appearance of pleasure and relief. Not only had he found a perfectly legitimate excuse—at least in his own eyes—for escaping from boredom but at the next Board meeting he had the pleasure of telling us we had taken wrong decisions in his absence!

Bees are the most considerate of domestic animals. They don't ask you to carry pails about in the slush and fogs of winter for they wisely go to sleep themselves and leave you free to do the same if you can. But when April quickens the sap in every living twig, when flowers appear and the soft airs replace the horrid blasts of March, when the days lengthen and the nights grow warmer—when, indeed, it is delicious to be out and about anyway—then bees give you the very best of excuses for not sitting at a desk. Moreover, they are insistent that you should be quiet, clean, gentle and unhurried: albeit they themselves, during a time when nectar is abundant, seem to work in a positive frenzy Sit down but a few feet from the hive and their frantic endeavours to pack one or two more trips into the hour distil a solemn, soothing hum which is as satisfying as to watch the direct, purposeful outgoing and the slower, loaded return. But, should the weather decide to return to March on a sudden, have no fear that the bees will share it with you.

The deep human instinct to look after some person or animal comes out in wayward forms. Our friend Professor Campagnac announced quite suddenly one day that he was certain he would make an inspired swineherd, and he nearly wept to think of the barren years in which he had taught at Liverpool University. He was to be seen scanning the *Farmer and Stockbreeder* and muttering to himself about 'good long backs' and 'well-set jowls'. Such maladies are highly contagious, and if Ernest had it badly his cook became delirious. She raved over the scraps the fowls were stuffing their crops with, vowing they would fatten a pig. She volunteered to feed the pig, to clean it out, to groom it and to deal in a silent and efficient way with its obsequies. When someone pointed out that pigs were always escaping she pooh-poohed the bare idea. She added that even if they—pigs, she said, always did better than a pig— escaped on a wet night she would scour Gloucestershire for them, and gladly. The pair of them worked on each other's feelings powerfully: his wife, Elizabeth, hadn't a chance. It was even suspected that Ernest had been practising speaking broad local dialect so as to pass with credit at gatherings of pig-keepers. Anyway, things were obviously working up to a crisis.

Finally, Ernest summoned me to a meeting at which he ex-pounded his fell design of a pig-club with three members: he was to be self-appointed head swineherd, I would find certain items of equipment and the clerk of the local council would know all the rules. A pigsty was easily built, a copper gave no trouble, and so on. Knowing men were discovered to whom pigsties presented no mysteries, the abode was completed and the small pigs were bought and imported somewhat unceremo-niously in sacks. From that moment Maud, the cook, forgot that the house existed. Her whole life was centred on the sty. True, she did manage to boil an occasional egg between cook-ing the pigs' meals, but she could not both clean the sty and the upper rooms. She had no wavering doubts about priorities, so her path of duty was crystal clear. The question of extending the telephone to the sty was discussed in a detached, unem-bittered way. It seemed the only possible solution, as telephone messages, although dealing obviously with matters on a lesser plane of importance, such as a German invasion, were still sometimes urgent. The grooming of the pigs was a ceremonial rite of profound significance, and they seemed to know it. Their little, wicked eyes twinkled as their hair was parted and their tails curled. And on Sunday afternoons all the neighbours came to visit them so as to report on these marvellous doings when The Eight Bells or The Red Lion opened.

As Christmas approached the pigs ate more and more. Having failed to get pig-potatoes Ernest never flinched as he dug up all his artichokes to ward off their ravening hunger. The feeding of Elizabeth and himself was utterly forgotten and he began to lose weight, in anticipation of the glorious meals which Maud promised him with glee. He had to say to his friends: 'Of course, you'll come and see us when we've killed our pig. Then we really shall have some food in the house. Now, of course, the pigs eat everything from the garden and it's hard to see where the next meal is coming from. Indeed, right up to now we've never known food so scarce. We've thought more than once of going away to a hotel for a few days' rest and regular meals—goodness knows, we both need it—but, of course, we can't leave the pigs. Maud couldn't possibly keep pace with them on her own and it would be unfortunate if she became discouraged and left, although of course she is hardly able to do anything in the house now. Really, when you come to think of it, we have to feed her so that she doesn't waste time on non-essentials. Of course, in a way we miss her as cook but what gets us down is the way she never talks of anything at all but those pigs.'

What a glorious day it would be when the pigs were killed! Our idea was to tackle this job before Christmas but, just as we and the third member of the club were about to do so, he suddenly discovered that it was illegal to kill a pig unless it had been fed by the owner or his servant personally for a specified time. There seemed no way out except to build a sty at King-combe and keep our pig there for a further period, so I tackled this, using bales of straw. The pig's favourite amusement was to wedge its snout between these and then heave, when it was at liberty in the garden. This usually happened at our meal time, so it cannot be said to have been popular. Meantime, Ernest could legally kill his pig and sit down mopping his brow after this had been done, having carefully disposed of the hat which we all assured him made him look a swineherd to the life. Maud rushed about with steaming buckets of boiling water and talked knowingly of the delicacies to come—

Date stone in wall, Kingcombe, 1941

Experiment in simple stone carving, 1942

Working on my Coronation souvenir table, 1953

One of three stone
benches, flanked
by large earthen-
ware pots, 1954

A stone table with
garden seat which
I designed in 1955
to use the tech-
nique of
oxy-acetylene
welding, its
calligraphic
pattern emphasized
by the stone wall
behind

Building the brick
arches to carry the
garage at
Kingcombe, 1956

chitterlings, faggots, black puddings, bath-chaps, sausages, tenderloin. There was a mountain of pigmeat but Ernest, in his emaciated condition, could not face gargantuan meals. Moreover, it would not keep indefinitely, though of course all that could be salted, such as bacon and ham, was salted. Elizabeth rang us up and asked us to come and see what a marvellous collection of bits and pieces would one day be ours when we killed our pig, but when we arrived she was full of complaints as to how she could be expected to cope with so much. It was illegal either to sell it or give it away and Ernest was a magistrate and scrupulous to a degree, so we returned to Kingcombe, baffled and hungry.

But pig-keeping on a small scale is an occupation which gets into one's blood and I understood when Gustav, the German prisoner who helped us on the smallholding, on being told by Toni that his tea was ready, rushed out with a bucket in each hand saying 'Pigs first'!

Handwork and odd jobs in a rural setting have never been more than fleeting experiences of mine. The insistent call of London was heard once more and I could not disregard it. Although I had serious reservations about leaving my wife and Mary to cope with so much work without my help, I came to the conclusion, after serious reflection, that any help I gave was more than counter-balanced by the mess and disorganization I caused. Women are very sweet in the way they discount such annoyances. At first it seemed that only occasional visits to London would be necessary, but as so often happens in life, the beginnings of an episode give little indication of where it may eventually lead.

PART III

The Larger Stage
1940–

CHAPTER 15

National Production: Utility Furniture

About the middle of 1942 I received a letter from the President of the Board of Trade, Dr Hugh Dalton, asking me to sit on a committee to advise him on the introduction of Utility furniture, which would be made available on coupons for certain categories of people who could prove need, such as those recently married, bombed out, etc. Mr Charles Tennyson was to be chairman—a good choice, I felt, for I had known him for some time and respected the work he had done in the cause of industrial design. The committee was well balanced: it included well-known members of the furniture trade, both employers and trade unionists, design and housing consultants and so on. And I was to be impressed with the way Miss Eileen Strudwick of the Board of Trade, who was appointed secretary, kept in touch with a situation which changed from day to day and even got on quite good terms with a somewhat disgruntled trade.

At our first meeting the President made it clear that he wanted us to ensure that the furniture should be soundly made of the best available materials and he emphasized that he wanted it to be of pleasant design. He spoke seriously of the possibility of a furniture famine unless immediate steps were taken to deal with the situation; and he left us in no doubt that he considered the job important war work and that he expected us to find a solution quickly.

We were given a good deal of information, particularly a long list of materials which were either unobtainable or in very short supply which included, of course, most of the things we needed: plywood, blockboard, hardwood, steel, cellulose, paint, linoleum, textiles and so on. It was obvious that any forecast of possible requirements was hazardous, because it was not practicable to make a census of the immense destruction of furniture caused by bombing. Any figures based on pre-war demand were therefore useless. We decided to put out enquiries for designers at once, asking them to submit examples of their work as a guide. From this selection of drawings the work of two men was thought suitable: H. J. Cutler and Edwin Clinch, both of High Wycombe. Their designs were simple and workmanlike and made it obvious that they had a sound knowledge of the trade. Meantime we had been attempting to set down what exactly we felt should be comprised in the first range, bearing in mind all the conditions. This wasn't as easy as it sounds, and in the early days there was a very real cleavage of opinion as to whether the designs should be standard or whether manufacturers should be given any latitude. It became quite clear however as we sifted the problem that nothing less than standard designs and rigid specifications would meet this exceptional case. Inspection became impossible unless inspectors knew exactly what they had a right to expect and were able to quote their source of information.

The acute timber shortage had become apparent early in the war and steps were taken immediately to limit the variety of pieces of furniture that could be made and the amount of timber in each. But this was a negative policy of damping down anything which bordered on luxury goods whereas we had to implement a positive policy of ensuring a supply of furniture of the best quality attainable, at controlled prices, to meet real need.

Our next hurdle was that some members felt that what the public bought before the war was well known, that that was what they liked and that was therefore what they should be given. This meant about ninety per cent imitation period furniture with only a sprinkling of good modern design. It was urged that the President had asked for pleasant furniture, but

the word had different meanings to different people. However, the basic rightness of contemporary design won the day,
for there wasn't enough timber for bulbous legs or enough
labour for even the cheapest carving and straightforward, commonsense lines were both efficient and economical. It was an
acid test and, naturally, some die-hards only admitted the
result reluctantly. It must have been a bit of a shock that a type
of design which had been pioneered for years by a small
minority—whilst the trade looked on and laughed—should
prove its mettle in a national emergency, but so it was, to the
amusement of some and to the amazement of others. In a trade
which was always pretty chaotic, with hundreds of fiercely
competitive small firms producing thousands of different
patterns, we were proposing to reduce the total number of
designs to less than a hundred, of a type that was unfamiliar to
many members of the trade, and to prohibit any other furniture whatsoever from being made. That's pretty drastic if you
like, but needs must when the devil drives.

In Clinch and Cutler we had picked two sound men who
sincerely wished to see standards in the trade raised. Only
those who saw the problem at close quarters can realize the
difficulties they were up against. Never once did they let the
committee down, although quite often it meant working
through most of the night. The standard they set in working
drawings undoubtedly eased the furniture into production
and very few snags appeared later on. Early in 1943 Utility
furniture began to appear in the shops and the prices—which
were not subject to purchase tax—looked very reasonable
compared with what was being charged for old stock and
secondhand pieces. The intelligentsia criticized it as being too
conservative, the trade as being too advanced, but I was encouraged to find shots coming from both directions: it looked
as if we were about right. I am never for forcing the pace, a
limited advance and then consolidation is a sound principle
both in war and peace.

I look back on the first range of Utility furniture with some
satisfaction. An immense step was taken in the right direction.

Bearing in mind the low standards of the trade before the war it was not reasonable to expect that we could reach at a bound those set by the best individual firm. We were also criticized because it was not designed for mass production, but it wasn't meant to be: owing to extreme transport difficulties it had to be made in the zone in which it was going to be sold. About half of the furniture trade of Great Britain is centred on London, so there was naturally a grave shortage of production in some other areas, where almost any firms which had reasonable woodworking experience, some of them quite small, had to be roped in. All the largest firms, and many of the most efficient, were working on aircraft or other special work of high priority. On the whole, the reception accorded to the new furniture by the trade was better than we had expected: we were not so optimistic as to have imagined it would be enthusiastic. Some of the daily papers seized on the fact that hardboard had been used for such parts as backs and drawer bottoms. 'Furniture made of cardboard' was news! But hardboard veneered on both sides proved a very useful substitute for plywood and it was the only one available which stood up to test. So I took a deep breath and sat down to think out whether, from the designer's point of view, we had done all we could.

What was the next step? I felt that to raise the whole standard of furniture for the mass of the people was not a bad war job, and it has always seemed sound to me, when in doubt as to people's requirements, to aim at giving them something better than they might be expected to demand. War-time conditions had given us a unique opportunity of making an advance. So many people in the trade talked of getting back to 1939, but I didn't want to go back, as the bulk of pre-war furniture was poor stuff, and I felt in my bones that there was a much greater proportion of the public than of the trade who felt as I did. Surely it might be possible to use the Utility specification as the basis of a quality mark in the post-control period, as I certainly should not be in favour of continuing controls longer than necessary. To this end, I felt it was essential to carry on intensively with research into design problems so as to be ready to cope with any eventuality. I therefore wrote a short report on the subject for the chairman, suggesting that a panel of not more than six designers be set up under the chairmanship of a knowledgeable man, perhaps an architect as he would be interested in metal, plastics and other materials beside wood, and that he should be given a seat on the Utility Furniture Committee so as to be able to state the designer's point of view.

The chairman and then the President considered my report and I was asked to see them. The President invited me to form the Design Panel and become its chairman which, strange as it may seem, took me by surprise. He said he hoped we should not be forced to make purely temporary furniture but he was much in favour of other research. If I took on the job I said that I should want to be assured that I should have a say in the constitution of the panel, that everything in connection with design would be referred to it and that reasonable funds would be available for making prototypes when such a course seemed desirable. This was agreed, I accepted and then I discussed the whole problem in detail with Tennyson.

It was clear that at this stage of the war I should find great difficulty in getting furniture designers of the calibre I needed. I already had Clinch and Cutler earmarked. Brian O'Rorke and Grey Wornum, both architects, attended several meetings but were too heavily engaged in other directions to carry on. Eden Minns agreed to come, but was called up into the Navy and was later sent to the Pacific. R. D. Russell—my brother Dick—was also in the Navy and was working at the Admiralty on camouflage. He got permission to attend for discussions occasionally, but before long was sent to India and Burma. Ian Henderson, who had had an interesting shop where he sold well-designed furniture and fabrics before the war, was in the Foreign Office and we had some talk about the problem. He thought he might get a three-months' release, if the application were made pretty high up. The size of the problem had not yet fully come home to me. I was thinking in terms of months rather than years; and so was the Board of Trade, which was talking of monthly contracts.

Then I got in touch with Jacques Groag, a Czech architect who had been a pupil and later an assistant of Adolf Loos and who had been helped to get to England by Sir Charles Reilly. It was a fortunate meeting, for Groag had an excellent sense of design and had done a good deal of furniture, though most of it was made by hand. The modern movement was in his blood and he provided exactly the right counter-irritant to the more prosaic outlook which might so easily have grown up owing to preoccupation with difficulties and shortages of every kind. It was fatally simple to take the easiest solution and accept the kind of detailing which the trade considered normal. Groag not only enriched our discussions by his imaginative outlook but he enriched our vocabulary by words whose rolling cadence delighted us, such as 'splendourous'! We were now able to push along a bit.

I urged that design research in two directions was necessary. Firstly, it might well be that an intensification of bombing would mean that the need of furniture was so vast that ordinary methods of production and materials could not cope with it. (This was in 1943.) And, rather than have people throw their clothes on the floor, we might have to make furniture which would be of a quite frankly temporary kind. On the other hand, we all knew that things would improve some day—plywood, blockboard, cellulose, steel and so on would again be available —and we ought to have blue-prints ready.

Consumer needs required study and I had some interesting talks with Francis Meynell, then in charge of this department at the Board of Trade. I also went to see Margaret Solomon at the Housing Centre, as I was anxious to find out as much as possible about how people lived, what they put in their furniture and so on, and she arranged for me to meet a group of housing managers at Toynbee Hall. I suggested that it might be possible to get together a group of local residents at Toynbee Hall and for our Design Panel to act as a sort of Brains Trust who could learn—and perhaps teach. We had a lovely meeting. Eileen Strudwick was in the chair and there was such a good-humoured, lively and keen audience. I tried to explain some of our problems and the chairman then invited questions, which came thick and fast. One woman said that in a blitz a piece of glass had gone through the end of her Utility wardrobe. 'You can't call that a piece of furniture,' she said, but she accepted our explanation. Then a black-eyed, hawk-nosed woman got up and said: 'What abaht this Utility furniture. Will it stand up to it?' I was asked to reply. 'Will it stand up to what?' said I. 'Well,' she repeated, 'will it stand up to it? My daughter's just got some—she was blitzed, you see—and when 'er 'usband 'eard about it—'e's been in India for four years— 'e wrote 'ome and said 'e'd seen some pictures of it in the pipers and some of it looked a bit spidery.' 'Spidery,' I said, 'I wonder what piece of furniture he was thinking of?' 'Well, I dunno, but the only piece 'e mentioned was the bed. And that's what I want to know so as to write to 'im. When 'e comes 'ome, will it stand up to it?'

There were many other questions, all of them practical, sensible questions about furniture in use in the home. This was very good for us, as we tended to become obsessed with the never-ending day-to-day problems of production methods and materials whilst the major problem of furniture in use was not pushed into the limelight every day. Yet after all, it is the one that remains long after the others are forgotten. We asked the audience to tell us exactly what they kept in various pieces of furniture. It isn't easy to design a sideboard which will serve equally well for a docker or a doctor. One old lady kept nothing but knitting in hers.

We learned other things in the East End too. We noticed in a shop window some pieces of Utility furniture covered with most appalling carving, rivalling the very worst exhibit at any pre-war furniture exhibition. Whilst an extra £5 or £10 was demanded for adding this the whole quality of the furniture had been destroyed. I could not help being amused a few months later to see a letter in the trade press lamenting the fact that carving was being wasted on utilitarian furniture when it obviously ought to be saved up until worthy forms could be enriched by it. It is curious by what devious paths one can reach agreement.

In fact, the committee had discussed the possibility of evolving one range with decoration. I sympathized with them to some extent as during the war it was not possible even to choose veneers—they had to be used as they came. I thought it just possible that Henry Moore, with his great interest in abstract patterns in several planes, might be able to make some suggestions. Tennyson and I met him to discuss this and found him most willing to be helpful but no more able to solve our problem than we were.

There was need for research in other directions too, in other materials, such as metal and plastics. At any rate such information as was available should be collected. And there was also the problem of textiles. Up till then we had been using textiles which were in stock, a reasonable thing to do, but the time was coming rapidly when special textiles would have to be woven. What designs should we use, old ones from the trade or new ones which took account of the severe limitation of types of yarns available, of dyes, looms, etc.? It seemed to me that we could no more go back to some of the dreadful pre-war moquettes than to 'drapers' jaco'. I must say I felt deeply that as we had to restrict people's freedom of choice so drastically it was incumbent on us to see that the designs were intrinsically good. Of course the reduction of freedom of choice was not so serious as appeared at first sight for, after all, there wasn't much freedom of choice before the war when in most shops the alternatives were bad or worse and you could have almost anything you liked except good design.

The making of prototypes raised many problems, for it was fiddling work which no manufacturer really wanted when he was harassed day and night by troubles of his own and particularly a shortage of the skilled labour which was essential.

It became increasingly clear that the committee could hardly have functioned without some design sub-committee such as the panel was. Much would obviously depend on my political sense, as the steering of better designs into production proved even more difficult than making them. We were attempting to interpret to the trade and to the public what was, in effect, a nationwide drive for better design. Although there was opposition, little of it was active as we never forced the pace and I never asked the committee to accept any design unless I really felt it solved the problem. I tried to keep my feet firmly on the ground and my eyes on our goal, seeking solid, not spectacular, progress. We were all much encouraged by the support given us by the more forward-looking manufacturers and retailers and by members of the public; and, I must add, by the Board of Trade, which I believe had never before employed industrial designers. The permanent officials, who treated us with tender solicitude, were rather at a loss as to our function, status, tastes or habits, and I was told that the more venerable members were even known to point us out to their friends as among the more peculiar manifestations of a state of total war! Anyway, they spared us the usual Civil Service ceremonial of a desk and carpet according to rank and we were left to accumulate an astonishing collection of furniture for our use, mostly discarded prototypes. We clung to this flotsam and jetsam like sailors to wreckage.

From the inception of the panel we had a weekly meeting at which the whole of the work in hand was discussed. There was a never-ending series of shifting bottlenecks in materials and a way round each had to be found. Such problems frequently affected design. Constantly we were asked to investigate the design position in a certain direction because of difficulties but after weeks of work the position might again have changed before production could commence. We were even told, quite seriously, just before D-Day that it might be necessary to use softwood for furniture but we pointed out that such a step could only be accepted if there was literally no alternative at all. Fortunately it was not necessary, but some preliminary investigation was done. No flying bombs altered our routine and I was amused to note that when the bomb-bell rang—which was pretty frequently some days—all typists and juniors were shepherded to the shelters. This left overworked principals to carry on in a vain endeavour to keep their work from getting out of hand, whilst they had also to write their own letters.

All this was somewhat frustrating to designers, because so little was coming out at the other end, although there was much in the pipeline. There may well have been times when members of the panel wondered whether I was putting our point of view to the committee, just as the committee may well have wondered what the panel was doing, but I tried to keep calm and see the whole picture. I hung on to the research we were doing into new types of furniture for production as soon as plywood and especially blockboard—so as to use flush doors—became available again. The committee wished to extend the existing range as there were some obvious gaps in it. It had proved a useful and foolproof range and was being made by about six hundred firms of widely different type. The good firms were making an excellent job of it, there were others who would as soon make a good as a bad job, and a minority who never had made a good job of anything and had, if possible, to be upgraded. Here the Board of Trade production officers in the areas played an invaluable part and it is true to say that their efforts contributed immensely to the success of the scheme. They encouraged the good manufacturers, helped the ones who had not a great deal of experience and sat on the tail of the few who were trying to evade their responsibilities.

The designing of industrial products is a team job and the team, when one works on a national scale, must be a considerable one. The committee, especially the technical members, who were always willing to be called on and gave helpful and disinterested advice, the manufacturers who did the job as well as they could in spite of the shortage of labour and materials and difficulty in replacing plant, the retailers who were both sympathetic and critical, the production officers who helped as I have said, and the other officials of the Board of Trade, the Ministry of Works, the Ministry of Supply, the

Ministry of Town and Country Planning, the Ministry of Health, the Ministry of Aircraft Production and the Ministry of War Transport, all these contributed to the design of Utility furniture. Perhaps no single group could keep the whole scheme pointing in the right direction so clearly as the retailers, by insisting on the goods delivered to them being up to specification. I know how difficult that is in a seller's market but there were many retailers who did take a lot of trouble to safeguard their customers' interests. In the Board of Trade, Eileen Strudwick, the secretary of the committee, always gave me excellent advice as to what was likely to be politically attainable and I found I was rapidly acquiring invaluable information on the functioning of a great department of State. This was to stand me in good stead later on.

Thinking ahead, it was obvious that demobilized men must have the first call on furniture and that demand would be considerable so that de-control could not take place immediately the war ended. The mass production woodworking firms employed on aircraft would be able to return to furniture making and to use their plants to capacity we should need a new range designed especially for them. We decided to work on the assumption that this might well be slightly smaller and lighter, so coping with the dual problems of small rooms and scarcity of plywood. My growing political awareness made me anxious to bring the trade into consultation as far as possible, as I felt it might avoid many problems at a later stage, so in discussing the matter at a panel meeting we decided to ask three or four of the large firms each to submit a sample bedroom, unpolished and made of the materials and by the methods each would like to use. The look of the finished article, at this stage, was not to enter our discussion. The rooms were duly made and we had long talks both with the manufacturers concerned and the technical members of the Utility Furniture and Furniture Production Committees. In the end we were able to evolve two rooms which, whilst achieving a reasonable standard of design, met almost all the production points raised. For instance, some firms always used the technique of planting their wardrobe door on the face of the carcass whilst others set it in. We realized how helpful it would be if we could think up more ways of using short ends, both of solid wood and veneer. The wardrobes, in which there was a panel nine inches wide on each side of the door, are an example of this. In one this panel was veneered in one piece from top to bottom, so using long veneers; in another it was cross-banded, so using short veneers down to nine inches and, at the same time, giving variety. In designing this range we had the great advantage that we could visualize the type of firm which would make it, for there were not many firms in the country with the right equipment for really large-scale production and only these would be designated.

This was a very important point. Before the war a furniture designer working for a firm knew their plant and methods intimately and he designed accordingly. He was in touch with the principals, or at least the works manager, who could make decisions rapidly. The firm would only sell in one market—high, medium or low—and could be certain of obtaining the specified raw materials exactly as required—next week, next month, next year. We, on the other hand, were designing for 600 firms who differed widely in every way—in size, location, tradition, equipment, technical ability, outlook and integrity. We advised the Utility Furniture Committee on design and the committee advised the Board of Trade, not a trading body, so that decisions were sometimes hard to come by in a hurry. And we were not thinking of one market or one locality, but of all markets in all localities: an MP in London, a docker in Liverpool, a fishwife in Aberdeen, a policeman in Birmingham, a solicitor in Penzance, a farmer in Merionethshire—these were our customers, to the tune of many million pounds a year. As to materials, as I have said, we could rely on nothing and alterations took place at very short notice. The Services, quite rightly, had absolute priority and the shifting emphasis of the war from Atlantic to Mediterranean, from Mediterranean to English Channel, from English Channel to Pacific, might destroy all our plans.

At the other end of the range we worked on new types of furniture which would not take appreciably more material but would absorb more of the skilled labour which we felt would become available. Everything pointed to an after-war position in which, at least for some time, materials were scarcer than labour.

Of course, people who break fresh ground anywhere generally stir up opposition but the kindly interest of the chairman was a great comfort to me and it never flagged, in spite of intense anxiety and bereavement on top of his wide business activities.

Since 1942 I had spent most of each week in London, going home by rail from Paddington at weekends, and as the Arts Club had been severely blitzed I had to get a room in town where I could. Although it seems extremely foolish in retrospect, I cannot remember spending a single night in a bomb shelter. Certainly it was noisy at times but generally I slept very well. I had the same feeling I should survive that I had had in the First World War, which had given me a hatred of dugouts and pillboxes. Towards the end of the war I had to do a fair amount of travelling on Board of Trade business, we still had illness at home which meant visiting various hospitals and occasionally there were other calls. For instance, about the middle of 1944 I heard that Harry Jones, my godfather, had had a stroke following the bombing of his house in Wimbledon and had been moved to his farm at Mayfield, Sussex, even though this was in Bomb Alley and his farm buildings there had been hit. So I went down to see him. It seemed he could not last very long and I was asked not to excite him, a somewhat odd request in view of the almost constant noise overhead. During a stroll before my bus was due a flying bomb approached, quite low and perhaps 150 yards away, closely followed by a fighter 'plane. The pilot manoeuvred the tip of his wing under the wing of the bomb and gently lifted it so that it took a dive into the ground, when there was a great explosion. It was a most skilful piece of work, in carefully chosen open country. On the way back, two flying bombs were seen approaching on either

O

side—one quite close and the other some distance away. The driver of the bus halted and, turning to the passengers with a grin, apologized for the delay but said it seemed better to let 'em get by as they appeared to be in a hurry!

Naturally, the end of the war in Europe came as an immense relief to all of us, but it was not marked by the hilarious demonstrations in London which I remembered in 1918. Although casualties in the forces had not been on the same appalling scale, bombing had brought the war right into the homes of British people and civilian casualties had been considerable. The clear division between front line and home base had become blurred and the general reaction seemed to be one of relief rather than rejoicing. From my office window in Page Street I could see the roof of Westminster Abbey, for which I have a great affection. It may seem odd, but once when there was bombing I found myself hoping that they would hit our beastly building instead of the Abbey, forgetting for the moment that we were in it! Fortunately the Abbey was not hit, though it has suffered severely from its guardians in other ways since then. When the news of victory came through my first thought was to walk across to the Abbey, which I found packed to the doors with a quiet throng of people who evidently felt the need for some kind of thanksgiving. The strain of incessant bombing and the devastation it caused were, I think, present in the minds of all and no one had any confidence that a state of total war would give way to a state of total peace.

The next day we started to review what the effect on the supply position was likely to be and to make the best plans we could. It was clear that the situation would not quickly become stable. The losses of shipping had been immense and the war in the Far East might go on for some while, although its outcome seemed certain.

At this time I was asked by an advertising friend of mine, Goddard-Watts, whether I would visit Scotland with him as he had to present a report on furniture to the Scottish Co-operative Wholesale Society. We spent nearly a week visiting their shops, from the large ones in the Paisley district to quite small ones in Lanarkshire, where the Society's pre-war Rolls-Royce caused quite a stir. The driver told us that the directors used them for a bit until they were handed over to the Undertaking Department—I have a feeling he meant the Rolls, not the directors. It was clear that the priorities were (1) food, (2) clothing and (3) furniture, so in the smallest shops the customer was given a rail ticket to visit the stockrooms in Glasgow, where the furniture was just as bad as in the English Co-operatives. The Society did, in fact, implement the first part of our recommendations, i.e. to commission a range of good designs from a skilled designer, and the works made quite a good job of it; but as no notice was taken of the second, to explain fully and with enthusiasm what they were up to, the operation did not pay off. I could cite many similar cases.

In our wanderings we went by the park of Hamilton Palace, built on an extremely rich coal seam which gave out. The contents of the mansion provided one of the exciting nineteenth-century art sales. The park was full of large pools where subsidence had taken place and the trees were dead and leaning at odd angles. Behind was a very grand mausoleum, but we were told that the coffins had been removed to the paupers' corner of the local churchyard as the building was in danger of collapsing.

We also made a short pilgrimage to Robert Owen's mill, as I wished to pay a belated, silent tribute to this great pioneer of more humane conditions in factories.

After the election of a Labour Government in 1945 Sir Stafford Cripps came to the Board of Trade. We were fortunate in having two successive Presidents who considered design important. One of Cripps' first acts was to set up a Directorate of Furniture Production, with A. E. Walsh as director. Production had to be pushed up at a steep curve and metal was visualized as a possible alternative to wood, which was still very hard to come by. My design team—which now included my brother Dick, Eden Minns, R. Y. Goodden, Neville Ward, Frank Austin, Cyril Rostgaard and Enid Marx—had been doing experimental work on this for some time. Cripps was extremely keen on the possibility of using the aircraft industry, which was booked for serious slimming, to produce aluminium furniture—although this scared the makers of wooden furniture, who felt that the vast demands of the moment could not last and that overproduction and price cutting might then reappear on an unprecedented scale. None the less, Cripps talked to me a good deal about the idea and ended by sending Walsh and myself to the United States to find out what had been done there. I was delighted at this prospect as I had met many Americans at Broadway and had heard so much of America from my father, who had been there twice. The voyage in the *Queen Elizabeth* was an astonishing experience to us, accustomed as we were to the deadly dull standard of living which wartime scarcities made inevitable, but to Americans, of course, it seemed quite normal.

We were received with great kindness and an obvious wish to be helpful which we found most encouraging. There is so much timber in the United States that it was only in porch, kitchen and office furniture that metal had been used to any extent. Porch furniture consisted mainly of various types of seating and tables, which presented few problems to us. Our troubles were in storage units and in these the kitchen and office fittings were made in ways familiar to us but not altogether suitable for less utilitarian purposes. So we followed up clues in other industries, including the producers of aluminium, but we found little to lead us to believe that aluminium could be an economic and acceptable substitute for wood unless the latter was almost unobtainable.

I was fascinated by my first glimpse of the States. Almost everything, even the language, was different and I noticed that practically everyone we met took it for granted that we would wish to stay for good. That we wanted to go back, and even to work for a Labour Government, struck many people as extraordinary. But they were always interested in discussing a new problem.

In 1944 I had received an invitation from the President of the

Board of Trade to sit on the Furniture Production Committee, which was to deal with post-control problems in the industry. Sir Charles Tennyson was to act as chairman of this committee also and a number of members of the Utility Furniture Committee would be members so as to establish a close link and prevent overlapping.

In 1945 I was also asked to sit on the Design Committee of the Furniture Trade Working Party, which was one of a number set up for different industries by the President to investigate conditions following the war and to make recommendations as to their improvement. The chairman of this committee, Jack Pritchard, whom I had known for twenty years, agreed with me that Cripps meant to take the reports of the working parties seriously and to implement their findings. Although I was feeling worried about the proliferation of committees I did not see that I could refuse in this case, as there were so few people in the trade who had made a prolonged study of its design problems. Jack Pritchard was one of them and would need support. Also, it seemed to me that such an opportunity of setting the trade on the right road might not recur for a generation or more. Fortunately, Eileen Strudwick was secretary of the main working party and of this committee, which—also fortunately—was a small one. She had become interested in design problems and this made her doubly valuable.

We started our peregrinations about the country, visiting technical and art schools, taking evidence on the methods of designing and related problems from manufacturers and retailers, from knowledgeable bodies such as the newly formed Council of Industrial Design, the Faculty of Royal Designers for Industry, the Design and Industries Association, the Society of Industrial Artists and so on. Of course we got much help from the Regional Officers of the Board of Trade. It was quite an interesting job as we tried to see a cross-section of the trade in each area. As it was usual, up to the First World War, for a cabinet-maker to bring his own kit of tools with him the capital cost of setting up a small workshop was not high and as most energetic men wished to be their own masters there were therefore many small firms. There was a good deal of price cutting, over-production and sweated labour, for the generally low rates of pay in industry made it difficult for working men to spend much on furniture. Under these conditions one could not expect to find in the trade a high level of intelligence, or even a willingness to co-operate. In Liverpool, a representative of the lowest end shambled into the room and, following the chairman's introduction, turned to me and said: 'So you're Mr Gordon Russell, are you? I came here today to see what you look like. I've been watching your antics for some time.' This was a lively beginning! When asked how he designed his furniture he went on: 'In my opinion there's far too much nonsense talked about designing. I do all of it myself and its never been the slightest trouble to me. For example, I chalk out a wardrobe design on the floor. I might put, say, a semi-circle on the door and if that goes well this year I'd put it upside down next year. Quite easy.' He spoke so naturally that I felt sure he was telling the truth, although he was not a person who inspired confidence.

Having got a pretty good picture of conditions in Britain we felt we could not make worthwhile recommendations without more information on technical training abroad. So we decided to look at Switzerland, where the standard of technical education was, we knew, high. I went to look at co-operative shops in Zürich, Basle, and Berne and eventually met M. Maire, the president. I told him I was struck by the high price of the furniture shown but shocked at the low standard of design. He replied that he realized this but that an attempt to sell better designs had failed—because, he thought, they had not carried out a consistent policy of educating the sales staff beforehand. I was to remember this, which tallied with my own views and experience.

The report which the Furniture Trade Working Party produced dealt with design more fully than those for most trades. I think the careful analysis we made was of value to the intelligent firms in the trade and, together with the Utility furniture scheme, had an effect in raising standards which is not fully appreciated even now. I was struck by the strong feeling in the good firms that the trade must not let pre-war conditions return. The design section was known to our committee as the Malvoisie Report as, in order to be quiet when drafting it, I sat up in bed for two days in the Baur au Lac in Zürich with a bottle of malmsey beside me! After more than twenty years I see no reason to wish to alter the summing-up in the Report, which was adopted unanimously.

'In the furniture industry design is so important that we have spent a considerable time investigating the position closely. In many industries, for example in the manufacture of aeroplanes, locomotives and many other technical products, it is the functional aspect of design which is of fundamental importance and though a certain beauty is often achieved, it is almost incidental. But in furniture the problem of design is not purely functional; furniture has to be lived with at close quarters and not only must it give efficient service, but it must also give pleasure. In our opinion, therefore, it is proper that this subject should occupy one of the most important parts of our report.

'We started by assuming that it would be generally accepted that there is such a thing as a standard of good design; that the industry has a responsibility to supply furniture of good quality, including quality of design; and that there is at present great scope for improvement. But our discussions have shown that this assumption is by no means common ground in the industry and that some firms would in fact strongly oppose it. We feel, therefore, that before proceeding to a detailed consideration of the problem of design we should state clearly the premises on which we have based our approach to it.

'The idea that good design must satisfy a number of well-defined conditions has long been accepted by those who have made a study of it, but this idea is still so generally unfamiliar that we feel justified in outlining its necessary conditions. We believe that good industrial design is concerned with form, colour, decoration, texture, fitness for its job, method of production, method of transport and saleability. It is not something applied at the end nor is it something different for the sake of being different. Conscious design must start at the inception of the article and go on steadily till the end. It is in the early stages that the basic shapes and many details are fluid. An opportunity missed then will not recur, and it is only the trained and imaginative industrial designer who is likely to be aware of its existence. Good industrial design under present-day conditions is the work of a group of technicians of whom the leader is the industrial designer. If properly trained he is the obvious person to express an opinion on function, form, colour, texture, finish, etc. He must work in the closest collaboration with the mill manager, sales manager and others. When a technically-minded artist has been stimulated by a problem he and his team will be likely to get the best attainable results out of the complicated industrial processes of today and the available materials, adapted to the ends which the object has to serve. For this reason it will be seen that good industrial design must of necessity be in tune with its own age. The copying of the forms of a past age which were designed for totally different conditions, materials and methods of production will get nowhere, whereas a knowledge of the past used as an inspiration for the future may be of real value. It is true to say that our heritage of furniture in this country is so fine that, if once we could find our way to the right road again, we might well become world leaders once more. We must learn again to think of design as an essential element of quality, as important as materials and workmanship.

'It is essential that a well-designed object should not only do its job with the maximum efficiency; it should also give visual pleasure. People however have widely different views on what gives them visual pleasure. To know what one likes is not necessarily to know what is good and what will stand the test of time. Just as writing is complementary to reading, without which it would serve no use, so industrial design needs its public. And *good* industrial design needs a *critical and appreciative* public.

216

'Any improvement in industrial design will increase the size of this public, already greater than many manufacturers and retailers believe, by making well-designed things more familiar to the mass of people. The interest aroused by excellent Service exhibitions, by cheap and good books, and by music should be borne in mind in this connection.

'We must emphasize that whether industrial design is deemed good, bad or indifferent is not merely a matter of opinion. It is a matter on which all those who have a trained aesthetic sensibility the world over will agree, in broad principle. To say that they have no right to do this and that they speak with no more authority than, say, a vagrant brought up in one of our great industrial towns is nonsense—such a man, it is likely, has never considered the problem and has hardly a single thing of beauty about him. It would be as reasonable to say that a man trained as an accountant is no more fit to air his views on book-keeping than an engine-driver. We accept the view that a very large proportion of the furniture made in this country before the war was of poor design and we cannot say too strongly that we feel that the inhabitants of our industrial towns should not be fobbed off with ugly things because they live in squalid surroundings, and because for the moment many will accept such things as natural. An increasing number is aware that something is missing in their lives and the furniture trade would acquire immense prestige if it accepted the responsibility of becoming leader of the more forward-minded. Moreover, such an attitude is essential in export trade where competition, although much more severe than at home, is easier to deal with on a quality basis than a strictly price basis.'

In conclusion I should add that the Furniture Trade Development Council which was set up as a result of the working party's recommendations and of which Jack Pritchard became director has had a considerable and beneficial influence. There is no doubt that the standards of the trade have greatly improved since 1939 and much of the credit for this should go to Sir Stafford Cripps. His belief that a careful enquiry into the way the trade functioned, followed by recommendations for improvement, has been abundantly justified.

The period leading up to VE Day and covering the next two years was a somewhat confused and frustrating one for me, as I imagine it was for most people. Obviously the Utility furniture scheme would not be required for long after the war ended but some form of control would be necessary. What form should it take? And what would be the future of the industry? These matters were the subject of many meetings at the Board, one of which sticks in my mind. I think it may have been in those horrible, bitter months early in 1947 when there were constant power cuts and hardly any fuel. I was summoned to Sir Stafford's office—the fruitily over-decorated chairman's room in the ICI building at Millbank which was the Board's temporary headquarters. It was a dull, overcast afternoon and he was sitting at his desk in a greatcoat with a large scarf over his shoulders and knitted gloves which made his fingers stick out at odd angles. I think he also had a hat on. The room was icy and was faintly lighted by a candle stuck on a plate. In a somewhat hollow voice he gave me his usual greeting, 'How are you, my dear fellow?' Tommy Handley of ITMA flashed across my mind—'Oh dear, Oh dear, you give me the Cripps' —and I hope I kept a straight face.

Cripps was also greatly interested in maintaining the standard of fine handwork and I had a number of talks with him on this subject. He appreciated craftwork himself but did not fully realize how difficult it was to sell it through the ordinary retailer, who seldom has a buyer or a salesman able to explain it to customers. He was anxious to promote a venture to export such work—although I had told him that I felt it to be far more important to have a really good gallery in London, where it could be well displayed and sold by knowledgeable people. In the spring of 1947 he arranged a small luncheon party to discuss his plan, but that morning I picked up a paper and read: 'Budget disclosures: Cripps takes over Exchequer.' All morning I expected a 'phone call cancelling or postponing the lunch but none came so I went along and found Lady

Cripps, Mr Harold Wilson, Mr Ivan Stedeford and one or two others. At exactly one o'clock Sir Stafford walked in, said he had had rather a busy morning and looked like having a busy afternoon so could we start at once—and at exactly two o'clock he left. Lady Cripps then asked me whether I was happy about an exhibition which was going to Copenhagen. I said I thought it was a pity not to send a selective exhibition to such a critical audience and she took this very seriously, said we must talk to Harold Wilson about it and buttonholed him, placing him between us in the back seat of his car. As he was taking over the Board of Trade from Cripps he had far more worrying preoccupations at that moment than an exhibition in Copenhagen. When we had dropped him at his office she asked me to come on to No. 11 to discuss the matter further. She felt that it would be a good thing to go to Denmark and find out on the spot what was happening, and asked me if I could go too. Whilst I was considering this delicate situation, which I felt sure the Board of Trade would interpret as an effort to short-cut them, Lady Cripps rang her husband's office, only to learn that he had gone into No. 10 to see the Prime Minister and was going out very shortly. 'Would you ask him to call as he goes out?' she said. In a few moments the door was flung open and Sir Stafford said: 'I hear you wanted to see me, my dear.' 'Yes,' she said, 'I'm worried about this Copenhagen exhibition and propose to go there with Mr Russell. You will be at Chequers this weekend. Is that all right?' 'Quite,' he replied, and the door closed. Fortunately Lady Cripps rang up next morning and agreed that it was impossible to alter the theme of an exhibition at the last moment so our visit was called off. One can only learn not to repeat a mistake. But I sometimes recall that strange scene—the Goya-like figure in the doorway and the somewhat forbidding portrait of Gladstone on the wall, the only Chancellors who have reduced the duties on light wines!

I had also been spending a good deal of time on discussions on another side of the Board, concerned with the formation of a Design Council which was to be set up under its aegis and with which, as things turned out, I was to become closely associated. And when I got home there were two completely different sets of problems at Broadway and Campden. Everything seemed to be in the melting pot.

CHAPTER 16

Broadway *Entr'acte*

The end of the war found us with a host of problems in the Lygon Arms and in Gordon Russell Ltd. The appointment, on demobilization, of Douglas Barrington to the board of the former enabled the same kind of reassessment to be made as that undertaken in 1919. The changes in the scene were even more startling. The work my brother had done between the wars—especially much higher training in the kitchen—had made it possible in the early 1920s to dispense with outside caterers for the hunt ball and other such functions. This was important as the demand for dances increased greatly after 1945. In order to reduce the amount we lost in the winter, Douglas believed that we were well placed to undertake functions such as cocktail parties, wedding breakfasts and so on. Such gatherings also served the useful purpose of encouraging local people to come into the inn and were valuable in spreading our high costs in the kitchen, where it is essential to have permanent, full-time staff. The fortnightly dances which were soon well established gave an air of gaiety and bustle to the place which kept everyone on their toes. These efforts led to a call for catering at functions in private houses, occasionally even thirty miles or so away, and this side of the business was also developed. A completely new demand also arose, for small residential conferences of up to fifty people, usually for higher business executives. Broadway is well placed for such purposes in relation to the industrial towns of the Midlands and very central and easy to reach from anywhere in England, and it is a place that people like to visit anyway. Sometimes these conferences have been on an international basis, as when the Board of Unilever brought their Dutch Board down to us, the first time they had met out of London.

As a result of development, the temporary canvas supper room now stood for five months in the year, instead of being put up and taken down three or four times. It was difficult to heat and was also a great fire risk. Moreover, the canvas was beginning to age badly and had become extremely expensive to replace. So in 1957 we built—to designs produced by my brother Dick's architectural partnership—completely new kitchens, gutting the existing kitchens and converting them into a permanent supper-dining room. We christened this the Russell Room and it was thought appropriate that I should carve a panel of stone bearing the name of the room and the Lygon coat-of-arms to be built into the wall at the doorway. In the adjoining room is a portrait of my father and a pastel drawing of my mother by Eric Kennington and a portrait of Don by Colin Hayes. The Russell Room is in the 1911 wing, at right-angles to the Great Hall, so that by planning the kitchens in the interior angle they were well placed to serve meals in either room. It could not have been foreseen at the time of building how important it would be, but it so happened that the windows on the yard side of the 1911 wing were all of the same height and general dimensions whereas on the garden side they were mostly small ones for larders or stores which could be replaced by large French windows giving access to the garden, a most convenient arrangement in the summer (see plate 16).

Although we had added many bathrooms before the war we still had not enough private ones to meet current demand so we did a good deal of work in this direction. Also we had much redecorating and replacing of carpets and curtains to make good, as this had been impossible in wartime.

Following the appointment of Douglas Barrington, Don was still in and out of the Lygon most days and liked to have a word with many of the guests, but he was also able to spend more time on outside affairs in which he had always taken an interest: the District Council, the Worcestershire County

Council—of whose Planning Committee he was to become chairman, the British Legion and Freemasons among others. But especially he took a leading part in the affairs of the hotel trade, particularly in the training of young people. As president of the Hotel and Catering Institute he was able to influence the setting up of training centres all over the country and to give practical help by taking trainees for short periods at the Lygon. This experience has proved of value to people now doing responsible jobs in the trade at home and abroad. His work in this sphere became well known and in 1964 he was asked to give a lecture at the Royal Society of Arts on the British Catering Industry, for which he was later awarded the Society's Silver Medal.

In our other business Dick Bee felt, quite rightly, that we ought to get back as soon as we possibly could to our real job of making fine furniture. He was a great stickler for quality. He felt that the combination of manufacturing and retailing which we had practised before the war, although it may have been inevitable at that time, was responsible for a great many of our troubles. He sensed that young people would now be far more likely than the pre-war generation to accept contemporary design and therefore it would not be such a heartbreaking job to sell through retailers. It seemed, too, that the market for contract furniture, with which we were in touch before the war, was likely to grow rapidly, so a small company, Russell Furnishings Ltd, was formed to cope with this. These developments called for a considerable increase of manufacturing and storage space. During the war permission had been obtained to build on the site of the blitzed barn, using the stone which remained there. Fortunately land at the back of the factory belonging to the Lygon Arms could be made available for the storage of timber. But apart from the question of space, plant and equipment needed overhaul and in most cases replacement. The only major item which had been added during the war was a battery of kilns for drying timber. These had proved essential as wood of a stipulated moisture content was not generally available in war-time and much of the precision work we were given to do was impossible without it. The kilns needed a good deal of steam, which was also necessary for the presses required for the increasing amount of veneering work. This equipment and the experience we had in using it were seen to be valuable in dealing with the larger-scale production which selling through the retail trade postulated.

As our two businesses were employing a substantial proportion of the available labour in the immediate neighbourhood any considerable expansion was ruled out. Moreover, the acute shortage of labour generally forced some mass production engineering firms, who could pay very high rates, to send buses each day for considerable distances to collect people to work in factory or office, thus depleting the force available for both of our businesses. For some time after the war, boys who were partly trained were called up for National Service, and although we took care to keep in touch with them not all rejoined us when they were released. In addition, with taxation remaining at wartime levels and even tending to increase, active private companies were greatly hampered in finding the necessary finance for expansion. But at least we were not the only people with problems.

CHAPTER 17

The Council of Industrial Design

Early Days and the Directorship

Early in 1944 I had been asked to see Sir Thomas Barlow, then Director General of Civilian Clothing at the Board of Trade, whom I had met in Manchester before the war. I found that he wanted to discuss a scheme for setting up a national body to promote higher standards of industrial design. This had been recommended by an official committee before the war but had resulted only in a small Government grant being given to start a National Register of Designers. It was clear that the Second World War had greatly accelerated the pace at which many countries which had been mainly producers of primary products were turning over to manufacturing an increasing range of goods themselves, a tendency much simplified by the development of machines which called for little skilled labour. It was also clear that the virtual liquidation of Britain's overseas investments would make exports more vital than ever, and that these would have to be of high quality so as to make the most of such raw materials as it would still be necessary to buy from overseas. Moreover, the tremendous impetus which the war had given to mass production, introducing new techniques and materials, inevitably meant much keener international competition so that good design as an element of quality would be far more important than it had been in the nineteenth century. Dr Dalton, then President of the Board of Trade, was aware of this and was also interested

P

in the subject from a social point of view. He felt that the country would realize that pre-war conditions had gone for good, a fresh start had to be made and therefore the time was opportune for reviving the project of a Council of Industrial Design. He also saw that Barlow, with his wide knowledge of industry and his experience in the Board of Trade coupled with the interest he had shown in design problems over a number of years, was just the man he needed as the first chairman.

Barlow was head of the great textile firm of Barlow and Jones in which, in 1935, he had set up a small design research unit, Helios, under Marianne Straub, an imaginative and well-trained textile designer. This was then a very forward-looking thing to do, especially in Lancashire. But he was an unusual person—a classical scholar, an authority on the work of Albrecht Dürer, a connoisseur of wine, especially Moselle, and a collector of beautiful objects of all kinds, including those of his own day. Here again he showed discrimination, for few rich men then bought any objects of art unless they could be guaranteed old. Barlow knew of the unusual pre-war practical experience I had gained in making and selling a high standard of modern design. He had heard a good deal about the success of the Murphy Radio experiment and, being in the Board of Trade, he must have known something of Utility furniture, which by 1944 was proving successful beyond anticipation. I had, indeed, built up a design reputation of sorts at the Board as I had realized that the situation was a delicate one and so had taken special care to apply my knowledge in a practical commonsense way. All this, allied with the insight I had gained into the working of the Ministry which was to father this experiment, made him feel that I could make a useful contribution to the early discussions.

It is one thing to be aware that a certain aim is desirable: it is quite another to set out exactly how that aim may be achieved. There was only a small group which thought a Council of Industrial Design a good idea, the majority regarding it as a waste of money. It is useful today to remember that at that time no country in the world had set up such a body and backed it with an adequate government grant. There were people in the Treasury and the Board of Trade who argued that public money ought not to be spent on such a project. Similar arguments had been used when the Council for the Encouragement of Music and the Arts, later renamed the Arts Council of Great Britain, was set up at the beginning of the war. Only the great prestige of Maynard Keynes and the obvious necessity for some diversion to keep up morale in wartime enabled it to be done. But why subsidize industry in peacetime? If industry wanted such a council why shouldn't industry pay for it? If industry was not willing to do so there could be no demand and therefore no need for it. And, in any case, if the goods made could be sold—and goodness knows order books were long enough—why bother what they looked like? The answer to these arguments was that industry as a whole was complacently unaware that anything was wrong with the goods it produced, that undeniably it was true that they could all be sold easily at the moment, but that the seller's market would pass, competition would greatly increase in world markets and then the suitability and look of the goods—their quality—would become as important as price and delivery. When that time came it would be no use trying to set up a council in a hurry, for an immense educational job had to be done—starting with reorganization of the whole method of training industrial designers, persuasion of industry to employ them, the creation of public interest in better designs and the consequent stimulation of a demand at home which would in time have an influence on export trade. It was essential that our customers everywhere should be convinced that Britain stood for quality—quality in its full sense of material, workmanship and design. The days of selling grey cloth, steel rails and coal were going or gone—as more countries became industrialized they would produce basic products for themselves—and our job in Britain was to realize that these countries would then have money to buy many specialized goods and services from us. Cases could be cited of

227

British goods which were quite inadequate in design and gave the consumer far less than he had a right to expect. Yet industry saw nothing wrong with them. Why should it be imagined that any sane man would pay high fees to a doctor when he was convinced there was nothing wrong with him, yet how often did he leave a nagging pain until too late? This was a common British attitude and it was invariably a pretty expensive one.

Barlow realized clearly that although he had the support of Ministers there was no way of telling how long they would be in office. Unless senior civil servants realized that the Council could do a real job of work which was of practical value the situation would be precarious, for it would not be possible to show results for some time. How to set about the job was the first problem and it was necessary to rely on our own judgment as there was nowhere to go for advice. Mistakes would undoubtedly be made. Resistance from at least some sections of industry was inevitable as however tactfully manufacturers were approached all of them had had a bellyful of controls in wartime and would resent any advice, especially from the Board of Trade. Indeed, it was quite possible that they might claim that on the one hand they were urged by the Board to export more and on the other hand the Council, which came under the Board, made this more difficult by exposing the fancied design shortcomings of their goods! It was obvious that the ice was very thin indeed and that the educational aspect was even wider than had been thought and would have to start in the Ministries most closely concerned. Grant-aided bodies are not usually popular with Government Departments, who look upon them as neither fish, flesh, fowl nor good red herring, so they are naturally the first victims in periods of great financial stringency.

When, following these preliminary discussions, I received a letter from the President inviting me to be one of the twenty-four original members of the Council I felt it was a challenge I had no hesitation in accepting. It might mean influencing for the better the thought of a whole generation. Francis Meynell, whose experience was also valuable in preliminary discussion, Allan Walton and myself—all Royal Designers for Industry— were the only designers appointed. I had been elected an R D I in 1940 and it is perhaps of interest to mention that Dick, elected four years later, and I are the only brothers who have so far been honoured by the distinction. Amongst the other members I particularly welcomed the appointment of Sir Charles Tennyson, whose support I had already come to value highly and who was well aware of the problems involved in the new Council's work, as was also Sir Kenneth Clark, the well-known art critic. It had been decided that a preponderance of members should be respected businessmen, something which I myself had strongly urged as being the only way to give the new body a standing with industrialists. Among these were several who had been interested in design problems for some time, such as Ernest Goodale, Josiah Wedgwood, William Haigh and Sir Steven Bilsland, who was appointed chairman of the Scottish Committee. Designers at that time had little influence in industry and were slow to realize that the only way to acquire any was to take a much wider practical interest in the running of the concern for which they were working and so qualify in time for a seat on the board.

The Council was launched in December 1944 and at its first meeting the President said:

'We must, therefore, make a sustained effort to improve design, and to bring industry to recognize the practical importance of this task. You have to arouse the interest of ordinary men and women. . . . If you succeed in your task, in a few years' time every side of our daily life will be the better for your work. Every kitchen will be an easier place to work in; every home a pleasanter place to live in. Men and women in millions will be in your debt, though they may not know it; and not in Britain alone but all over the world. . . . Industry itself will have much cause to thank you. Our export trade, and our volume of business at home, will both be the greater if our goods are planned and made, with skill and imagination, to meet the user's real need, and to give pleasure in the using.'

The Council's terms of reference were 'to promote by all practicable means the improvement of design in the products of British industry' and the following main functions were specified:

'(a) to encourage and assist the establishment and conduct of Design Centres by industries, and to advise the Board of Trade on the grant of financial assistance to these Centres;

(b) to provide a national display of well-designed goods by holding, or participating in, exhibitions and to conduct publicity for good design in other appropriate forms;

(c) to co-operate with the Education Authorities and other bodies in matters affecting the training of designers;

(d) to advise, at the request of Government Departments and other public bodies, on the design of articles to be purchased by them, and to approve the selection of articles to be shown in United Kingdom Pavilions in international exhibitions and in official displays in other exhibitions; and

(e) to be a centre of information and advice, both for industry and for Government Departments, on all matters of industrial art and design.'

I had a number of talks with S. C. Leslie who had been appointed director. A Rhodes Scholar from Australia with pre-war publicity experience, he came to the Council from the Ministry of Home Security, where he had spent most of the war as Director of Public Relations. He therefore had a wide knowledge of advertising and publicity and of the working of Government Departments which was to prove of great value in the first major job the Council was given to do. It owes a great deal to him for the tremendous drive with which he tackled the inevitable problems and the skill he displayed in selecting people, at very short notice, to cope with those sides of the work with which he was not altogether familiar.

Almost the first thing Barlow asked me to do was to go to Sweden with Francis Meynell and Dick Ryder, who was then on the staff of the Council, to represent Britain at the centenary celebrations of *Svenska Slojdforeningen* (the Swedish Society of Industrial Design) in 1945. It was my first flight and the first time I had been out of England since 1939. I had then also been to Sweden, where I had acquired many friends since my first visit to Scandinavia in the early 1920s. We flew in an old Dakota and were royally entertained by the Swedes, including a splendid dinner in the Golden Hall of the Stockholm Town Hall. It was a most exciting interlude after the grim, dull war years and I was able to discuss many matters of mutual interest with Swedish designers.

Within twenty-four hours of taking over as President of the Board of Trade in 1945 Sir Stafford Cripps walked into the offices of the Council in Petty France and told Leslie that he wanted the Council to stage a considerable exhibition of British goods, for which special funds would be made available. This presented the newly formed body with a splendid opportunity, but also a tough problem in rapid recruitment of the sort of staff who are very difficult to find in a hurry. It set about its task with several aims in mind: to arouse greater interest in design in the minds of the general public, as consumers; to intensify the interest of manufacturers and distributors in industrial design and their awareness of the desirability of rapid progress; to give encouragement to British designers of all kinds; and to stage a prestige advertisement before the world for British industry, industrial design and standards of display. A major snag was that the exhibition had to be got together at short notice and as most firms were then turning over from war to peacetime production and materials were still in short supply no one had a clear idea of what well-designed articles might be available in a year's time. Under these conditions it was decided that the wisest thing to do would be to stress light-hearted, gay décor and display so that, if the worst came to the worst and in some sections it should prove impossible to find more than a handful of exhibits, the show would not be a flop. After the wartime slogan 'Britain Can Take It', the title 'Britain Can Make It' exactly matched the mood of the moment. James Gardner's imaginative approach to display allied with the skill of the consulting architect, Basil Spence, who has since become famous for more permanent work, contributed greatly to the success of the exhibition. But any well-staged show could hardly fail to have been a success at that time, for nothing of this kind and scope had been held in London for seven years and it offered the public a foretaste of the fruits of post-war production. Crowds poured into the Victoria and Albert Museum which, having been emptied of its normal contents in wartime, had very appropriately been made available for the purpose. From September 1946 until the end of the year nearly one and a half million people visited it, paying a shilling each. A grant was made to enable the Scottish Committee of the Council to launch a similar exhibition, 'Enterprise Scotland', in 1947. This was equally successful and more than doubled its estimated attendance—some 456,000 people were admitted—in spite of the fact that the entrance fee was also doubled. That its first big ventures should have been so singularly successful gave the Council confidence in tackling its difficult job.

Meantime, in 1946, Barlow asked me to become chairman of a committee set up to report to the Minister of Works on the improvement of design in the Ministry's purchases, a somewhat delicate operation but one of considerable importance in view of the immense amount of equipment passing through their hands each year. The report we made may have given encouragement to those in the Ministry who were anxious to see it pursuing a more enlightened policy. Certainly a great change has now come about, considerable progress having been achieved under Sir David Eccles, whose imaginative approach to Coronation decorations in 1953 demonstrated this for all to see.

In 1947 my wife and I snatched a couple of weeks holiday in

Switzerland and sat about in the sun doing nothing for the first time for what seemed centuries. In Lugano we ran into Bill and Dorothy Haigh. He was an original member of the Council, one of the kindest of Yorkshiremen and a staunch friend. In our saunterings we discovered finocchio in the fruit and vegetable market, which we always visit. And in a shop we saw an astonishing basket, quite large and shovel or fan shaped. Remembering the coat-of-arms in the splendid brass of Sir Robert de Setvans (1306, at Chartham, Kent), three seed (winnowing) fans, I felt sure it must be for winnowing corn at very isolated farms in the mountains, and that is what it turned out to be. I was delighted that my interest in heraldry, by enabling me to recognize an object I had never seen, had given me a sidelight on peasant life in Switzerland. When I got back I heard that Leslie had been asked to return to White-hall to take charge of the Information Division at the Treasury. This was a great blow to the Council, which received an urgent request for his release from Sir Stafford—a request which could hardly be refused. We advertised, but it wasn't easy to find a man with the right qualifications, and after some time Barlow asked me whether I would be prepared to apply. I was still working at the Board of Trade but imagined I should be released shortly, so I told him that if he felt I could be of more service to the Council as director than as a member I would, if approached, certainly consider it seriously as I was deeply aware of the potential value to the country of such a body. On the other hand, I realized that if it failed to win the confidence of industry it might prove the graveyard of the hopes we had for improving design standards. I added that I had already been working five days a week in London for nearly five years and as I was a countryman at heart and my wife and I were determined to keep our house in the country this was a serious deprivation. Shortly afterwards I had a letter from Barlow asking me to meet the Council, which had interviewed several candidates and was seriously disturbed that, at a time when a new impetus was essential, it had been without a director for several months. The result was that I was offered the post. Obviously Barlow had checked that I would be acceptable to the Board of Trade and apparently I had a clear récord as I had been awarded a CBE earlier that year! Yet it was with a certain secret satisfaction that I was able to inform the Council that my training had been an entirely practical one: I had no other qualifications of any kind, not even a university education. I was 55, a time of life when many men begin to think about retirement rather than starting on an entirely new kind of job, but my family's propensity for changing jobs won the day.

At about this time I was asked by the Minister of Education to sit on a selection panel to choose a new principal for the Royal College of Art. I enquired what plans there were for the development of the College, which was then spread all over South Kensington. It had been due for rebuilding early in the century, but plans had been stopped in 1914 by the war and although further consideration was given to the matter building was again stopped by the Second World War. The Minister replied that it was felt desirable to appoint a principal and hear his views. I then asked whether notice would be taken of these and, as I expected, had a somewhat non-committal reply, but I felt the time was ripe for a strong principal who would goad the Ministry into action. By a fortunate chance I was in Newcastle shortly after this for the Council's first Design Week and was invited to dine with Robin Darwin, who was Professor of Fine Art at the University of Durham but had previously been on the Council's staff for a brief period, when he was responsible for preparing a useful report on the training of the designer. He is a good cook and after some excellent salmon I enquired whether he was putting in for the Royal College job. He said he was happy where he was and didn't think the Ministry would do anything about reorganization, but I felt they would and, as I was sure there were times when he hankered to be back in London, I urged him to consider it. As it turned out, his appointment as principal of the College— a post which he was to fill with conspicuous success—and mine as director of the Council were announced on the same day and appeared in adjacent columns of *The Times*. We were able to forge a close link between the two bodies, to the great advantage of both, for it was the Council's job to persuade industry to employ the more highly trained designers which the reorganization of the College would provide. This link was further cemented by the appointment of two people who had been with me at Broadway, Professor R. Y. Goodden (now vice-principal) to the School of Silversmithing and Professor R. D. Russell to the School of Furniture Design.

On September 1, 1947, I took over my new job, on a half-time basis for the first month as I had to clear up my work at the Board of Trade. The first thing I did was to call on Mrs Lovat Fraser, then chairman of the Design and Industries Association, Milner Gray of the Society of Industrial Artists, and Kenneth Luckhurst, secretary of the Royal Society of Arts, to assure them that I should greatly value any support they could give me. I also visited John Farleigh at the Crafts Centre and Cleveland Belle at the Cotton Board's Colour, Design and Style Centre in Manchester, and spoke at the Art Workers' Guild. It has always seemed to me a matter of great importance that such bodies, whose general aims are similar, should be on friendly terms and the highly individualist approach of the artist does not always make this easy. I am delighted that five such bodies are finding a home in the imaginative Carlton House Terrace scheme, which Roland Penrose of the Institute of Contemporary Arts has worked so hard to bring about.

My accession provided a fine opportunity for an attack on the Council from all sides. I got the backwash from Utility furniture and from 'Britain Can Make It'. Manufacturers not unnaturally disliked the idea of controls and of their goods being selected by an outside body. Not all the Council's selectors for the exhibition had been as tactful as they should have been but of course many of the articles submitted were not well designed and had to be rejected. Most firms had long order books immediately after the war and firmly believed that if a thing sold well it must be well designed. Retailers felt that their ability to select what the public needed was being challenged. Designers said that the Council's selection was too timid, whereas manufacturers complained that it was too revolutionary. Several people who obviously felt that a great error had been made in not putting them on the Council came to see me and outlined how the job ought to be tackled. One or two of these, over a period of several years, attacked as a matter of principle every single effort the Council made. It was inevitable, also, that some of the business members of the Council were apt to think it ought to be a sales promotion body, pure and simple. Criticism of the standard of British goods seemed treason to them when it was obvious that export sales were needed desperately, a view with which I could not help sympathizing. The Press—especially the trade Press—saw a heaven-sent opportunity to back up the various factions by belabouring the Council. My experience at the Board of Trade made me realize that if several important export trades ganged up and went to the President with a united front saying that the Council was discrediting profitable export lines by pointing out faults in design it would be extremely difficult for him to resist such pressure. This might lead to restrictions which would make it impossible for the Council to function and failure would be most popular with a large number of industrialists, who would immediately proclaim that they had pointed out the folly of the whole operation from the start— as was indeed true. In retrospect this time seems a most hazardous one, but it was at least stimulating and I always tried to calculate the odds. I saw that it was essential that our parent body, the Board of Trade, should be convinced that we never took a step which could not be justified so that if a serious rumpus blew up we should at least have their sympathy even if they could not give us their full support publicly. Altogether I didn't have a dull moment while I was trying to select my staff but I took some consolation from the fact that the sniping came from all sides! My army experience stood me in good stead, and I hope I managed to appear fairly imperturbable. Occasionally, too, I came across something which entertained me, such as a heading in a trade paper: 'FBI backs CID'. This, of course, was intended to indicate that the Federation of British Industries was giving us support. But I couldn't help wondering whether my American friends would interpret it as an attempt by the Federal Bureau of Investigation and the Criminal Investigation Department to circumvent international crooks!

In the *Queen Mary* returning from America the year before, I had met Paul Reilly, son of Professor Sir Charles Reilly, principal of Liverpool University's School of Architecture, who used to come to see us at Campden before the war. During the voyage I saw a good deal of Paul, who had been sent to New York for six months to work on a plastics paper by a publishing firm who hoped to start a similar journal in England. He was a very keen and lively person with just the right architectural and journalistic background and I decided to offer him the senior job of chief information officer. Although he was under contract to his firm they were quite unable to get an allocation of paper and whilst they were anxious to keep him on in hopes of securing this he hated the idea of not doing a real job. He therefore said that if he could get his release there was nothing he would like to do more than join the Council's staff. Fortunately this proved possible and the Council could not have found a more devoted worker. Mark Hartland Thomas joined us as chief industrial officer and, with Dick Ryder (exhibitions) and John Weyman (administration), completed my main team. John Weyman had been the first member of staff to be appointed and fortunately proved to be that somewhat rare bird, an accountant with an interest in design.

I had thought it odd that the Council's terms of reference did not mention the retailer. I knew well, from experience, how difficult it was to sell better standards of design, yet such standards could only be nourished by sales. It was useless to expect manufacturers to produce better things unless they could be sold. In the durable consumer goods field at least, if the retailer would not present them with enthusiasm the manufacturer was forced to advertise them nationally and so bring customers into retail shops asking for them, but this could only be done by the largest firms. I therefore proposed to have three (later expanded to four) staff divisions of the Council, each with a corresponding committee: industrial, to stimulate supply; information and exhibitions, to stimulate demand; and administration, to deal with internal organization, finance and staff. This proved a good and enduring pattern.

Meanwhile, I escaped to Kew Gardens and drafted a report on development for the Council and it is interesting to record that my main points were accepted:

(1) That the Treasury and Board of Trade should not judge the Council by the number of Design Centres set up. Much more preparatory work would be needed in the industries to be served.

(2) That the Design Centres already established should be encouraged to serve as models likely to stimulate other industries to set up their own Design Centres.

(3) That a series of Design Weeks on a large scale in industrial towns, based on the experience already gained, should be organized in order to arouse interest in the provinces and to supplement the Council's activities in London.

(4) That the Council should work with, and give every encouragement to, existing voluntary organizations with aims similar to its own.

(5) That every effort should be made to convince manufacturers that good design is as much part of good management as costing, salesmanship or welfare.

The Council's terms of reference had laid some stress on the encouragement of individual industries to establish their own Design Centres, as had been done voluntarily—and with some success—by the Cotton Board in 1940. These centres were to be financed jointly by the Government and the industry concerned in very much the same way as Industrial Research Associations. It was envisaged that they would study the problem of design in relation to the products of the particular industry and collect and disseminate information with a view to raising standards. Detailed discussions had been opened with a large number of industries and two Centres—Jewellery and Rayon—had been decided upon. The Council was also associated with a move to establish a Crafts Centre, which was to be financed and governed on similar lines to an industrial Design Centre. It was clear, however, that industry as a whole was by no means convinced of the usefulness of such centres and I felt that a great deal more groundwork would be neces- sary before they could be established with a fair chance of success. To impose them on industries under the aegis of Development Councils, which were extremely unpopular as they were being financed by a levy, would, I believed, have been fatal. I think experience has shown this view to have been correct.

Whilst I was still working only half time at the Council before taking over fully on October 1st I had a most disturbing letter from the chairman, dated September 28th. He said that his doctor had told him that, as he had been greatly over- worked during the war, he must lay off for three months and reduce his commitments permanently. Under these circum- stances he felt he had no alternative to resignation. This really was a body blow, for not only did I have a great affection for Barlow but it had been at his personal request and with his promise of backing that I had agreed to take on the job and although I had had few illusions about the difficulties, it was now evident to me that industry would resent any form of advice, direction or control even more than I had anticipated. Although I had worked in the Board of Trade for several years it was not at his level, as I realized with startling clarity. However, I must own I was almost in tears when I was told, a very short time afterwards, that Barlow had taken on the chairmanship of the District Bank. Our new chairman, Roger Edwards, proved a most valuable support to me at this critical juncture. He was an original member of the Council, a director of the Co-operative Wholesale Society, self-made, completely honest and fearless.

In such a situation little boats keep close to the shore and I

repeated to my staff my determination to make friends where-
ever we could—or at the very least not to make enemies.
Nothing pleased me so much as a letter commending our
service. I realized that businessmen might know little about
design, but they were usually pretty good judges of sincerity
and efficiency and I argued that if we were honest and efficient
they might well come in time to believe that our views on
design were worthy of their attention! I took a deep breath
and tried to carry on regardless of the battering from outside
but earnestly investigating complaints.

I was greatly influenced by Trevelyan's *England under Queen
Anne*, and the way in which Marlborough realized that his job
was perhaps even more political than military. I liked also to
think of Walpole sorting out his letters until he came to his
gamekeeper's and then, having heard how his pheasants were
doing, turning to the affairs of Europe. And I have to admit
that when the regular pink list, beautifully composed and
illustrated by Ted Ardizzone, of wines just purchased for the
Senior Common Room at the Royal College of Art or some
catalogue of plants or books arrived, my secretary, Eileen
Reynolds, knew it was useless to plague me with the latest
breakdown. I had taken Eileen over from Clem Leslie and she
proved a great support under these trying conditions. She
would come in and, finding me reading the latest attack and
muttering unfathomable blasphemies, would say: 'Come on,
say it!' And once she appeared with a file on some subject
which had cooled off for the moment and said: 'What is LSDL
you have written on this?' 'Let sleeping dogs lie,' I said.
When, in 1949, Eileen had an opportunity to go to India I must
admit I was somewhat despondent. But Rosamund Hogg, who
had been working in the Council for some time—originally in
the director's office—and therefore knew the background,
rapidly got the hang of the job and was a cheerful and utterly
reliable prop throughout the period of my directorship.

Whilst all this was happening it was essential to implement
the plan for a series of Design Weeks. The first tryout, at
Newcastle-upon-Tyne, had clearly shown that much more local

interest had to be stirred up beforehand, also that a supporting exhibition was needed. This must be designed on a unit principle so that it could be rearranged easily to fit the widely differing accommodation available in each area. It was essential, too, to seek the active co-operation of every local organization impinging on our work: the municipal and education authorities, the local chamber of trade, groups of architects and designers, Townswomen's Guilds, Rotary Clubs, youth clubs and so on. Retailers, also, must be encouraged to stock and show some of the things in the exhibition as this might lead to some permanent improvement. The art gallery, which was often the only possible location for an exhibition, was visited by few people in many provincial towns. This situation has fortunately changed a great deal in the last twenty years but it will be clear that in 1947 the Council was anxious to prove that it was a practical, down-to-earth body which could assist manufacturers and retailers to sell goods and that its functions were not cultural only, which might be implied by staging our exhibition in the local art gallery or museum.

Dennis Clive, who was in charge of the Design Week programme, therefore spent a good deal of his time talking to city councils. Usually we found the Mayor very willing to co-operate and give a luncheon to the Press and a few local bigwigs beforehand. Sometimes the Mayor opened the exhibition, sometimes we persuaded a nationally-known local figure to do this. It meant quite a lot of travelling for me as I had, of course, to be present and sometimes it was necessary to address not one but several groups and to broadcast. It was valuable, too, to have the support of any of our local Council members. This was a two-way traffic, as it was also a useful method of educating them without appearing to do so! Over a period of some two years we held Design Weeks in Cardiff, Manchester, Birmingham, the Potteries, Nottingham, Bristol, Southampton and Bradford, with a travelling exhibition, 'Design Fair', as the focal point. The cost of this programme and the time involved was considerable, and although we had many applications we were unable to extend it to cover smaller

Q

towns, much as we should have liked to do so. But between Design Weeks it was possible to send small exhibitions to a number of other places and we were also able to encourage keen retailers in such towns to put on shows of their own with our help and advice. Meantime, the Scottish Committee sent an exhibition, 'Enterprise Travels', on a thousand-mile tour of Scottish cities and towns. We were well aware of the much greater problems such an effort presented in the north and endeavoured to give them all the help we could.

In 1948, being on the Council of the Royal Society of Arts as Master of the Faculty of Royal Designers for Industry, I put forward a proposal for an exhibition sponsored by the Society, the Faculty and the Council of Industrial Design. The theme I suggested was 'Design at Work', showing how various firms set about designing industrial products by collaboration with members of the Faculty. The exhibition was duly held, at the Royal Academy of Arts. Edward Halliday, who was currently painting a portrait of The Duke of Edinburgh and whom I had originally met when he had compèred the first broadcast I did in 1934—one of a series on design subjects—was interested in what I had told him of the proposed exhibition and said he would mention it to Prince Philip. This he did and the result was most encouraging, for not only did the Duke express interest but said he would like to visit the exhibition. I was greatly impressed by the searching questions he asked and his obvious wish to be well informed on a subject that, apparently, was new to him. Halliday brought him to luncheon at the Arts Club afterwards so that I could talk to him quietly and this was the beginning of ungrudging support of the Council which has been of immense value. He realized from the first what many industrialists were slow to grasp, that our work could become of national importance. He found time to discuss any matter where his help would be useful and, most important of all, he gave his personal support publicly at a time when I was harassed by much sniping from outside.

There was at this time a growing demand both at home and abroad for articles and talks on how the Council worked. We began to get visitors from overseas who were interested in setting up similar bodies in their own countries. I tried to give them full information, being careful to point out that our work was largely pioneering and we were constantly adapting it in the light of experience gained; also that conditions in other countries were often vastly different and therefore the pattern might prove of little use. To explain what we were doing, I went to Darmstadt, Oslo, Stockholm, Copenhagen, Milan, Rome and Zürich among other places. In Stockholm, where I have many friends, I was later asked to address the Annual General Meeting of *Svenska Slojdforeningen*, of which the late King Gustav of Sweden was president. He sat in rather a grand chair just in front of me and after the address I was asked to take him to see the supporting exhibition of British goods staged in special showcases in the open air in a nearby square. As we left the building one of the laziest trams I have ever seen approached, with another coupled behind. The King and I stood on the kerb while this obstruction slowly passed us and I could not help thinking it was odd that in Scandinavia trams took precedence over Kings! He showed considerable knowledge of the subject on which I had lectured —which was not surprising as his son, Count Sigvard Berna-dotte, is a well-known industrial designer.

In 1948 I had an invitation to visit New York again, to discuss matters of mutual interest with the directors and staff of the Museum of Modern Art and to sit on a jury to judge an international competition for low-cost furniture which the Museum was organizing. This was an enjoyable break from the anxieties and annoyances of the Council, which I left in Paul Reilly's capable hands whilst I was received in the most charming way by old and new friends. I found that whereas foreign competitors had been required to submit drawings only, Americans were asked to send a prototype as well. There were a great number of these and in order to accommodate them the Museum had hired space in a storage warehouse which was as like a feudal castle as anything in New York. Built of brick, about four storeys high, it had no windows but apparently it had been considered that to add steel doors—perhaps they were dummies—on each floor would make it appear quite impregnable. On entering, there was a steel roller shutter large enough to admit a lorry and another similar one about thirty feet ahead—the equivalent of a portcullis but, so far as I remember, there was no moat or drawbridge! We met there one afternoon and were asked to return at ten the next morning, a Saturday. When I did so there was no sign of life whatever. I rang the bell, and rang again, but there was still no reply. A driver drew up with a large truck, got out and came across the road with that delightful, loose, shuffling walk which I regarded as a speciality of cowboys in Westerns. I was really in America—fine! As he came up I rang again but still nothing happened. Then he said: 'They don't work Saturdays.' I said I thought they would let me in if I could make my presence known. 'I'll try once more,' I said, and as I pressed the bell I gathered from the look he gave me that he took rather a poor view of European intelligence. But at last I heard steps. Then the inner shutter was pulled up and down. More steps, and up went the outer one. Recognizing me from the day before, the doorman signed to me to enter. 'Where can I park my truck?' said the driver. 'We don't work Saturdays', was all the reply he got as the shutter closed once more.

I fell in love with New York and found just walking around the city a never ending source of entertainment. Outside the church on Fifth Avenue were several of the most gigantic paving stones I had ever seen; and one evening I pulled up short with astonishment when I noticed that the sidewalk was covered with the unmistakable, clear yellow leaves of the maidenhair tree. Many hundreds of these trees have been planted in New York and seem to stand the bitter winds between the high blocks remarkably well. I wonder if they would thrive in London? On the subway I saw a man with a paper cap just like the carpenter wore in *Alice*. I was told he probably worked in a newspaper printing room and it was made of the first sheet off the press. Standing in Park Avenue with trains roaring under the pavement and traffic roaring on the road I heard an even greater rumpus. It was the New York fire brigade, preceded by men on motor bicycles with wailing klaxons. In front of me was a vast skeleton building on which the riveters were at work once more—perhaps it had been stopped by the war. Two men met on the sidewalk and greeted one another. Above the hellish racket of riveting one shouted at the top of his voice: 'Say, boy, it's good to hear that noise again', and I realized that in New York it is as exciting to hear riveting as it is to hear the first cuckoo in England. When I told a friend of my father's with whom I was dining that I had walked through Central Park he was somewhat taken aback and I gathered that he regarded this as a risky form of exercise after dark.

Edgar Kaufmann most hospitably put me up and when, poor mutt, I asked whether it was a contemporary copy of a Claude in his flat he said it was alleged to be a Claude, and well authenticated. There seemed to be absolutely nothing that couldn't happen in New York! I stayed with Kaufmann's father and mother at 'Falling Water', the house Frank Lloyd Wright built for them cantilevered over a stream in an oak wood in Pennsylvania. The large dining space interested me greatly. The walls over the stream were almost entirely glazed but at the back the room had been dug into the rising hillside and the rock taken out had been used as building stone. A considerable outcrop of it had been left in the floor and in the dim light it gave an extraordinary primeval quality contrasting with the very high degree of sophistication elsewhere. Around the house was a group of smaller houses in which friends could be put up and just come along to dinner with their hosts—a fashion set, with considerably more formality, by Louis XIV at Marly.

I especially wished to see something of the Tennessee Development Authority project so I went down to Knoxville and was fortunate enough to meet a Swiss architect, Rudi Mock, working there. He most kindly showed me around the area and introduced me to one of the engineers, who took me along with him on his monthly inspection. We visited three of the immense dams. From the top of the highest the power-house at the base looked like a match-box, but when we went down and entered it I was delighted at the orderliness and beauty of colour and forms in this vast machine hall. Here, it seemed to me, was a valuable lesson in how the machine could be harnessed gracefully to the service of men and nothing of this kind could possibly have been done until our own age. From this hall we walked into a passage which led to the very heart of the concrete dam, perhaps 500 feet at right-angles to the face. There was complete silence but for an occasional drip of water. At intervals there were recesses to accommodate accurate instruments which recorded any slightest movement since the last monthly inspection. Each was carefully checked. At the end of the passage we turned at right-angles once more, walked a similar distance and came out of this modern pyramid into the sun. I liked the way that engineers, architects, landscape architects and interior designers worked alongside in the same building, which resulted in a far more integrated plan than we usually seem able to achieve. When I returned home I went to tell Lord Citrine, then in charge of the Central Electricity Authority, what I had seen and he asked me to visit several of the new British power stations and report back. This I did and I hope it may have encouraged the Central Electricity Generating Board to make use of the services of the considerable number of landscape architects they now employ. As a proud Honorary Associate of the Institute of Landscape Architects I am pleased to be able to report such real progress.

Just after my return from the United States I was saddened to hear of the sudden death of Allan Walton, which left Francis Meynell as the sole practising designer on the Council as I had become director. Some three months later Meynell resigned as he disapproved of the Council's publishing its own magazine, *Design*. As he had been in the Board of Trade during the war and his wife was the senior civil servant who had been much concerned with the setting up of the Council and in fact attended its first meeting with the President, I had no way of estimating what the damage caused by this action might be.

Naturally the situation gave me a great deal of anxiety. There was hardly anyone on the Council except the chairman and Tennyson to whom I could talk freely and it only needed a trade recession to seriously affect our ability to do the job for which we had been set up. But we were already embarked on a major national project which was to do much to establish the position of the Council.

CHAPTER 18

The Council of Industrial Design

Towards the Festival of Britain, 1951

When, in October 1947, Mr Harold Wilson became President of the Board of Trade, one of his first acts was to inform the Council that the Government had decided to stage in 1951 a considerable exhibition to celebrate the centenary of the first international exhibition which was held in the Crystal Palace in 1851. We were able to call on Mr Wilson for a good deal of support in the preparatory period as he remained at the Board until just before the opening in May 1951. He knew that one of the Prince Consort's main aims in 1851 had been to improve the standard of design of British goods, and as this remained our aim for the centenary we were not slow to point out that, although we were confident of increasing the pace, it was not a job in which results were likely to appear overnight. When he came to address the Council we had no doubt that he felt the job we had set out to do was important, although he had not the crusading zeal of Sir Stafford. Lord Ismay was appointed chairman of the Grand Council. I had known him for some years and greatly respected him. His wife came of a well-known Broadway family and they lived at Wormington Grange, a few miles away. When I went to see him he reminded me, with a smile, that much of his courting had been done from the Lygon and he well remembered my father ticking him off for keeping him up one night when the porter was ill! The director-general was Gerald Barry, whose knowledge of journalism

248

and interest in architecture augured well for the success of the project. I was asked to meet him to discuss the responsibility allocated to the Council for 'a first rate design display which will include consumer goods, civil transport, certain classes of capital goods and some handicraft production'—as distinct from a separate science exhibition. On thinking over the matter it seemed to me that a pavilion of industrial design did not make sense and that the whole exhibition ought to take account of how both it and the things shown were designed, otherwise we might find clumsy wcs and basins in the public lavatories, all sorts of lettering in different pavilions, the cheapest park chairs for seating—in fact a general impression that lack of co-ordination had produced the particular brand of chaos in which Britain tends to specialize. But this meant giving up the Council's complete sovereignty in one pavilion for responsibility, somewhat loosely defined, over all—not an easy point of view to put forward to a group of businessmen administering a Council which was not yet accepted by industry. Edwards strongly supported the wider view, as he always did, and carried the day. But how could our plan be implemented?

It was first necessary to decide on the site of the main exhibition—and even following the blitz it was not a simple matter to find at least thirty acres, easily accessible, in an area as built up as London. The 1851 exhibition had been staged in Hyde Park opposite Knightsbridge Barracks and large elm trees had been enclosed in the huge glass pavilion, the ancestor of prefabricated building. There were good reasons for not using the same site, one of the strongest being the difficulty of dealing with transport in the immensely more complicated traffic conditions which had arisen since 1851. Eventually, by a process of elimination, a site on the South Bank of the Thames opposite to Whitehall and close to Waterloo Station was approved.

Next, it was essential to formulate a general layout plan, allocating space to the various pavilions, gardens, etc. From that point individual architects took over their own assignments, making every endeavour to harmonize their work with the master plan of Hugh Casson—whose idea of using White-hall Court, all beflagged, across the river as a backdrop to the exhibition was, I thought, a stroke of genius. A theme had to be worked out and written for each pavilion and these had then to be interpreted in terms of display and goods by the display designers appointed. Until this work was complete it was impossible to decide what exhibits, fittings and furnish-ings such as notices, furniture, floor coverings, lighting fittings and so on would be required. This stage might well be reached very close to the opening date with no time to shop around. Foreseeing this, Hartland Thomas put forward the idea of a 1951 Stock List, an illustrated and sample card index under trades of all the well-designed articles his team of industrial officers could search out in a systematic survey. This entailed a great many meetings with industrial groups and trade associa-tions so as to enlist maximum support. There were some seventy categories, ranging from locomotives to table ware, from liners and sailing boats to henhouses and garden tools, and the index finally proved so interesting in itself that it was decided to exhibit it on the South Bank under the title 'Design Review'. The combing process resulted in the dis-covery of some fascinating industrial techniques and other new developments which we were able to include. When the individual display man came to us with his list of requirements we were able to tell him what ought to be available and to en-sure that one maker's goods were not shown in six pavilions and another's nowhere. If the articles were chosen from photographs the designers naturally wanted to see them, but they were not always in stock as we could give no guarantee that they would eventually be shown. At every stage delays were possible.

It was vitally important to the whole future of the Council and its work that the process of selection should be carried out entirely without favouritism and in such a way as to win the confidence of industry and despite some inevitable criticism, it was clear after the Festival that relations with industry had been strengthened and improved. I was particularly anxious that the selection should aim at achieving a good standard of design in every field and should in no way represent the taste of a small clique, and to this end I sent the following directive to my team of industrial officers on June 9, 1950:

> 'There seems to be a feeling in many quarters that the exhibitions in 1951 will show only "the very latest thing ever". It is, of course, most important to illustrate up-to-date developments in British industry as far as it is possible. But the months necessary to prepare the catalogue will make it absolutely essential to freeze selection, and not dilly-dally because better designs may be in the offing. These can well be shown in "Design Review".
>
> As I see it, the exhibitions should aim at showing the high level that current British industrial production can reach on a selective basis. It has been said over and over again that these will not be exhibitions of stunts, made specially for display in 1951 without any thought that they will ultimately be made for sale. They will be real goods to go into real shops and so be available for real people. This may not be an earth-shattering statement, but it is British commonsense and should get us somewhere by permanently raising the standard. The other method tends to lower standards by making the so-called designer seem a wild and reckless person.
>
> There are at least three categories of articles which have shown remarkable continuity of good design:
>
> (1) Articles so dominated by function that, as their use has remained constant, their shape has varied little through centuries and has even dominated the material. Fishhooks and pins are cases in point—the Roman bone pin carefully shaped by hand is certainly larger than our mass-produced metal pin but the shape is almost identical, "as like as two pins"!
>
> (2) Articles where the form has been brought to great perfection by small improvements over years, the use

of the article remaining constant and the material the same. Some of the ''parish designs''—used indiscriminately by manufacturers in the Birmingham area come to mind, pottery teapots, baskets, hand-tools and others.

(3) Designs where the pattern has appealed so strongly to several generations as to transcend the dictates of fashion. Floral prints are an example—some of the most popular have not been out of print for over one hundred years.

Although sales by themselves are no proof of good industrial design—large sales of stunt articles can be ensured by aggressive advertising for short periods—there must surely be something of fundamental value in an article which sells in large quantities over a long period of time.

It is essential that we should aim at achieving a good standard of design in every field—not merely a personal preference which may degenerate into the taste of a small clique.

At this most important stage in selection will all industrial officers try to look at their trades with new eyes and see whether prejudice, familiarity or misunderstanding of what we are after may have led them to overlook *any* articles of *good* design?'

How many people have borrowed a locomotive? We had a special section of locomotives for which we needed one made for export. The firms concerned—there were only a few as British railway companies had from the first built their own, so there was no home market—were most anxious to be helpful but the problem was to find an engine which would be finished by the middle of March, as large trees had to be planted in front of it, and whose owners would be willing to lend it until October. The owners, in most cases, had been waiting a long time for delivery owing to the war and were not prepared to accept still further delay. At last we found out that one of a batch of fifty for Indian State Railways would be complete by March and, as far as the makers were concerned, could be borrowed. Would the owners lend it to us? We wrote and wrote again, but in India at this time it was not easy to find out who was responsible for what. We cabled and cabled. India House was sympathetic but unable to help. Meantime the exhibition designers were getting restive, for if the locomotive, a very large and fine one, could be borrowed it would be necessary to reinforce the roadway from the entrance at a cost of £2,000. At last we got the O.K. from India. But then it transpired that because it was a broad gauge engine it could not come down from the North British Locomotive Company in Glasgow under its own steam. It was also too large to put on a wagon, owing to tunnels. It could not be sent by road as there was no road which had not some bridge unable to bear a load of 120 tons. Air was obviously not practicable, and to send it by sea meant sending also a special floating crane to handle such an outsize load, which was not normal in the Port of London. This would cost over £1,000 and although we might just have managed to find this, we knew that when it became known other manufacturers would also expect us to pay carriage. So we went round with a hat to all the makers of components, who met us generously, and she came after all. As I gazed at her—she was a beauty—I wondered how many people could possibly have guessed at the blood and sweat involved in getting her in place!

The last hectic months before the Festival was due to open proved a time of great strain, not least to George Campbell, seconded from the Treasury to keep a constant check on expenditure. He seemed to be losing weight and I said to him one day: 'George, I can't understand you Treasury blokes. You make one hell of a fuss if we want to transfer expenditure from one subhead to another—virement you call it. You tell me you never get any time off. Don't you ever have a meeting cancelled?' 'Oh yes,' he said, 'of course we do occasionally.' 'Then why don't you take your own medicine and tell your secretary that the meeting is off, that obviously you can't transfer your time to another job and you're going out—to tea in the park?' He said it was a brilliant idea which had never occurred to him but he tried it on the next appropriate occasion and it worked like a charm: he came back feeling years younger!

In the grim struggle to open on time there were amusing episodes. The man erecting the skylon display feature came down from his perilous perch blue with cold in a March gale and slipped up on a broken duckboard. Quite seriously, he said to his mate: 'If someone doesn't mend that bloody thing there'll be a nasty accident.' And we liked Hugh Casson's gentle reminder that a good time and a half was had by all!

The opening day of the South Bank Exhibition proved cold and misty—there was even, I think, some rain. There had been an impressive service in St Paul's the day before, and The King and Queen came to perform the opening ceremony. My most vivid memory is of Sir Winston Churchill—who, with his great sense of occasion, was wearing his medals—going up the escalator in the Dome of Discovery by himself whilst we applauded him from above.

But this was only one of a number of exhibitions both in London and all over the country, including two in Scotland, land and sea travelling exhibitions—the latter in a converted aircraft carrier, the *Campania*—and 'Ulster Farm and Factory' in Belfast. Gerald Barry and I attended the Royal Opening of this, one of a number of visits I paid to Northern Ireland during my time at the Council.

Finally, the Council was responsible for the selection, collection and eventual return to some 3,500 firms of approximately 10,000 industrial exhibits in the Festival's six official exhibitions. Additionally it took every possible step to see that these were properly displayed, numbered and captioned, cared for and cleaned. It provided much of the original research and planning necessary for the preparation of themes for the exhibitions, it recommended display designers from its Record of Designers, it arranged live handicraft, industrial and sporting demonstrations, supplied information for catalogues, publicized all aspects of the Festival relating to British manufacturers and edited and published an official

Festival publication on industrial design, *Design in the Festival*, of which some 95,000 copies were sold.

The collection, safeguarding and return of all exhibits was quite an operation in itself and this most important job which, if ill done, might have created great friction with manufacturers, was coped with smoothly and efficiently by (Major General) Jack Benoy, whose knowledge of logistics had enabled him to cope with the transport side of the invasion of Africa. This had seemed to us admirable training for another operation requiring imaginative and meticulous planning. But he had a considerable shock on the last evening of the exhibition when the flag was hauled down, and without any previous warning, all the lights were turned out for a minute, with every pavilion crammed with people! Pilfering of small exhibits had been much in our minds from the first but on the whole the precautions we took proved adequate.

The Council also organized, through a committee chaired by John Gloag on which industrial, trade union and design organizations were represented, an international design congress of which the theme was 'Design Policy within Industry as a Responsibility of High Level Management'. It was a landmark in the Council's history because it brought many leading industrialists together to discuss common problems of design policy for the first time and because its discussions revealed a notable measure of agreement on the basic principles of a sound design policy. Three conclusions were outstanding and the Council accepted them as the natural starting point in its future discussions with industry:

(1) A sound design policy involves giving responsibility to someone at Board level who has sufficient authority and belief in the importance of design to supervise the formulation and execution of policy.
(2) Designers must take their place in the development team on an equal footing with engineers, research staff, salesmen and other specialists, and they should be paid according to their status.

255

(3) Good design is indivisible; it should extend to all activities of a firm, including its publicity material and auxiliary services.

The Scottish Committee of the Council also had special responsibilities related to the Festival. The Exhibition of Industrial Power held in the Kelvin Hall, Glasgow, and Scottish representation in the 1951 Stock List gave it the opportunity for an intensive approach to Scottish industry generally; and the 'Living Traditions of Scotland' exhibition of architecture and the crafts in Edinburgh—one of the best exhibitions of its kind I have ever seen, for which Wyndham Goodden, the Committee's chief officer, was responsible— was its major contribution to the Festival in Scotland.

We all felt rather sad that the Festival should have become to some extent a political issue so that, when the government changed at the end of 1951, there was no possible hope of extending it for another year. Had this been done, I believe the impact would have been tremendous, even if the South Bank Exhibition only had survived.

CHAPTER 19

The Council of Industrial Design

The Design Centre

When a comparatively small body has to set almost every other effort aside to cope with an event such as 'Britain Can Make It', or the Festival of Britain, there is bound to be a following trough to such a tidal wave. I have described how the first of these exhibitions happened so soon after the Council's formation that its permanent organization was not completed. The growth was almost entirely an exhibition growth which was, of course, lop-sided for normal conditions. After the Festival of Britain conditions were entirely different. Although the Council had been working on this great event for three years it was only during the year before the opening that almost everyone was concentrating on it in one way or another, although the industrial division's work was, of course, almost entirely angled on it. The Festival of Britain, like the earlier exhibition, provided an excellent opportunity for furthering the Council's long-term aims of convincing industry of the need for and benefits to be derived from improvements in industrial design. The exhibitions division too was much concerned with the Festival, but at the same time it was arranging a number of smaller exhibitions, showhouses, etc., up and down the country, for we were deeply conscious of the need not to restrict our activities to the capital but to take our message into the provinces at any available opportunity. The information division was developing a wide range of services

R

aimed at the retail trade, education authorities, the Press and general public. Three main lines of approach to the retail trade which have proved enduring were gradually developed: short residential courses for salesmen, buyers and managers and the arranging of exhibitions in stores either by the Council or, increasingly, by the management with the advice and assistance of the Council, and the encouragement of higher standards in window displays. The education section built up a lecture panel of several hundred professional lecturers up and down the country who could be recommended to interested enquirers. It also offered a wide range of publications on design topics, mainly concerned with home furnishing, a free monthly bulletin of design events up and down the country, *Design Calendar*, and various visual aids. A library and photographic and slide library were also developed; and, primarily for industry and designers, there was the monthly magazine *Design*. Press and promotion offices were fully occupied in handling publicity for both normal and Festival activities.

After the great Festival effort we all felt a bit spent and it was obvious that unless a clear-cut plan for the future could be put forward the staff would become restless and frustrated. The problem was how best to capitalize the interest created by the Festival. At this juncture, owing to the national financial stringency, we had to accept a reduction in our grant and decided that instead of paring all our services it would be better to make one big cut. To my intense regret, the axe fell on our educational services, because they were long term. Money was not available for publications, exhibitions, etc., and the Council had to develop means of working in collaboration with retailers and others so that they bore the main cost whilst the Council provided the 'know-how', although the lower the Council's share of the cost the more difficult it became to insist on high standards of advertising, display and selection. But the Council took the reasonable, short-term view that we should have to show quick results if we were to get much sympathy from our parent body.

When Dr Edwards was appointed chairman of the North Eastern Gas Board with headquarters in Leeds, he naturally felt he should retire from the Council as he would be able to spare little time for meetings in London. By sheer hard work he had certainly helped the Council to survive some perilous years. Edwards understood from the first that things could not be designed by a committee, a point which some Council members seemed to miss. He liked to settle policy and having picked the best available person to carry it out let him get on with it. Meantime, he made every effort to ensure that a reasonable grant was available to do the job. I liked working with him, as he always said exactly what was in his mind but never refused to listen to any carefully weighed opinion. Early in 1953 the President of the Board of Trade appointed Mr Walter J. Worboys to succeed him as chairman. Worboys was not a man who did things by halves. He was a director of Imperial Chemical Industries and had been a member of the Council for several years, he believed in it and was determined that it must have another big objective and the thing which stuck out a mile was the need for a permanent exhibition gallery of its own in London. This had been included in the Council's terms of reference and as early as 1945 consideration had been given to the desirability of establishing a Central Pavilion for Industrial Design—as recommended too by various official committees before the war—and authority had actually been given by the Board to make preliminary en-quiries about sites, although it was then obvious that building would not be feasible for some years. Temporary exhibitions were certainly valuable but a permanent, changing, selective exhibition in London as a national shop window for the most interesting current designs from the British consumer goods industries would really put the Council on the map.

It seemed that sufficient groundwork had now been done to make this a practical proposition; indeed, the increasing number of good designs coming from British factories and the competitive search of home and foreign buyers for higher standards of design now made imperative such a national

Design Centre if full advantage was to be taken of the advances already made. This was in line with my original thinking that a national Design Centre might pave the way for individual trades to set up their own. It would be the logical and culminating development of the many displays, great and small, national and local, with which the Council had previously been concerned and it would serve as a springboard for further activities, particularly in provincial centres of industry. The Centre would be of value to all sections of the community: to manufacturers it would both provide publicity for their products and enable them to see exactly what, in the Council's eyes, constituted good, modern design; to designers, many of whom have all too few opportunities of seeing design trends in goods which will be sold alongside their own, it would give the opportunity of seeing up-to-date developments; to home and overseas buyers it would give a lead on good design which would help them to cater more successfully for a growing demand; for architects, interior designers or purchasing officers with the problem of furnishing or equipping a large building, it would provide in one place information which it might previously have taken weeks to collect; to school teachers and students it would provide stimulating ideas; to overseas visitors it would show a cross-section of the best contemporary work in Britain; to housewives it would offer a selection of goods of enduring value; and for the Press—particularly the women's Press—it would provide a useful source of copy, which again would help forward the Council's work.

But it would obviously be a difficult thing to bring off. In the first place, it would be necessary to convince our parent body that it would be valuable to industry before we could expect a grant. It would certainly cost a good deal of money, even if—as was proposed—a considerable part of the running costs was found by charging exhibitors for space. This in itself presented a very sticky problem. 'Britain Can Make It' and the Festival of Britain had been selective exhibitions and industry did not much like the idea of selection by an outside body, but at least no charge had been made for showing their goods. We had no doubt that there would be much criticism of a plan to select and charge too and that it would need a great deal of hard work to sell that idea. And, when sold, it would obviously make it more difficult for us to maintain the necessary high standard, so making it quite clear that no firm, however large and influential, could be said to have bought its way in. Nor would it be easy to agree a basis of charging which would be acceptable to the smaller firms which usually produced the more interesting designs whereas the mass producers, if they wished to come in at all, would obviously be prepared to pay much higher rates. Whilst there was likely to be a good deal of public interest initially, resulting in high attendances, we did not know how this interest would be maintained over a long period in the absence of large-scale advertising, which we knew we should not be able to afford. Our revenue could have come partly from a charge for admission but we rejected this as being almost certain to reduce the exhibition's educational value by discouraging students, women shoppers and so on, thus restricting attendances, which would, of course, be the yardstick by which the exhibitor would judge the worth to him of participation. We had been successful up to date and we had no wish to blot our copy-book, but I felt quite sure it could be done.

Worboys was very successful in dealing with the Board of Trade and the Treasury where, by good fortune, the senior permanent staff, Sir Frank Lee and Sir Maurice Dean at the Board and Sir James Crombie at the Treasury, were both imaginative and sympathetic to the work of the Council. After much discussion with them the plan was approved, subject to the Council's financing a minimum of half the running costs from receipts, the Government matching this sum up to a limit to be agreed. The Council was also to make an appeal to industry for a contribution towards the capital cost of establishing The Design Centre. This was a further hurdle, but our Council members did valiant work and the appeal, which was addressed mainly to suppliers of raw materials and services rather than to manufacturers whose products would be eligible for exhibition in fact brought in nearly £27,000, which we regarded as an expression of confidence in our efforts.

In October 1953, Mark Hartland Thomas had resigned in order to resume practice as an architect and this led to fairly major changes in my team: it was decided to appoint Paul Reilly deputy director in charge of the industrial division and a new chief information officer, James Noel White, was recruited.

We spent much time looking at various premises and at last found 28 Haymarket—a new and ugly building but on an almost perfect site, in the heart of the West End of London about 150 yards from Piccadilly Circus.

Two hectic years ensued, in the midst of which—in the New Year's Honours List in 1955—I was created a Knight Bachelor as 'designer and artist'. Under this guise, I believe the honour was a recognition of the part the Council as a whole had played since I became its director. I found the ceremony in the Palace a moving one, especially as it was conducted, with great grace and skill, by a woman. The Queen, as she tapped me gently on the shoulder with the sword, murmured a few words about the Council of Industrial Design and I felt gratified that her reaction, as usual, would be that of a great many of her subjects. Shortly afterwards I had a letter from Heralds College asking me to go there and sign the book, which proved to be a vast tome. After a few words of congratulation Richmond Herald asked if I would like to commission a coat-of-arms and I said I would think about it. As I walked down the steps I noticed a small van parked on the other side of the road. On its side was the inscription 'Richmond Herald'. This, I thought, is the end—but then I realized in a flash that I was quite close to Fleet Street!

By means of a long series of meetings we sought to gain the support of trade associations for The Design Centre. I preferred small and quite informal meetings at which I could get into direct touch with individuals who could say what they felt and I would not just be addressing an impersonal gathering.

Two fairly large ones, however, I remember clearly, the potters at Stoke-on-Trent and the furniture trade in London. I was warned by the industrial officers concerned that both trades disapproved of our ideas *in toto* and were out for my blood. Oddly enough, I found it stimulating to go into a room full of hostile people, say what was in my mind as tactfully as possible, listen to and answer criticism and leave them apparently either stunned by the further proofs of idiocy on my part or convinced: I could never quite make up my mind which it was! But at any rate there were no rotten eggs; and no apathy, which is always far more difficult to cope with.

A vital part of The Design Centre and tool in arranging it was 'Design Review' which, although reduced in coverage, had been retained as one of the Council's most important links with industry and had already proved useful to those concerned with the selection of well designed goods in the trades it covered. So here I must say a word on selection policy, over which the Council was more or less constantly under fire at this time, still is on occasion and I suppose is always likely to be. As I have already said, I have no wish to be a design dictator and during my time at the Council I always strenuously avoided being associated with any measure which might make it appear that we were restricting the freedom of manufacturers to sell anything they cared to produce. Our job was to persuade them that a standard existed and that it was worth their while to up-grade their production so as to attain it. It is sometimes said that there is no such thing as good or bad design, that it has no real measurable standards, that it is, in fact, just a matter of personal taste. But it is readily accepted that there is a standard of, say, honesty, or driving, or housing, so why not one of design? Finally it seemed that we must try to put into words what we were trying to do and I think I cannot do better than quote the definition we evolved, as published in the Council's Annual Report for 1953/4:

'The principles governing acceptance or rejection of products submitted by manufacturers for ''Design Review''

263

are a major concern. Though rules of thumb and narrow definitions are neither feasible nor desirable, the general principle can be stated that the object is to promote good design as comprising good materials and workmanship, fitness for purpose and pleasure in use. These attributes can often apply as well to a traditional design as to a modern one and it is well known that Britain has won a world-wide reputation for her traditional designs; but this reputation could not have been won had earlier generations not had the courage to experiment and to add their fresh ideas to the national heritage. Therefore, while accepting the claims of many traditional designs that still measure up to today's requirements from the point of view of the user and of the maker, the bias of the Council's propaganda has always been towards encouraging fresh thought and design in both the old craft-based and the new technical industries, whether the inspiration for a good design is original and contemporary or basically traditional.'

When the opening day came, April 26, 1956, we had got sufficient support from the forward-looking firms in industry to be assured of a reasonable selection and it was encouraging when the Duke of Edinburgh, who performed the opening ceremony, wished us luck as we entered upon what he hoped would be 'an industrious, adventurous, controversial, vitalizing life'.

In 1956 the Council also organized another major Design Congress—having decided that this should be a quinquennial event. This was addressed primarily to British industry and took as its theme 'The Management of Design'. In so doing it particularly wished to bring home the relevance of this to the capital goods and service trades in addition to those concerned with durable consumer goods. The division of the theme into three sections—Case Histories; The Role of the Designer; and Implications for Management—took careful account of this.

The Council of Industrial Design

Wider Horizons

With the Design Centre open and running satisfactorily it proved possible for me to accept, in the next eighteen months, three invitations to visit countries which were new to me—Russia, Canada and Sierra Leone.

My visit to Russia was in July 1956, when I was invited as a member of the Fine Arts Committee of the British Council to join a small party headed by Sir William Coldstream, Slade Professor of Fine Art at University College, London, which was to investigate the possibility of an exchange of exhibitions of fine art and industrial design. I was, of course, to advise on the latter. We flew to Moscow and, arriving there at night, were driven past the marvellous Kremlin group of buildings to our hotel. The next morning I woke up to gaze through a curtain of runner beans in flower at the golden onion-shaped domes glittering in the sun and I had to pinch myself to make sure I was awake! I liked this custom, which seemed to be quite usual, of planting beans in window boxes and training them on strings to the wall above. It was akin to a Swedish idea of planting them in a large circle with the strings tied to a central pole to form a fairy-like bell tent, delightful for children to sit in on a summer day. When I saw a symbolic notice warning motorists to take care as pigeons were being fed I felt I should like the Russians—who inspired my admiration, too, by the way they had coped with the problem of litter, a national disgrace with us. They have a splendid, perhaps Eastern, sense of colour which is notable in the theatre and was, I imagine, at one time quite usual in the peasant's dress. The Lapps certainly used marvellous reds and blacks—perhaps all people who live in snow for much of the year find colour essential to keep up their morale and quite practical in case they get lost. The utterly dull mud-coloured clothing seemed a poor substitute for these departed glories. It is a phase we have gone through in the West but from which we seem to be recovering, I am glad to say.

Our hosts were attentive and thoughtful. Although it must have been obvious to people in the street that we were foreigners we did not see any signs of hostility, even when our guides made us crash the long queue for the Kremlin or some gallery. Museums were beautifully kept and well attended. In Leningrad we were allowed to go in the Hermitage an hour before it opened to the public, which we greatly appreciated. I spent three wonderful days there but could well have spent three weeks. There were more than 300 galleries open, the largest being the reception hall of the Winter Palace, which could hold over 1,500 people. Among things of special interest was an immense dinner service made by Wedgwood for Catharine the Great, decorated with a whole series of paintings of English country houses; and a group of ingenious machines made by London clockmakers for Peter the Great. The work of excavation and preservation seemed to be of a high order. By injecting some kind of plastic into wood carving which had been reduced to charcoal it became possible to reconstruct considerable areas of a burnt-out building. And there was a marvellous tomb-barrow from the Altai Mountains which, immediately after it was completed, had evidently flooded through a tunnel made by a tomb-robber and frozen so that the whole contents, including *appliqué* wall-hangings and a splendid carpet, had been preserved in perfect condition for more than 2,000 years in a natural refrigerator. I was surprised to find that there was such a fine collection of French Impressionist paintings and we were shown the method of storing on sliding racks some 1,000 paintings which could not be exhibited. The rare treat was only made possible by the paucity of good industrial design outside.

I had, first of all, asked the Ministry of Culture if they could give me any information on where I should go to see well-designed goods. They showed me a number of hand-made gifts, hand-painted boxes and so on, but when I explained that I wanted to see interesting machine-made goods they seemed rather foxed and lost interest. The carpet in their hall, which I imagined they had chosen, gave me a clue to what I might expect! I then visited a cabinet-making workshop, an engineering workshop, various stockrooms, the large department store GUM and several shops. As one would expect, their machine tools were often much better designed than consumer goods which at that time had had very little attention. In any case, they were in short supply and consumer demand was not encouraged.

My wife likes to buy baskets abroad and I had seen some fine ones being used in the fields for gathering delectable looking fungi. To get one of these seemed impossible and, although I was accompanied by at least six people all of whom were most anxious to be helpful, the only suggestion was that I should visit GUM where I did eventually get an indifferent one.

In view of my interest in railways I asked to see the 'Red Arrow', which runs between Leningrad and Moscow. At the main station we went into what I can only describe as the Station-master's Drawing Room—a large room which must have been a pre-revolution survival, with heavy and dull Victorian decoration and French windows on to the platform. I was surprised to find that there were several classes in the 'Red Arrow', and everything was very clean and shipshape. I climbed up into the cab of the engine to shake hands with the driver, who took much trouble to show me everything.

When I got back to the hotel at about midnight I had a 'phone call from a Press man who wanted to see me. He came up to my bedroom and asked me many questions. When I said I thought the view of Leningrad from the river, with the lovely curve of eighteenth-century houses painted in the most delicate colours, was as fine as anything I had seen in any city I knew, he said with some passion: 'They should have been destroyed!' I realized that to him they were just aristocratic symbols and I wondered if I should ever learn to keep up with sillyologies.

We were taken to see Peterhof Palace and gardens—Peter's Versailles—which left me unmoved with its gilded sculpture and copper trees and birds. But since then I have seen plans of smaller gardens which I would dearly love to visit, as they appear to be fascinating combinations of the formal and informal which particularly appeal to me.

As ever, I looked at floors—and Russian floors are worth looking at. In the wonderful little church in Red Square there is a floor of cast iron slabs about two feet square, rusty brown in the corners and silvery grey in the doorways where it is worn smooth. And in the Kremlin there are semi-precious stone floors of onyx, malachite and, I think, agate—irregular pieces, fitted together marvellously—and wood floors elaborately inlaid.

We were not invited into a Russian house and had the feeling when we lunched at the British Embassy that it was closely invested, but the small marooned community remained cheerful.

On my way home I stopped at Helsinki, looked up several Finnish friends and dined with the eminent architect Alvar Aalto, an Honorary RDI, whose warm friendliness was just the right tonic. He showed me his plans for the city and I greatly admired the steady way in which work was being pushed ahead in spite of their somewhat difficult neighbours.

Later in 1956 I had a letter from the director of the National Gallery of Canada, Alan Jarvis. He was a Rhodes Scholar, had been one of Stafford Cripps' private secretaries and was for several years a member of the staff of the Council, and he wanted me to undertake a lecture tour right across the Dominion explaining what the Council was and how it functioned. The aim was to promote interest in a body of a

The Council of Industrial Design

similar kind which had just been set up in Canada and it was
hoped that I would attend the opening by Mr Vincent Massey
of the Design Centre in Ottawa and meet some of the principal
supporters.

I had been to Montreal once before and had then dined with
an architect whom I had known when we were both boys
living at Repton. By a strange coincidence, I was asked to dine
in the very same house by the then occupier, the UK Trade
Commissioner, and I was able to introduce him to the architect, whom he had not met before, at a Canada Club luncheon! I flew from Quebec to Vancouver, stopping to lecture
at various large towns on the way. I was particularly glad to see
the new theatre at Stratford, in its beautiful open setting. It
was not then finished but has, I understand, been successful.
And in Vancouver I was taken around by Wells Coates, an
architect and RDI who had settled there. Quite close to the city
was much fine virgin forest yet I noticed in several houses that
there were open fires of 'logs' made of wood waste, very
dense and heavy, which even in this country of forests were, I
suppose, cheaper than real logs! I was pleased to find a growing
interest in painting and should have loved to spend more time
in the West and to visit Seattle and California but I was to be
given a medal by the Parsons School of Design in New York so
dallying was out of the question.

I had been disappointed that in flying over the Rockies
there was such thick cloud that nothing could be seen, but
flying over the Pyrenees on my way to Africa in the following
year it was clear, unbelievably clear. The brilliant green valley
bottoms showing as small streaks with a silver thread in the
centre within a red-brown pattern of parched hillside was one
of the most extraordinary scenes I remember from the air,
as dramatic in its way as the approach to Chicago by night.

As the Lion Mountains rise steeply almost from sea level
and are covered with dense tropical forest, and Sierra Leone's
airport had to be built across a lovely bay from Freetown, I
enjoyed the leisurely approach by water, on the open deck of a
launch, which gave time to savour the remarkable African

269

landscape. I had been asked by the British Council to attend the first Arts Festival to be held there, and so great a number of widely different events had been arranged that it proved impossible for me to see all of them. But I liked what I saw of Africa and its cheerful people.

The most ordinary events took on a fantastic character. I was taken to see a woodworking shop and noticed a lot of doors, all framed up and glued but without any wedges in the through-mortices. My English guide was as astonished as I was and told me that normally they did not make doors, only furniture—which, incidentally, was made to Utility designs and specifications sent out by the Board of Trade. These doors were, apparently, for a Minister who was building a house for which the frames had been made on the site, every one to a different size. Native huts did not have doors so the workmen had no experience in coping with them. My guide said that if he were to ask the man making the doors why he had not inserted wedges before glueing up he would merely think that someone had trodden on the Englishman's shadow and he wanted charms put in to keep witches away! It was necessary to give the most explicit directions—for instance, that bookshelves must be level.

I was taken over the gaol by the governor. There were well-organized training workshops: tailoring, smithing, carpentry, etc. I noticed that the outer walls were quite low on the inside and asked whether many escaped, to which the governor replied that his problem was not so much to keep people in as to keep them out! Directly the rainy season started it was a custom to commit a petty crime so as to come in for a month or so, be well fed, sleep in the dry and be taught a trade.

Beautiful basketwork and weaving in narrow strips was still being done but vegetable dyes had been replaced by aniline dyes in harsh colours.

I lectured in Freetown and was flown up country in a tiny 'plane from which, when the pilot circled round to show me some diamond workings, I feared I might fall out! On arrival at my destination I found that the students had moved about thirty tons of timber out of an iron-roofed hut so as to have a lecture hall. It was a terribly hot and sultry night: I was wet through, and after talking for a quarter of an hour I was worried to see several students at the back of the room go out. My chairman whispered: 'They will be back shortly—they are feeling the heat!' I was so encouraged to find that I could stand up to the conditions better than local people that I managed to finish and answer questions without fainting.

On the next day I was taken by the Forestry Officer to see some of the virgin forest. The roads of red laterite became treacherous after a shower of rain and where they descended steeply and turned at right-angles to go over a bridge there seemed almost invariably to be one or more wrecked cars in the river. The lorries were usually named and I particularly liked one with 'Best Girl No. 2' painted on the side. When we reached the turning place in the forest there was an immense pyramid of drums of petrol and a smaller one of oil. Between them was a miniature native hut and going to look at it I found, under the palm-leaf roof, a blazing fire with a large can of water over it supported on three stones. I went back and asked my guide why the hut was there, to which he replied that it was for a watchman to prevent theft of petrol. 'Don't worry about theft,' I said, 'the whole lot will go up any minute.' Rushing over, he yelled for the boy and at last a grizzled old negro crept out of the hut. 'Put that fire out' was shouted at him, but he looked as if he didn't understand, dodged behind an immense tree and made off at the double. We put the fire out but I was mystified and that evening I told the story to the Resident Magistrate with whom I was staying. 'No,' he said, 'not odd, he thought you were going to eat him! There was a fire and a pot handy.' I found this hard to believe but he asked me to come out on his lawn where, pointing to the vast forest stretching as far as we could see, he said: 'Who can be sure that cannibalism and slavery no longer exist?'

My departure from Freetown was quite an occasion. The Governor lent me his launch, impeccably polished and with a crew of three or four. I was almost piped aboard and as I was the only passenger a chair had been placed on the deck with an immense umbrella over it. I thrive under such conditions—which, however, gradually faded. Air France seemed workaday and the bus at London Airport brought me back to reality and my desk with a jolt.

Although The Design Centre had recently been our main preoccupation at the Council, the years had, of course, seen other developments. Some were comparatively small, though interesting, like the work of the Coronation Souvenirs Committee, chaired by Miss Audrey Withers (then editor of *Vogue*), which endeavoured to ensure that a higher standard of souvenir was available in 1953 than would otherwise have been the case—though this did not revolutionize the trade's standards as may still be seen in almost any gift shop. The central selective exhibits which the Council was invited to stage at several of the furniture trade's own annual exhibitions were another such activity. And in 1954, the bicentenary year of the Royal Society of Arts, on whose council I was then sitting for a second time, I put forward the suggestion that the Society should institute a Bicentenary Medal to be awarded each year to one, 'who, in a manner other than as an industrial designer, has exerted an exceptional influence in promoting the development of art and design in British industry'. The suggestion of thus honouring the patron was approved and I was delighted that the first recipient was Sir Colin Anderson, a distinguished member of the Council, whose work as a director of the Orient Line in improving the overall design standard of their ships was a pace-setter to this important industry. In the following decade the recipients also included Sir Walter Worboys and Mr Paul Reilly.

The Council's terms of reference provided for its advising 'at the request of Government Departments and other public bodies' on the design of their purchases. The importance of this field of activity was never underestimated, although it was realized that nothing would be gained by attempting to force the pace, and strenuous efforts to be helpful were made whenever help or advice was sought.

The Council can claim to have influenced for the better the standard of design in such things as furnishings purchased through the Ministry of Public Building and Works, street furniture—for which it accepted certain responsibilities in relation to the Ministry of Transport and the Royal Fine Art Commissions, and quantity-produced farm buildings on which it has now been working for some years in collaboration with the Ministry of Agriculture. But the history of its efforts to improve the design of postage stamps is a less happy one.

At an early stage in its life it was asked to set up a committee to advise the Postmaster General on this matter and Sir Francis Meynell, who as typographical adviser to the Stationery Office for some years had brought about a remarkable improvement there, agreed to take the chair.

The design of postage stamps calls for a very high degree of skill for apart from the need, in many instances, to convey an idea by some form of symbol which will tell on a minute scale, it is also governed to some extent by the necessity for protection against forgery, by the importance of being able to recognize each denomination instantly under widely different conditions of artificial and natural lighting and by the need to prevent re-use through failure to spot cancellation marks. Because our country pioneered the introduction of the postage stamp and the first had on it the Queen's head but no country of origin, we have the unique privilege of continuing to use the sovereign's head instead of the name of country. To complicate the designer's task still further, he often had little time to complete his task and it was sometimes then discovered that he had not been given a clear brief as to what he might or might not include.

The recommendations of the Council's committee were considered by the Postmaster General himself and his officials and ultimately by the sovereign, whose personal views were always sought before printing commenced. This was not a mere formality. In one case, I remember, King George VI vetoed a design, not unreasonably, but on an issue that could hardly have been foreseen, and the designer had to work for thirty-six hours on end to cope with the situation created. The earliest stamps, which portrayed the head alone, were fine examples of design but the decline of portraiture led to a deterioration early in our century. This lack of interest stimulated a demand for other subjects which has been encouraged by the insatiable avidity of stamp collectors, but to keep a balance on such a small surface as a stamp between, say, a landscape and the sovereign's head raises design problems of an acute kind.

To evolve a long-term policy and make it work was difficult owing to the constant and rapid changes of the Minister in charge. Yet unless such a policy could be laid down it was almost impossible to get together a small group of specialist designers—with others coming in at intervals to ensure variety. For the problem of designing small things like postage stamps, and indeed coins and bank notes, of which only a com-paratively small range is necessary but production may be in hundreds of millions, is in some ways more difficult than the problem of designing thousands of widely different things to be produced in smaller numbers. It calls for an exceptionally intensive study of production methods by the designer, allied with technical skill and imagination, and the necessary ex-perience can only be gained by a comparatively small number of designers working fairly continuously in the one field. In the case of coins, of course, the demand for new designs occurs so rarely that more public interest in well-designed medals could have a powerful effect, by enabling designers to keep their hand in. The introduction of decimal currency provides a rare opportunity for advance in this field of design.

Just as I was retiring as director of the Council, Meynell decided that he was unable to continue as chairman of the committee owing to pressure of other work and I was asked to succeed him. I had been an *ex officio* member from the first so I was well aware of the difficulties, but at that stage we seemed to be making some progress and certainly we found the Post Office officials anxious to be helpful. But as it proved difficult for me to attend the increasing number of meetings, often at short notice, Sir Kenneth Clark, an original member of the committee, took over from me after two or three years, later himself relinquishing the chair to Mr James Fitton. But the policy of greatly extending the number and frequency of special issues—and, on occasion, the by-passing of the committee—has made it almost impossible for it to function in an effective way.

I deplore the discourtesy shown to the Queen by the reduction of her portrait to balance a football in a recent issue; and when there is usually too much detail on a stamp it is hard to see why the printer's name should appear—we have got on quite well without it for over a hundred years.

A more encouraging example of a new approach to design problems may be cited in British Rail—a nationalized industry. When we heard in 1955 that they were to be given £1,240m in order to bring the system up-to-date we spent a considerable time investigating how railways all over the world had tackled their design problems. We felt that it would be tragic if vast sums of money were spent on poorly designed equipment. In rolling stock, for instance, the railways seemed to have been satisfied if their new coaches were an improvement on the last lot, but the public compared them with motor cars and aeroplanes in which seating, for example, had been studied carefully. And whereas the life of a car or 'plane was five to ten years, railway rolling stock had a life of twenty-five years and some of it, owing to the war, had been in service far longer. We then published a special railways number of *Design* and sent copies to all members of the Railways Board.

Shortly afterwards General Wansbrough-Jones, Sir Brian Robertson's number two, asked me to go and have a talk with him. He told me they were impressed with the arguments we had put forward and were considering the formation of the proposed Design Panel, to which I replied that if it was to work smoothly there were several points to consider. The job would have to be done from inside as any attempt to impose it from outside would be likely to meet with opposition as so many railway families had given devoted service for several generations. It was important to stress that no blame attached to the engineers, whose training took little account of the side of the job for which industrial designers were qualified. Therefore such a panel, which should not be large, should consist mainly of top railway staff, and it should be made clear that it would carry weight by appointing as chairman a senior member of the Board who believed in the importance of the job even if he was not knowledgeable. Then an experienced man in design matters, who would need to be both tactful and of forceful character, should be appointed as chief executive to work directly to the panel. He should establish a close liaison with the architects' department, which was doing excellent work, and, of course, with all chief engineers, public relations men and so on. He would need a few design staff later, but there must be no empire building. All design problems must be referred to the panel—and there were design problems in everything the railways used from timetables to teaspoons, from locomotives and rolling stock to ships. The first step was important: at an informal meeting the chairman should explain to top staff what was intended, seek their full cooperation and ask them, in turn, to see their own top staff.

I was asked to sit on the panel, and on a small committee to select the design officer from a short list. George Williams, one of the most experienced industrial officers at the Council, told me he would like to apply as he was both an engineer and an industrial designer, a rare combination. He proved to be the successful candidate. I told him it would be a tough job but certainly I would give him any help I could, although his leaving would be a great loss to the Council. On the other hand, he would be carrying on his previous work in the most practical and valuable way. I felt that the training of people for jobs such as this ought to be one of our aims at the Council. Industry would naturally turn to us when trying to fill them and we ourselves were unable to offer high salaries or promotion beyond a certain point. Williams proved successful in a difficult job and when, after nearly ten years, he died suddenly the man appointed to succeed him was Jim Cousins, also an experienced officer from the Council—this time an architect.

The results of their work are appearing in a great number of British Rail activities. Not all great organizations have made such consistent progress and much of the credit should go to Lord Beeching, whose belief in the value of the panel's work was shown by consistent backing. I was glad to be able to quote to him cases in which a higher design standard had shown savings in cost.

There are, of course, similar bodies which could give a considerable push in the right direction by adopting such methods to promote the application of a consistent design policy throughout their organization.

The work done for the Festival and the development of 'Design Review' had demonstrated the value of such exhibitions and the unique ability of the Council to handle them, for no other body had the machinery and experience to stage *selective* exhibitions. This, and The Design Centre itself, led to opportunities which were of great importance to the Council for further collaboration with Government Departments—particularly the Board of Trade and Central Office of Information—the Federation of British Industries and others in staging exhibitions overseas showing the best standards of current British industrial production. There were, of course, exhibitions for which no official sponsor for a British display could be found because the context was neither strictly commercial, in which case it would be the responsibility of the Board of Trade, nor purely cultural. The Milan Triennale was one, and another—a single event—was a special international exhibition H.55 (Halsingborg 1955) arranged by the Swedes. I had the honour of being asked to serve on the Honorary Committee for this; and Britain was one of several countries which were invited to take space in a special section to show the best examples of interior design. The Council failed to secure an official grant and it was only by means of a private fund raised through the public-spirited action of Sir Kenneth Lee, an ex-member of the Council, that it was enabled to arrange a British exhibit. This proved to be one of the main attractions in the section. Later the Council decided to extend its work overseas by stimulating the interest of retail stores, particularly in Europe, in staging special exhibitions of British goods selected from The Design Centre. Two of the first such displays were held in Holland and Denmark.

At home, too, the Council did not rest on its laurels following the opening of The Design Centre, despite its immediate success. It was obvious that it could never reach the masses from this one London address; that with a turnover of some 3,500 exhibits a year only a small proportion of manufacturers were represented from the industries covered; and that the number of home and overseas buyers visiting the exhibition could be greatly increased. The evidence of shop windows everywhere underlined the size of the task. Constant propaganda work and the success of the Centre would extend its influence but how could the Council do this in a more direct way, with strictly limited funds? One means it adopted was an extension of the work already undertaken with individual retail stores. In a limited number of towns selected stores were encouraged to stage major exhibitions under the title 'The Design Centre comes to . . .', assistance being given by the Council but the stores bearing the main cost. Linking events were organized so that the occasions became somewhat similar to the earlier series of Design Weeks, but these exhibitions had the advantage of being supported directly by stock in the shop. The first was held at Newcastle-upon-Tyne in September 1958 and was followed by The Design Centre comes to Wales, to Southampton, to Manchester, to Southsea in the following year. Subsequently, a pattern of collaboration with local retailers, chambers of commerce, newspaper proprietors, etc., for the showing of an exhibition on an independent site was also worked out. The issue of detailed information on special features in The Design Centre made it possible for these to be copied by stores, and quarterly lists of exhibits in the Centre were also offered to retailers to encourage their display.

As another means of gaining widespread publicity in shops for products exhibited in the Centre, the Council introduced a distinctive black-and-white quartered triangular label for attachment by manufacturers to those of their products which were eligible. The success of this scheme may be judged by the fact that nine years later, when it had been extended to cover all goods selected for 'Design Index' (as 'Design Review' was renamed in 1958), some sixty-two million labels had been sold.

The setting up of Building Centres in provincial cities led to an enquiry from Bristol about the possibility of setting aside space there for a small, changing exhibition of articles selected from 'Design Index' and a complete copy of the Index itself. As this is subject to constant revision, the servicing problem was quite a formidable one but it was surmounted—a duplicate being required at about the same time by the Council's Scottish Committee in Glasgow for its Design Centre, opened in 1957—and the experience gained proved valuable in coping with further enquiries from Nottingham and Manchester. Similar overseas centres with copies of 'Design Index' could be valuable.

In 1957 the Council instituted annual Design Centre Awards, selected by an independent panel of judges from products exhibited in the Centre during the year. Prince Philip demonstrated his continuing interest by agreeing to present certificates to the successful manufacturers, as he has done annually since. Later he suggested that in alternate years the ceremony should take place in a great provincial industrial centre and this was first done most successfully in Manchester in 1964. Additionally, he himself generously initiated in 1959 a special award, The Duke of Edinburgh's Prize for Elegant Design, to be given personally to the designer for 'a contemporary design in current production distinguished by its elegance'. The winning design is chosen each year by an independent panel of four judges appointed at the invitation of the Duke of Edinburgh, who sits as chairman.

A further landmark in the Council's history was reached in 1958 by a limited extension of work into the capital goods industries, the first move being a one-day conference on the role of the industrial designer in the engineering field organized in Birmingham in conjunction with The Engineering Centre. The importance of these industries in export trade had been fully recognized but with limited funds the Council had previously felt that it could most effectively tackle its task, in the short term, by concentrating on the durable consumer goods industries, leaving capital goods on the one hand and the fashion trade on the other for later attention—apart from inclusion in such special events as the Festival of Britain and the Design Congresses and through the magazine *Design*.

It was with pleasure that in 1959 the Council learned that its work had been recognized internationally by the award to it of the *Gran Premio Internazionale la Rinascente Compasso d'Oro* 'as the oldest and most efficient government organization for the development and popularization of good design'.

This was the note on which my directorship of the Council closed, for in 1957, when I had been director for ten years, I had told the chairman that I felt it was time for me to think about retirement. The Council had a tremendous long-term job to perform but it was firmly established and had proved its ability to do valuable work, at home and abroad, for which no other organization was equipped. It was on good terms with its parent body and with industry and commerce as a whole and it had as focal points for its educational activities a permanent showplace in London, The Design Centre, and its monthly magazine *Design*. We had decided, however, that it would take some time to ensure a smooth transference of responsibility to my successor, Paul Reilly (see plate 18), and had agreed to allow a period of two years for this.

So the time for my departure arrived at the end of 1959, when the chairman's period of office was also coming to a close. In my time I have worked under a number of chairmen but I can think of few who put more enthusiastic and consistent effort into the job in hand than Walter Worboys—now Sir Walter, for his work had been deservedly recognized in this way in 1958, to the pleasure of all at the Council. He was well aware of the difficulties that beset us but at no time did he give any hint of the possibility of failure. His successor was to be Sir Duncan Oppenheim, chairman of the British-American Tobacco Co. Ltd., a keen amateur painter and a discriminating patron who was already chairman of council of the Royal College of Art so that the link between the two bodies would be closely maintained.

I had every confidence that my team of top people would continue to push forward with enthusiasm on the lines we had all had a hand in devising. Paul would be leading them, James Noel White had been appointed his deputy, Philip Fellows had quite exceptional experience in charge of exhibitions, Alec Gardner-Medwin was head of the industrial division, and Michael Farr, the editor of *Design*, was promoted to take over the information side. We all, I think, felt quite keenly the breaking of a long period of friendly and fruitful collaboration in which the many attacks from outside had made us rely on each other far more than would have been the case in an easier task. The foundations had stood up to test. Of course there was still bound to be sporadic criticism, which is not an unhealthy sign, but we were no longer shot at with zest from all quarters as a matter of course.

Had the Council failed to win the confidence of industry continuance of its work would have been impossible. It could, however, be claimed that many sections of industry, and of commerce, now realized—albeit with some surprise—that it was capable of doing a valuable job of practical use to them which would become increasingly important. It had been shown that an outside body which looked at the problem in an objective way could select an industry's products for quality more satisfactorily than a trade federation, in whose displays each member felt he had the right to participate. Whilst such selective exhibitions, large and small, at home and abroad, permanent and temporary, play a great part in the Council's educational work they have, at the same time, both a direct commercial purpose and a prestige one, demonstrating as they do that Britain has many lively, go-ahead firms.

Our hunch that we could both select products for exhibition in The Design Centre and charge exhibitors had proved correct. Public interest had been well maintained: in the three years attendances were 2,497,651, averaging 2,206 for every day in which it was open, and in the eleven years which have now passed 8,877,770, averaging 2,558 per day. These figures are of course, those by which the exhibitor judges the worth of showing his products and provide the incentive to improve designs so as to make them eligible for inclusion.

It is also perhaps worth noting that in the financial year 1959/60 the Council managed to augment its Government grant of £181,500 by earning £148,709 from its services to industry and commerce, rising to a grant of £369,400 supplemented by earnings of over £276,000 in 1966/67. But the Council was set up to do what is essentially an educational job and undue pressure to increase its earnings—which I regard as a serious possibility—could make it impossible for it to do this properly. It might lead to concentration on activities which are self-financing or positively revenue-earning at the expense of others which could be more beneficial to its long-term aims. It could well affect the hard-won respect of industry and commerce, for whilst I firmly believe that people tend to value more highly things for which they have to pay there is a grave risk of doubt arising as to the Council's integrity in selecting if the raising of prices for exhibition in The Design Centre should limit unduly the items available. Unless extreme care was exercised, standards might be debased. Certainly the range of exhibits would be narrowed and as the most interesting designs often come from the smaller firms with low advertising budgets the basic purpose of the Centre could be defeated. Emphasis on money-earning projects at the expense of others of perhaps greater relevance to the Council's aims could affect the morale of the staff, resulting in resignations and possible difficulty in recruiting others of equal calibre. Also, the Council's programme of work in the provinces could be reduced and so lay it open to the charge of concentrating unduly on the metropolis. I think it is important that these dangers should not be underestimated in the years ahead.

I was much touched by the many letters and marks of

appreciation which I received on my retirement. My friends at the Arts Club entertained me to dinner and presented me with a charming old silver tankard; and the President of the Board of Trade also arranged a small dinner party at which he invited me to accept membership of the Council for an in-definite period. Whilst I greatly appreciated the honour of becoming the Council's scheduled ancient monument, I said that I would not attend a Council meeting for a year, for I had seen many cases where a retiring chairman or director felt it was incumbent on him to turn up each day and breathe down the neck of his successor, a kind of aimless vanity which in-variably leads to trouble. But I told Paul that I would always be ready to discuss any problem or to do any particular chore if asked.

The Design and Industries Association announced that they wished to arrange a more formal dinner at Fishmongers' Hall and had asked the Duke of Edinburgh if he would grace it with his presence. This he did and the amusing speech he made added greatly to the pleasure of the evening. There were staff parties too and many other junketings. To mark my retire-ment, Council members generously gave me a cheque and I used this to build an English oak staircase which I designed myself—admittedly an unusual parting gift—and my staff in London commissioned Peter Collingwood to design and weave a splendid woollen hanging which covers the wall of its first half landing. The staff of the Scottish Committee gave me an old cut-glass decanter of beautiful shape on which they had had a special inscription cut. Such things which can be seen day by day in use give me far more pleasure than rarities which have to be locked up.

I had been proud in 1952 to be made an Honorary Designer of the Royal College of Art and so particularly appreciated being 'promoted' to the rank of Senior Fellow following my retirement. The Society of Industrial Artists also chose to mark this moment by presenting me with their Design Medal, which is awarded annually to a professional designer of any nationality for outstanding achievement in commercial or industrial design. In presenting this, the president of the Society said that my efforts to promote the work of other designers had been so successful that people might overlook the fact that I was myself a designer!

It would be foolish to pretend that I was not gratified by these attentions. But I remembered how Max Beerbohm went to see Beerbohm Tree in his dressing room after a successful first night. Tree was wading through a sea of messages and said 'Max, I do love praise', to which Max replied that good honest flattery was an acceptable substitute so far as he was concerned!

CHAPTER 21

A Consultancy

I had now done a seventeen-year stint of public work, which would not have been possible had I not had some private income of my own. As I had not been willing to live in London I had had to meet the additional living and travelling expenses involved; and at the same time I had found that in a period of inflation the pay of staff in grant-aided bodies always seemed to lag behind that of civil servants who, in any case, themselves earned less than was usual in industry. Thinking over my situation, I felt sure that if I were to set up my own industrial design consultancy practice in the right way—based on Kingcombe—I should find that I could earn at least as much under more congenial conditions and be able to share more time and more of the work at home with my wife. I had set my heart on completing the house and garden, which had been postponed in 1937 owing to the increasing threat of war, particularly as this would simplify its running. Some work, at least, was becoming increasingly urgent and it was highly desirable that it should be financed out of income. I also wished to find time to finish this book while many of the events were fresh in my mind. Everything pointed once again to a completely new type of job but at least I felt I had acquired a certain expertise in coping with this family tradition of starting afresh!

I outlined my plan to Rosamund Hogg, my secretary, who had been with me for ten years and had always given me stalwart support. She had already told me that she intended to find a job in the country but I pointed out that whilst she was sure of a good job if she stayed with the Council there was a considerable element of risk in my plan. To start a new kind of consultancy at the age of sixty-seven is not normal practice. But, like me, she had found the job at the Council a gruelling one and felt the need of a change, even if it was only a change of work and environment. I was delighted, therefore, when she decided to continue with me as her knowledge of the whole background would be invaluable in the type of work I had in mind. So I fixed up an office at Kingcombe, my wife found her a flat in Campden and we made a start in March 1960.

My plan was to set up a kind of consultancy such as I did not think existed. I had no wish to start designing again for industry and I did not want to control a large office but I felt that there was a need for someone with wide and varied experience of all kinds of design problems who could give top-level advice on how to tackle a particular design job, or a reorganization of design policy. There has been a marked tendency since the war for large companies to swallow smaller ones by take-over bids. From the point of view of productivity as an end in itself, irrespective of what is produced, there may be something to be said for this. But so often any small company which had the beginnings of a design policy got no sympathy whatever from the larger group. The boards of these giant combines, who appeared to spend much of their time planning or resisting further take-overs, usually consisted of accountants or financiers with little knowledge of the actual process of manufacture and even less of design. Some of them were beginning to think that there might be something in 'this design racket', but they had little idea of what the next step might be. During my time at the Board of Trade I had acted as interpreter, with some success, perhaps due to the fact that I always tried to see the point of view of both sides and then not only to endeavour to reach a solution which was reasonable but also to explain it fully so that it could be seen to be reasonable. This took much time, tact and thought and, of course, a certain expertise which it had taken me some years to acquire. And my time at the Council had greatly broadened my experience in such matters. I came to realize that the interpreter was the missing link and that without him, in many firms, there was little hope of making an advance. The sad thing was that when, with many misgivings, a firm had taken on a designer and the experiment had broken down they would seldom admit that there had been faults on their side. On the contrary, they were convinced that their misgivings had been proved correct and it was often quite a long time before they could be persuaded to repeat the experiment, under different conditions. I knew only too well that in such cases, however straightforward a design problem might be, there were very few designers tough and persevering enough to sell the idea to the board once again. Further, if the board could not be induced to give full support any proposal was almost certain to be shot down at managerial level. At this point expert disinterested advice could save much waste of effort and, quite frequently, nearly irreparable damage in staff relations. Apart from this, certain committees and juries needed a design adviser of wide experience who was well known. The Railways Board Design Panel, on which I had served since 1956, was one example; and another was to be the Bank of England Banknote Design Committee. And there were more temporary panels, such as that with representatives from nearly a dozen countries which I chaired for the International Wool Secretariat to select the Woolmark. This has since become widely known and it pleased me to get unanimous agreement for a design which I think excellent, in a case where not only complex problems of reproduction on a minute scale in weaving as well as printing were involved but also registration as a trade mark in countries all over the world.

As director of the Council it had also, of course, been necessary for me to do a great deal of voluntary work and not all of this could be dropped when I left London, even had I wished to do so. I continued to serve on the councils of the Royal College of Art and the Royal School of Needlework, for example, and was later asked to become a member of the National Council for Diplomas in Art and Design when it was set up under the chairmanship of Sir John Summerson in 1961. I had also been a trustee, since its formation in 1957, of the

Digswell Arts Trust, an interesting experiment initiated by an old friend, Henry Morris, who as chief education officer for Cambridgeshire had pioneered village colleges. He strode into my office one day to say that he had got a large old house near Welwyn Garden City which could be divided into flats and studios for artists and craftsmen, the idea being that this would give great practical help to promising students in that awkward gap between leaving an art school and becoming established. Living and working in a community, they would be inspired to some extent by each other's work and see their own in a wider context than might otherwise be the case. I hope this scheme may serve as a model for others elsewhere. I had also been approached, directly my impending retirement was announced, by the Design and Industries Association to see if I would take over their presidency. And later I was invited by the Art Workers' Guild to become its Master for 1962. I accepted with pleasure and said I would like to make my address at the beginning of my year of office instead of at the end, as had been the custom. It seemed to me that it was so important for all craftsmen to look forward, especially in a rapidly changing world, whilst taking care not to accept every change as an advance, and I wanted to stress this.

My consultancy practice grew rapidly, and allied with such voluntary work, it meant that my dream of keeping out of London except for one day a week did not prove practicable—although I have had rather more time at home, even if this has been mostly in my office. Of course, I have also been able to give more attention to our businesses in Broadway, where there were further changes.

In February 1956, at the height of the preparations for opening The Design Centre, my mother had died. I had tried to get down to see her every weekend and, if possible, to have a meal with her or take her out for a drive. Many people used to visit her in her sitting-room, where she gave audiences, and she remained cheerful and lively, with a very good memory, until she was nearly ninety-two. Although she was two years older than my father she had outlived him by more than eighteen years and had become so much a part of the Broadway scene that I could hardly bear to think of it without her.

The business which she had helped my father to develop had to be carried forward and we had further pressing problems to cope with at the Lygon. Our work in increasing and improving our kitchen accommodation had been closely followed, as we planned, by more space for serving meals. But our drive to increase bathrooms had in fact slightly reduced bedrooms for in the 1911 New Wing we had to take blocks of three bedrooms and convert the centre one into two bathrooms. It was clear that kitchen and dining-rooms ought to be balanced by more bedroom accommodation and we had no doubt that the demand existed. In 1960 we therefore commissioned my brother Dick's firm to design a further block of rooms—the Garden Wing—to extend the New Wing to the back lane. It had a much needed store on the ground floor and fourteen bedrooms above, each with bathroom. We spent quite a time investigating the kind of fittings which would be most convenient for a guest staying, as a rule, only a night or two. Douglas Barrington went to look at hotels in a number of countries and our conclusions were then interpreted as built-in units by Gordon Russell Ltd., the aim being to group these so as to have the maximum amount of clear floor space. We also paid particular attention to lighting. My peregrinations have taken me to many hotels. Often I have found a badly-designed domestic bedroom suite arranged with the bed on one wall, wardrobe on another, chest of drawers on the third and dressing table on the fourth, so that any free floor space was in the corners of the room where it was practically useless. The lavatory basin often had a mirror which was either too small or fixed too low for a tall man like me to shave in comfort, and for good measure the electrician had often placed the light so that one's head was between it and the mirror. These are small annoyances but they add up, and to me they are signs of that lack of integrated design which is a distinguishing feature of our age. It has been our ambition at the Lygon to see that the old part of the house should be treated with sympathetic con-

T

sideration whilst incorporating modern amenities, and that additions should not ape the old but show careful and discerning attention to the problems of our own day and attempt to solve them in an imaginative way. This principle will again be applied to the Orchard Wing which is to be completed in the spring of 1968. In order to collect up-to-date information whilst this was being designed and to sell our services abroad— for, in spite of constant Government obstacles, the hotel and restaurant industry is one of the country's largest earners of foreign currency—Douglas Barrington spent eight weeks in 1967 in America and also attended travel agents' meetings in Paris, Stockholm and Stuttgart. The combination of good wine, food and service in well-designed pleasant surroundings combining the best of new and old work in both buildings and furnishings is not common and we should be the last to claim that we have all the answers. But at least we realize that unremitting and skilled attention is required to maintain the standards set by my father.

From the furnishing angle, the Lygon is fortunate in being able to draw on the experience of Gordon Russell Ltd., which has not only the skill to tackle beautifully made single pieces but also has wide experience of production in considerable quantities for universities and other public bodies as well as for domestic use (see plate 17). Examples of the former are the table which the Queen presented to President Eisenhower during her State Visit to the United States in 1957 (see plate 17), and the lecture bench and lectern which the Duke of Edinburgh, as President, gave to the Royal Society of Arts in the same year. Both of these were designed by R. D. Russell, who became Professor Emeritus when he retired from the Royal College of Art in 1964 and has since done an increasing amount of designing for the firm.

When I left the Council, Paul reminded me that I had often said that we were starting at the wrong end by trying to convert hard-boiled businessmen to better design and that we should start in the schools. Now, he said, is a wonderful opportunity of putting that excellent idea across. I was hoist with my own petard! At the behest of the Council, in the autumn term of 1961, I spoke to the sixth forms of thirty-four public schools, including Eton, Harrow, Winchester, Rugby, Marlborough, Stowe, Sedburgh, Christ's Hospital and Repton—where I found that the art master was living in our old home! It was not at all easy to plan a tour which worked geographically and fitted in with the schools' preferences as to date and it proved an exhilarating if somewhat exhausting job, with such rewarding audiences!

Then in 1962 the Government of India asked me to spend about two months there under the Colombo Plan in order to advise them on the setting up of four schools of industrial design. Oddly enough, the Treasury medical section, to which I had to report, was in the Council's first home, Tilbury House, Petty France, where I had worked for eight years. I arrived in Bombay at the end of September and was welcomed there and kindly looked after by my ex-secretary, Eileen Reynolds, now married to Charles Biddolph.

I visited Delhi three times, also Calcutta and Madras. I went to Bangalore—where I suddenly came upon Sutton's Seed Trial Grounds, the same board that I had passed most weeks by train at Reading! And to Mysore and Ahmedabad, the great textile centre where, on the clean yellow sand bordering the river, which shrinks to almost a brook after the monsoon, cloths of splendid colours—red, yellow, green, blue—are put out for sun curing and form a vast but quite unselfconscious abstract pattern which is most marvellous to behold. At the back of it all, in the brilliant clear light, fluttered the washing of the city, forming a wonderful haze in which the dhobiwallahs picked their way, their chattering a far background noise not unsoothing to the ear. I had dinner in Ahmedabad with a much-travelled and cultured mill-owner, Mr Gautam Sarabhai, chairman of India's National Design Institute, who had a remarkable collection of ancient Indian bronzes in his house and, outside, a splendid bronze cooking bowl, some six feet in diameter, from a monastery.

Whilst I was in Delhi the Festival of Divali was celebrated.

There were huge paper effigies and myriads of lights, and delightful traditional patterns in rice paste were traced on thresholds. There was a day of mourning on the anniversary of Mahatma Gandhi's assassination and a service at his cenotaph. I said I would like to go to this and was told it would be very crowded unless we went early. So at 5.30 we started and, leaving the car, followed a steady trickle of people through a field. We arrived shortly at a place where shoes and socks were discarded and from there made an exceedingly painful pilgrimage over a cinder track. Religious music was being broadcast and we walked round the tomb, which was covered with flowers. Looking up, I saw Pandit Nehru and members of the Government sitting on the ground in the front row of a large congregation. I think I was the only Englishman there. It was a dignified, simple and sincere ceremony and I was told that throughout the day increasing queues came to pay their respects, yet it retained the intimate quality of an Armistice Day service on an English village green. I also visited Gandhi's little house, perched high above and overlooking the river at Ahmedabad, which is now kept as a national museum.

I had been interested in Mughal gardens ever since I came across Mrs Villiers-Stuart's book on them. The use of water and light, and of sweet-smelling white flowers so as to tell at night, and even, on occasion, the use of scented water in the fountains of open pavilions, together with a central space for musicians, all indicated a highly imaginative approach. My Indian friends told me that Lord Curzon was the first Viceroy to show an interest in Indian buildings and started an Ancient Monuments record—an immense task which has proved valuable. When they saw how real my interest was, especially in the astonishing difference between Mohammedan and Hindu buildings, they took great trouble to see that I was shown fine things as we travelled around. Descended from a nomadic people who lived in tents and made their way over vast deserts, the Mughals were accustomed to steering by the stars and so became mathematicians, studying geometry in order to plot their courses. In Delhi, I visited the wonderful masonry structures of tremendous size for recording the path of the sun with great accuracy. The largest sundial had some forty steps on the gnomon and its shadow was cast on immense quadrants faced with marble and accurately engraved in degrees. These were built by the Maharajah of Jaipur early in the eighteenth century. The marble quarries of Jaipur have been famous for centuries and I was fortunate to be able to have a lotus bowl made to my design. It has a slight pinkish flush— most beautiful when wet—and I am told it is harder than any Italian marble. Both mathematical precision and the lightness of the tent are reflected in Mughal architecture. The lovely carpets they hung inside their tents were translated into wonderfully selected and inlaid marbles in their permanent buildings and even the carved decorations on them became two-dimensional and reminiscent of woven work, but always of less importance than the shapes on which they were placed. The Hindus, on the other hand, seemed to regard ornament as an end in itself and the more of it the better. In many buildings there were no strong controlling lines and I longed for at least one plain surface as a foil to so much decoration. The carving was often excellent, but one could not take it all in.

The buildings that I found most interesting were all in the first category: the Fort and Taj Mahal at Agra, the Red Fort, Mosque and Hamayun's Tomb at Delhi, and the great layout in red sandstone at Fatehpur Sikri with its marvellous little fretted white marble tomb in one of the immense courts, which was paved with squares of different coloured stone so that chess could be played with girls as chessmen. By getting up early, I was able to visit the wonderful botanic gardens in Calcutta, where I saw the giant water lily and lotus growing in the open and the extraordinary banyan tree, covering an immense area, whose new stems dropping forty feet from the larger branches are as straight and symmetrical as steel piping. The Indians themselves were proud of the garden below the great dam at Brinvan, near Mysore, and I was taken to see it; but the poetry which was so enthralling a part of the earlier gardens had, to me, been neglected by the engineer. The early gardens were surrounded by walls, rectangular in shape and divided into four by canals, 'the rivers of Paradise', often with a raised platform at the junction, as in the garden of the Taj Mahal. I was anxious to see this marvellous building by daylight and moonlight. The Keeper of the Monument, who has an office in the great gateway, was kind enough to let me spend there the hours until the nearly full moon appeared. Here was a series of most interesting photographs of the building going back a great number of years. The earliest of these showed how the original planting had been completely altered by the inevitable Victorian shrubberies which had bordered the long canals, the last dull effort of the nineteenth-century landscape school. However, Curzon had seen how important the original planting had been in that the formality of the alternate cypresses and flowering almonds, under-planted with many kinds of bulbs, were like a frame of jewels to the placid water, fretted at time by the showering sprays from the lotus bud fountains. Having seen *Canna* spot-planted in the beds of English parks I was astonished at their beauty when, relishing the light and heat, they were planted by the hundred in Indian cities. My well-informed guide then took me to see the building and the garden from every aspect by moonlight. I shall not forget the view of it from one of the mosques: I could just distinguish the silhouette against a velvet sky and as we walked I noticed that there were semi-precious stones inlaid in the upper part of the walls, set at slightly different angles so that they twinkled exactly like the stars. At Seringapatam there is a small tomb building of most exquisite workmanship. The doors, beautifully inlaid with richly-engraved ivory, are as wonderful in their way as the doors of pierced and carved marble with peg hinges which I saw elsewhere.

I was also taken to see the earliest English church in India, next to the Fort in Madras. This had gravestones of English-men going back as far as 1635, with wonderful capital letters which looked as if they might have been copied from a legal deed. Wellington had been governor of Madras in his twenties and the records had been carefully preserved in the museum. The amount of claret and port these chaps drank in such a climate was astonishing, but most of them died of cholera or fever before they were forty. I found that the same care had been taken over relics of Queen Victoria in her great marble memorial in Calcutta.

The Viceroy's (now the President's) palace in New Delhi is part of the vast development by Lutyens, who was a highly skilled landscape architect. The garden layout was planned on a rather flat site, with a good deal of water but little shade and no artificial lighting. This seemed odd, as any large groups in daytime would need shade and fans, and if advantage were taken of the cool of the evening lighting would be necessary. When the President took over, an electrician had been called in who, in the tradition of his kind, trailed steel pipes over Lutyens' fine stonework and hung bulbs in small trees! It seemed a pity that a fine opportunity for imaginative artificial lighting was missed.

Everywhere I went I was shown kindness and consideration. I can only hope that my report has proved of some use to this great country which, like ourselves, is faced with so many problems today.

Towards the end of my stay I also went to Karachi to address a design conference and found that although there seemed to be difficulties for Indians visiting Pakistan and vice versa I was made welcome in both countries.

I travelled some 8,000 miles in India, mostly by air, and spent quite a lot of valuable time waiting at airports as air services were curtailed following the Chinese invasion in the north. On the last day two Indian friends lunched with me in Delhi in brilliant sunshine. And with delicate courtesy I was escorted to the airport in the evening by several people with whom I had worked. As Bahrein airport was closed, we arrived in London two hours early; so, as my wife had arranged to meet me, I waited at an airport once more— but for the opposite reason this time! It was November and there was an early fall of snow on the ground but we got to Kingcombe in time for lunch, a contrast with lunch the previous day in Delhi.

Early in 1962 I received a letter from the Royal Society of Arts which informed me that the Society's council had decided to award me the gold Albert Medal for 1962, 'for services to industrial design'. I felt honoured to recall that in the previous year it had been given to Professor Walter Gropius, the distinguished architect and designer who started the Bauhaus at Weimar just after the First World War and whom I had met several times both here and in America, where he had since settled.

Prince Philip presented the medal to me at a luncheon given in the Society's house on May 23, 1963 (see plate 18), and when, in replying, I pointed out how well qualified he himself was to receive it—for it is given 'for distinguished merit in promoting arts, manufactures and commerce'— he said, in one of his amusing asides: 'Who's giving this medal, you or me?' I had meant every word I said so was delighted to learn later that, after some hesitation due to his being President, he decided to accept it for 1963— at the earnest request of the council, who felt the award to be most appropriate as it had been instituted in 1863 as a memorial to his predecessor, the Prince Consort, who had also, for eighteen years, been President of the Society.

The Russell brothers—Gordon, Don and Dick—at the opening of the
Russell Room, Lygon Arms, 1957

Discussing a problem in the factory with the works manager, Adriaan Hermsen,
whose skill as a cabinetmaker made him aware of the contribution to quality
production that could be made by the machine

17 English walnut table incorporating a
replica of the master plan for the 1944
invasion of Europe made for
presentation by Queen Elizabeth II and
The Duke of Edinburgh to
President Eisenhower on the occasion
of their State Visit to the USA, 1957
Designer: R. D. Russell

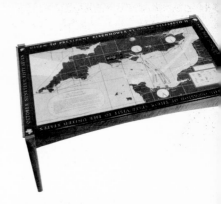

2,000 chairs in English
oak made for Coventry
Cathedral, 1960
Designer: R. D. Russell

Below left: Dining room
in rosewood and
mahogany, 1965
Designers: W. H. Russell
and Trevor Chinn
The chair, designed by
W. H. Russell in 1950,
has become a classic

Below right: Study
bedroom for the
University of Sheffield,
1962
Designers:
Desk —R. D. Russell
Chair—W. H. Russell

Prince Philip, as President of the Royal Society of Arts, presenting the
Albert Gold Medal, May 23, 1963

In the Design Centre with Sir Paul Reilly, my successor as Director of
the Council of Industrial Design

19   Kingcombe from the North West
Feeding the fish from the front porch

Lunching with my wife and daughter, Kate

21   The herbaceous border and wall built in 1950

Pools in the garden

2   Looking up and down the main garden stairway during construction

23   Endpiece

Kingcombe Again

Kingcombe had been roughly treated during the war and no redecoration had been done. The unfinished corner of the house had had only somewhat sketchy weather-proofing and part of the roof had already blown off. The garden had become a smallholding, inadequately maintained, and part of the house was still let. My wife and I often walked round what our pre-war Irish nannie had been pleased to call 'the eshtate' and wondered how we could possibly make a start. Michael Hope, whose family had spent a good deal of the war with us, said that Kingcombe was a microcosm of a town in that it had its West End, its workshops and even its slums! We could not help agreeing that it was a true, if somewhat depressing, picture.

I decided to get Frank Smith, a local mason, to come up on Saturdays and that I would work with him in an endeavour to bring back some order into paths and walls near the house. I enjoyed this straightforward work which, so unlike my London job, clearly showed what had been done at the end of the day. But often I had to bring writing or reading home with me, and so found I could get outside for only a short time. This put me in the position of supervisor, which was not nearly so pleasant a change as doing some of the actual work myself. I have always had a strong feeling that working with my hands—even tough, physical labour on occasion—is the perfect complement to brainwork and the worries and anxieties it tends to cause. Just as the man who finds it easier not to stretch his brain becomes dull-witted with age, so the man who takes no physical exercise finds on retirement that his heart will not allow him to make a start. I suppose none of us achieves a balance which is completely harmonious and satisfying but it does seem important to try. At the end of the year the amount we had accomplished seemed to me to high- light the size of the task. This implies that the house and garden are large, which is not the case. Our problem was that neither had been completed before the war and both to com- plete and maintain them by weekend working was quite a job. The appalling cost of building, especially highly specialized building in stone on a difficult site, ruled out the possibility of taking one bite at it but by 1950 our work began to show. I was quite proud of a stone retaining wall 110 feet long and 7 feet high, every stone in which I laid myself with a scratch labour force, including my son Robert, during a short holiday snatched from Festival of Britain preparations (see plate 21). When this was done we were able to level and re-seed the main lawn.

The next big job was to get a kitchen garden nearer the house and a proper kitchen yard and outhouses. I decided to combine the outhouses with a turning place for cars and garage above, at road level—a somewhat urgent matter as Kingcombe Lane had been widened during the war to take a shuttle service of lorries carrying stone for aerodrome run- ways and the growing, and faster, traffic after the war made it dangerous to back into the road up the incline from our small garage. Also, there was no adequate turning or parking place for anyone who came to see us. My long garden wall had meant hard work, rough on the hands, but it was simple and straight- forward to set out, and the subsequent careful checking of levels and batter presented few problems. But a building on two floors, which the fall of the site made essential if hun- dreds of tons of filling were not to be called for, was a different matter. Not only had the upper floor, at road level, to carry the weight of cars but a turning space beside a public road —and just beyond cross-roads—was quite likely to prove convenient for the odd heavy lorry.

The job began to look like engineering, weekend engineer- ing at that, with primitive tackle. The more I thought about

298

it the more it seemed to me that the Romans had found the perfect answer to this problem by the use of semi-circular arches and vaults. Ever since I first saw the Pont du Gard—and perhaps before—I have been bewitched by the sight of arches. To see vast stones tossed up into the air and so balanced as to make the whole mighty structure appear to stride across the valley savours to me of magic. My wife and I spent hours looking at it in the sun and ended by dining in a little hotel nearby. Some time later I came across Rousseau's description of a similar visit. He, too, lost all sense of time and lamented the distress his disappearance would cause his mistress, who had warned him of the young women of Montpelier, but had not mentioned the Pont du Gard. Still, as he says, one cannot think of everything! The other Roman aqueducts, those which Louis XIV built from Marly and the still more grandiose project which ends at Maintenon, railway viaducts, the arches below the old Adelphi and even our oddly placed Marble Arch —all were enchanting to me. I planned one day to build an arch myself and here was an opportunity. One can build an arch of stone on a small scale, which is not possible for an amateur in the case of other engineering marvels, which I find equally fascinating to visit: web-like structures of steel, such as the Clifton suspension bridge or the Forth or Severn bridges. The calculations required and the intractability of the material, let alone the fact that they are not made up of any simple modular unit, preclude modest experiments appropriate to a domestic background.

The collapse of a singularly inadequate timber ramp from the road to our kitchen premises just before the Christmas holidays precipitated action and I announced to a slightly bewildered and incredulous family that I should build forthwith against the wall of the house a permanent flight of stone steps, under which I should contrive a commodious space for ash bins. I did not at this stage disclose that the space would be covered by a vault to carry the upper steps or my family would have seen through my new-born interest in severely practical affairs at holiday time.

The mild and fine weather favoured us. Eight steps brought the work to the springing line of the arch and the next day I completed the projecting wall at the far side of the recess. Meantime I had worked out in my head a form of centering to support the arch until it was completed. I had to use such materials as were at hand. The span and depth were both but four feet, yet my solution would have astonished Vitruvius. With rough props I formed a wooden platform at the springing line and on this I placed the gabled top of a bee-hive, over which I sprang a dozen newly-cut osiers. These formed a good curve and I laid my thin unworked stones directly on them. I toiled like one possessed and as the weight grew I feared a collapse but, strangely enough, it held.

Surveying our triumph in the fading light my companion, the gardener, remarked that he had heard there were blokes in London who thought building in stone was dying out but, he added, 'they ought to come and see what ordinary chaps in Gloucestershire could do when they set their minds to it'. The first irreverent reference was no doubt to the president of the Royal Institute of British Architects and other eminent persons, though I had not hitherto suspected him of studying the correspondence columns of *The Times*. But it was the 'ordinary chaps' which stuck in my gullet. I had come to think I was almost the sole repository of the distilled engineering experience of Imperial Rome! Ordinary chaps indeed!

I really was rather proud of my work, accomplished without spending a copper on plant! This was a cardinal point with me in all building because expensive plant deteriorates, especially in the winter, and hiring for a day's work each week is very costly.

My next vault was a bigger span—about eight feet—and I wanted it to be semi-circular. I had three centerings made of rough timber. These were set up on dry bricks as before, and some very old corrugated iron sheets were then lashed to them with wire, and plastered with lime mortar so as to fill the corrugations—otherwise I found that the bricks or stone were apt to tilt into them. Again I found this method quite satisfactory and when two courses of bricks had been laid and the mortar had hardened the centering could be used for the next arch as soon as the wall had been built to carry it (see plate 15).

In the middle of the building I constructed a large reinforced concrete rainwater tank—for which I did hire a concrete mixer. This tank provides an immensely strong central pillar for the reinforced concrete slab over the vaults which, covered with old granite setts from Birmingham, forms the floor of the turning space at road level. All the rainwater from this side of the house, and a great deal from the road and paved space, discharges on to it and drains into the tank, which holds about 3,000 gallons. It is then carried to the garden by gravity, in polythene pipes. We find it invaluable in keeping the garden supplied in a dry summer for, with our own spring providing the household supply, there had not always been water to spare for garden use as prolonged dry weather reduced the flow.

Our arches became more and more professional to look at and I grew more ambitious. A small one was built of empty wine bottles laid on a curved plywood sheet and grouted with cement mortar. The last has a span of 14 feet and forms an excellent cool cellar which isolates the end wall of the house from the hillside from which our spring issues. It was built in a way which may not have been used in England for a thousand years. We dug a wide trench 14 feet from the house wall, throwing up the soil on to the space between. When we came to stone, with a good deal of water issuing from it, we built a rough wall. Then we formed the soil into the shape of vault required and built directly on it. Finally, we excavated about thirty tons of soil—which was exactly what we needed to fill below the top soil in hollows of the new kitchen garden. As the wall had not reached down to the final floor level owing to the spring we then built a stillage for barrels, which also acted as a dam so that we could collect as much of the water as possible and add it to the household supply. I may perhaps claim to be the only Englishman who, since the war, has built such a vaulted wine cellar with his own hands. Unfortunately I have not yet been able to fill it with wine.

This work could hardly have been done unless I had known exactly what I wanted to do and how to do it and had been able both to supervise it and do much of the work myself. It was not done in this way out of cussedness! Each job was considered carefully so as to use any materials in hand, always bearing in mind the irregular times of working and the lack of special tools and plant. Inevitably it meant a good deal of experimentation and improvisation, always allowing what seemed to be an ample margin of safety. This was, I imagine, the way in which mediaeval cathedrals were built. Occasionally, as at Beauvais, their soaring vaults collapsed and then there must have been much heated argument as to what had gone wrong. My smaller efforts have a low factor of risk and, so far at least, there are no signs of trouble, even though there has been at least one ten-ton lorry on the turning space.

When I left the Council of Industrial Design I decided to complete the house with what labour I could get. My previous skirmishes had been, as I have said, one-trade practice but the work on the house would, I knew, be complicated. It would involve masonry, bricklaying, joinery, plastering, tiling, electrical work, slating, painting, carpentry, plumbing, asphalting—in addition to labouring—a formidable list even in the hands of a competent professional builder. It was not a big job but it was certainly an awkward one. A cellar had to be excavated, owing to the fall of the ground, and there were three floors above with a half-landing difference in level on the two sides which had to join up with the earlier work. My team consisted of two Irish labourers, who lived in a tiny cave —a real cave—in a quarry about half a mile away and who were good workers but singularly irregular in their habits; the mason, Frank Smith, who had worked for me at odd times over several years and who was capable and, on the whole, reliable although he would sometimes disappear without warning for a week or two to do a job for a neighbour; a really first-rate joiner, Bill Pither, who was generally rather hard pushed as he had a feeling that he ought not to turn down any job that was offered; an excellent plasterer and tile-setter, who could only come on Saturdays; a good plumber; and an electrician who was not easy to get hold of. My brother Dick advised on the plans and made some valuable suggestions. As an Honorary Associate of the Royal Institute of British Architects I felt it was incumbent on me to do much of the planning, but I cannot claim that this was responsible for my promotion to Honorary Fellow a few years later! I was also able to do some of the actual work, such as walling.

It can readily be understood that organizing this team and keeping them supplied with the necessary plant and materials was tricky. My wife acted as builder's foreman when I was away and Rosamund took progress clerk's duties in her stride.

I employed several techniques which I have not seen elsewhere, including the use of empty wine bottles instead of hollow clay tiles in suspended reinforced concrete ceilings and the use of cabbage leaves in the shuttering of the kitchen window lintel. Cabbage leaves seemed particularly appropriate in this situation and their waxy surface gave the concrete a polish against the matt background of the wooden shuttering. I had hoped to use water lily leaves in the same way but, alas, winter intervened. I have always been interested in the texture of concrete and some forty years before had used special basketwork panels in a lintel, suggested by the use of osier hurdles by the Germans as shuttering for pillboxes during the First World War. My lintel has weathered beautifully and still gives me pleasure. The kitchen has a large window facing north-east with a fine view, and on the south-east side there are clerestory windows which extend to the adjacent pantry. These are above general ceiling level, in order to clear a flat veranda roof outside. They give ventilation at the highest point and well diffused light; and they have the additional advantage of brightening the kitchen with sun until after midday without any noticeable increase of heat. They also enable use to be made of the wall space below. The outside wall of the kitchen contains a cavity to take a dustbin for compostable waste. The bin can be removed from outside, whilst inside a close-fitting lid above the bin and beside the sink enables waste to be dropped in readily. This saves much walking and the bin can be emptied at intervals. My pride in this was somewhat shattered, however, when I read that a somewhat similar arrangement was found in the ruins of a house two thousand years old in Upper India! In a passage upstairs I laid the usual red flooring quarries, using cement joints about an inch wide with cast lead, slightly domed circles inserted at the intersections. I cast these myself from the capsules of wine bottles which I had saved. I get particular pleasure in finding a use for something which is normally thrown away, though in America this will sound like heresy!

It is always a considerable problem to do any major building work in a house which is occupied and I fear it was a great trial to the women of the place. On the other hand, how many builders relish the idea of the client living on the site? At Christmas 1961 we had half a kitchen with one wall of polythene which flapped in the wind, a situation which, a few weeks later, did not simplify arrangements for Kate's wedding breakfast. She had met Ken Baynes when they were both working for the international graphic art magazine *Graphis* in Zürich. As a young designer trained at the Royal College of Art and proposing to start a practice in London, we had many interests in common.

The work was finished at last and is generally approved. In spite of the continuous pressure of the job on top of a rapidly growing amount of office work I got a great deal of enjoyment from doing it and even managed to work in a few extras which pleased me. One of these was carving the Kingcombe Cat in a block of stone which had been built in for such a purpose nearly forty years before! Another was a floor of Derbyshire marble which we polished *in situ*. And in the new guest room, which has a large window at one end with a wide-ranging view, I thought it would be interesting to panel the walls in white-painted wood with the upright rails coinciding with the ceiling joists, on the undersides of which similar rails would be planted to support small vaults of plywood covered with hessian and painted a fine blue, chosen by my wife with great care.

We live in an age of specialists who often intimidate ordinary mortals and prevent their 'having a go'. With growing productivity it does not seem likely that there will be a demand for such jacks-of-all-trades in industry, but perhaps greater leisure and do-it-yourself will be a powerful incentive outside. It is in the hope that my experience may encourage others that I have written about this work in some detail.

With the completion of the house I was able to turn my attention to the garden. We had already got the new kitchen garden into working order. We had planned it with some care, including a herb border close to the kitchen and, beyond, a compost pit for the conversion into humus of all waste other than foul weeds. Directly the kitchen garden was cleared in the autumn I sowed mustard seed, which was cut with a scythe when about a foot high, compost spread on top and the whole dug in. This greatly improved the soil, which was not old garden ground.

The paths are fairly wide, formed in about eight-foot lengths of concrete left rough from the screed, which gives a pleasant non-slip texture. Between each length a ten inch gap was left. To close each end of this a blue engineering brick was laid and the gap then filled with brown pebbles set in cement mortar. Should a small settlement occur the crack will be at one end of the joints and so will hardly show; and the whole makes a much more seemly path than concrete alone.

The lie of the ground enabled me, by the use of some filling, to tilt it slightly towards the south. As we are fairly high and crops mature about a fortnight later than in the Vale of Evesham nearby this small point saves several days, a matter of no small importance in the bed of asparagus, whose season, so eagerly awaited, is all too short.

Our gardener left us in 1939 for a war job and since then our outside help has been mostly part time and almost all unskilled. During the war we had first a German and then an Italian prisoner, followed, for several years, by a steady elderly man with some knowledge of vegetables. Since he retired my wife has done a great deal herself, with valiant help from Mary,

u

otherwise relying almost entirely on Irish labourers, who come and go, together with a sound gardener who, as he drives a van at night, gives us a few hours very occasionally.

In these circumstances, Toni keeps her eyes open for any likely help. One Saturday afternoon she noticed a Pole who had just missed the Evesham bus. He had on a natty suiting and thin pointed shoes, but no matter. She asked him if he would like to put in an hour or so in a garden. When I gave him a spade he looked at it as if he had never seen such a tool before and when he started to use it I thought he hadn't. My wife asked him what his job was. He said he was a hairdresser, so she gave him a pair of shears and he made a tolerable beginning on the yew hedge. This was one of the jobs that our eldest son, Michael, did very well with mechanical clippers until he became a busy economist. Oliver, our youngest boy, showed no interest in gardening but, like my wife, was fascinated by languages, from Italian to Swahili, and got a bronze medal from the Royal Society of Arts for Russian whilst still at school.

Another man was of an entirely different mould. Red-faced, cheerful and bucolic he was a good worker and as lively as one of Shakespeare's clowns. I commented on his polished shovel, as clean as that a navvy used to cook his bacon on. I noticed that, whenever possible, he preferred it to a spade. 'Ah,' he said, 'when you work on the roads you want to keep your own shovel at home: other blokes don't often look after it as well as I do. And it comes in handy for special jobs like, say, grave-digging. I've often thought that what I'd like more than any-thing is an acre of my own ground to work on and one or two graves to dig each week. Just to keep me going in beer, like. Why, t'other night I went into the Eight Bells with my shovel and one or two of them grinned at me. "A bit of the usual evening work, eh, Bill? Bet you don't finish it afore closing time." "Make it a pint apiece," I said, and off I goes—after a quart to start with. And I came in well ahead of time with a tongue like a hay-rake. Those pints what I didn't pay for tasted grand.' Here he stopped and eyed me thoroughly. I thought he was angling for a pint, and perhaps he was. 'Funny thing,' he said, 'after such a rushed job he isn't going to be buried there after all. His family decided to put him alongside his missus in Bournemouth. Yes, fact, Bournemouth of all places. Easy digging there—all sand I'm told—but you might have to shore it up. Now you wouldn't like the one I dug here would you? It wouldn't take me long to lengthen it! He was a small bloke and there's no point in wasting effort. But of course you're not an RC so that wouldn't work. Unless someone's pretty nippy they'll have to pay me to fill it in. But it'll be a lovely job getting it out next time, if they don't cut the rate! I wonder who will go in it after all? Jimmie Hunter I shouldn't be surprised: he looks very poorly. Ah, I keep my eye on the sick-list!' I don't have as much time as I would like to talk to these chaps, who, in these days of mass entertainment, are often well worth listening to.

As I am away a good deal, and when here am likely to be either in the office or engaged on constructional work, it would be foolish to imagine that we have either a tidy garden or a high standard of cultivation. But I find the work of absorbing interest and whenever I travel I try to look at some gardens.

As a designer I realized at an early stage how different garden design is from that of industrial products. Two sites are never exactly the same—soil, aspect, contours and so on all vary—growing trees and shrubs alter in size year by year and in colour and texture month by month and annual and perennial plants show widely different colours according to the season. Winter has its own special beauty for then one sees more clearly the structure of trees, and the colour of the bark of dog-woods and willows tells against the greys, soft greens and browns. In furniture I was interested in old and new, hand and machine made, and I soon saw that there were many different aspects of gardening. I was bored by the arguments which went on at one time as to the merits of formal versus natural gardens. I like the best of both. The architect or landscape architect and the horticulturist each have an essential contribution to make in layout and planting. A good garden must have good bones and it must be planted with sympathy and knowledge. It is seldom that one man is trained to cope with both of these and it is certainly true to say that whilst in England the growing of flowers is generally up to a pretty good standard, the design of gardens is, as a rule, no better than the design of industrial products. And why should anyone imagine it would be? Many gardeners are quite unaware that there is such a profession as landscape architecture. And even if they were, a serious problem remains, for whereas industrial products are made in large—sometimes very large—quantities to one design every garden is individual and if it is of any size it needs a great deal of consideration on the site to discover on the one hand the *genius loci* and the plants which grow happily and on the other what the owners have in mind. Such skilled advice is necessarily somewhat expensive but, as in building a house, one is unlikely to get a good result by doing without an architect.

Certainly today there is an increasing tendency to employ landscape architects for large schemes such as universities, power stations and hospitals. In such layouts there is almost certain to be a fair amount of levelling or excavating and if the landscape architect works with the architect from the inception of the plan he will in many cases be able to suggest a re-arrangement of contours which will enable the unwanted soil to be used to advantage on the site, not only saving considerable sums in cartage but making it possible to plant trees at once. This can be of great practical value, as soil and trees combined can form good windscreens and also mitigate the noise from nearby roads. Owing to high taxation and labour costs the large garden as it existed before 1914 is no longer feasible. The smaller garden of today gives less scope for imaginative treatment but its more intimate scale makes its detailing extremely important to get satisfactory results. Here, as in industry, much depends on how knowledgeable and interested the patron is.

The word 'garden' means so many different things to different owners. Often it is accepted as a place to grow the largest possible flowers in the brightest possible colours. It may be reduced to the limit of labour-saving by the planting of shrubs and the use of paving, gravel or even asphalt instead of grass. Or it may squander labour by the devotion of an owner whose passion in life is to grow plants which do not naturally like the soil or situation. Or, of course, it may be a garden to sit in, to play games in, to swim in, to let children or dogs loose in. To me a garden should be first of all a work of art, taking account of the owner's interests, a work of conscious design— perhaps the most fascinating there can be. It must be thought of as complementary to the house, which must have at least some architectural merit. And the whole entity must be related to the landscape in which it stands.

The war provided for me a period of gestation, if a somewhat hectic one. Returning to more normal conditions, I decided to simplify the pre-war garden plan quite a lot—to have fewer flower borders and much more space turned over to woodland —beech, elm and ash in small coppices underplanted with bluebells, daffodils, snowdrops, primroses and such-like wild flowers which are as lovely as anything one ever sees. The ground is treated quite differently on each side of the house. A small and intimate sunk pool garden at the entrance, formal lawns and yew hedges on the south-west side with coppices beyond, a coppice of elms and a series of pools on the south-east (see plate 21) and the kitchen garden on the north-east. The water comes from a spring in the hillside, cool and delicious, and the first small tank is my watercress bed. It is a great luxury to be able to cut it absolutely fresh.

The stairway at about the middle of the garden (see plate 22) divides the lawns from the beechwood. The stairs go down in six flights of five, each with landings between so that one can pause to take in the splendid view. They are flanked by small cascading tanks, whose water is the lifeblood and, with the birds and the wind, the music of the garden. The stairway leads down to a long grass terrace of recent construction, which forms a frame to the garden and below which, in a field, are several unusual trees. At one end are chestnuts with great elms above, all rather shady and mysterious, shutting out the view. As one walks along the terrace the view opens out, with Campden and its fine church tower in the valley and a wide landscape beyond. Continuing and looking back one has a view of the hills without a single house. Further along one gets delightful glimpses of the countryside through a carefully thinned coppice of elms full of bluebells. So many surprises in a distance of less than two hundred yards! From the top terrace of all, at road level, one looks over the lawn, yew hedge and bosco of flowering cherry trees and lower terrace to a wide view, bounded at each end by the old elms. The foreground is kept quiet and green, so as not to compete with this (see endpapers).

The use of artificial light and water in gardens has been revolutionized by electricity, but I don't feel the freedom which is now possible has been adequately explored. To make such gardens as Versailles and Villa d'Este at Tivoli meant diverting rivers, building aqueducts and canals to supply the fountains. Cost rules that out today and in any case constant streams of water are only suitable in a hot country: in England we do from time to time get hot spells when it would be delicious to have the sparkle and sound of water but we certainly don't yearn for it in a misty November. The direct-coupled electric pump enables us to use it when we wish but so far we don't seem to have got beyond the 'tiny jet with plastic nymph and instant pool' stage. At exhibitions there have been experiments, as there should be. The water mobile at the South Bank in 1951 and the Dutch pavilion at Brussels in 1958 both showed imagination of the right kind. In the latter the theme of water, so appropriate for Holland, was admirably worked out and there were some attempts, not all of them successful, to use light and water elsewhere in the exhibition. When fountains and fireworks are combined at Versailles on July 14th an extraordinary fairyland is created, made all the more mysterious by the drifting smoke and the various crackles and bangs against the background of splashing water. The *chadars*, or carved marble water chutes on an inclined plane, are a delightful feature of Mughal gardens in India, as is the charming custom of carrying a thin sheet of water over a wall which has recesses in it to take small oil lamps, which contribute a flicker to the movement of the water. The use of parabolic jets and lotus bowls was introduced to Spain by the Moors who, coming from a parched country, were skilled in the use of water. The hiding of water in pipes has destroyed our reverence for its mystical quality in its primitive form of gurgling brooks or deep still pools. It has become a commercial product delivered, without fuss, at so much a gallon. Theodor Schwenk in *Sensitive Chaos* is able to view it still with wonder. However sophisticated we become we cannot exist without it and therefore, in common with earth, air and fire, it should be treated with proper respect.

In England, the use of large sheets of still water, placed with admirable skill in relation to the contours of the site, was one of the triumphs of the landscape school. The edges were softened by rushes and other wild water-loving plants, such as our exquisite marsh marigold, rushes, wild iris or purple loosestrife and where the bank was steeper a judicious planting of indigenous trees, perhaps under-planted with male ferns. We have much to learn from a close observation of nature's way—she usually disposes her treasures in broad masses. In such a setting many exotics seem out of place, but are quite at home near the house, as if they needed a friendly hand in a country they are not quite sure of.

My experiments in the use of water range from the formal through the semi-formal to the completely informal—all, of course, on quite a small scale. The square pool at the entrance (see plate 19), with its marble lotus bowl and single jet, and the series of tanks flanking the stairway are examples of the first; a canal on which I am now working, built on a slight curve with grassy banks level with and bounded by the lower terrace, will be an example of the second; and a series of landscaped pools carefully planned to sit naturally in the falling contours comes into the third category. Provided these are waterproofed, we have enough spring water to keep them full. All have provided opportunities for the use of local stone, some of it carved, and various treatments of concrete.

The sculpture of Henry Moore or Barbara Hepworth looks splendid when well placed in a garden but it is out of my reach, unfortunately. Yet there is a certain satisfaction in creating humbler works for oneself. Having started during the war cutting one or two inscriptions I went on to some garden benches. Then I let myself go on a larger job—a Coronation souvenir table in a rather luscious baroque manner such as this grand occasion seemed to demand (see plates 14 and 20). Since then I have done other things, all of which help to give an individual quality to the garden. They show that someone cares a great deal and gardens react quite strongly to affection, of which the symptom known as green fingers is a manifestation. I have to admit that all this work of mine has a certain *naiveté*, such as one sees in country tombstones of the sixteenth and seventeenth centuries. The carver of these did not follow carefully an architect's full-size drawing: he took a piece of stone, saw what was the best way to shape it and with a fragment of charcoal from his wood fire set out his design. My method is exactly the same. And the beauty of it is that this can be done in the open air or under a primitive lean-to roof with the simplest of tools, costing a few shillings. The work can be left at any point and taken up again next hour, next day, next week, with perhaps a delightful interlude studying how a mediaeval carver solved a particular problem.

Similar in character are the fine hand-thrown pots planted with flowers like begonias or geraniums such as one sees everywhere in Italy or Southern France. These can form a delightful substitute for bedding out. We like especially to use them on steps. Equally, of course, they make possible the creation of a garden in a few square feet of yard or on a tiny flat roof. In England such pots are not easy to find but some nice ones are made at a small pottery at Wrecclesham, near Farnham (see plate 15), and the Rural Industries Bureau may know of others.

Of all the occupations in a garden what can be more rewarding than planting a tree and then watching it grow?

Each one shows so clearly the care that has been bestowed on it and one gets to know it as one does a person. St Francis' Brother Fig Tree is very real to me. Encouraged by my friend Cecil Pilkington, I have looked after the pruning and general cultivation of my trees myself. The pruning knife I use, which is commonly sold in the Vale of Evesham, has not altered in at least eight centuries: a manuscript of the twelfth century shows the pruning of vines with exactly such a knife. Its fitness is so demonstrable that the shape can hardly be developed further and it is pleasant to think of anything constant in such an unstable world as ours. Some of my trees are sizeable: many will see another generation before they reach maturity, but what of it? I have had the pleasure of planting and cosseting them. The older I get the more time I spend on the preparation of a site and the smaller I plant, this being especially important in a windy place. The second point, as William Robinson noted, is to mulch for a year or so and keep down weeds rather than trying to water. In a small coppice of beech planted two feet high the trees are now over thirty feet and I have three or four hundred ash, taken out of herbaceous borders as seedlings, which are now over twenty feet high. That I shall not see these in their prime does not worry me at all. How much the poorer I should have been without the planting our forebears have left for me to look at. There was doubtless much to be said against the enclosures and the great estates of the eighteenth century, but the sweep of imagination of these landowners, who housed themselves in such a civilized way and would gaily landscape-plant half a county, is something to marvel at. Even today, when the trees are past their best and have in many places been hacked by lesser men, the projects appear remarkable and designed with consummate skill.

I have been much encouraged in my gardening efforts since I learned from *Trees and Shrubs Hardy in the British Isles* by the late director of Kew Gardens, W. J. Bean, that Ernest Henry Wilson, one of the greatest of plant collectors, was born in Chipping Campden in 1876. From Birmingham Botanic Garden he went to Kew and then made two expeditions to

China for the great nursery firm of Veitch. He made a further two visits to that vast unknown country under the auspices of Harvard University. Then, after working in the Arnold Arboretum, near Boston, Mass., for two years he was sent to Japan and on his return was appointed assistant director, taking full charge in 1927. He introduced some 1,200 species of trees and shrubs and Mr Bean said that the full value of his services to botany and horticulture have probably not been equalled by any other collector. It pleases me to think of him as one of our Cotswold worthies.

Epilogue

When I receive a notice of an old people's outing from the Friends of Campden I sometimes wonder why it has been sent to me, for I have to confess that I simply don't react as I am told an Old Person should—unless, of course, one of Lear's Old Persons. It seems, as usual, that I am a bit of a nuisance, for I can't be neatly docketed and put into the right pigeonhole. I have friends of all sorts and all ages. I simply can't work up a spluttering tirade against young men with long hair, or young women with short skirts, or bald-headed old men, or coloured people, or drug takers or even people who really like what appear to me to be bad designs. Its quite obvious that there is something very odd about me!

Yet when I look back I have to admit that my lifetime, which, as I say, doesn't seem to me an exceptionally long one, has witnessed far and away the most astonishing changes of any similar period in the history of mankind. From the horse to the bicycle, motor car, aeroplane and sputnik, from the oil lamp to atomically generated electricity, from the Mills bomb to the H bomb, to say nothing of television, radar, electronics and computers.

The technological changes which are taking place at an ever increasing pace have not, unfortunately, been balanced by a corresponding growth in the humanities and therefore our age, which is supremely confident that it can do anything, is uncertain what it wants to do and hasn't even got time to sit down and think about it. Is it really so much more important to make a slum of the moon than to abolish our slums? And what is the sense of spending hundreds of millions to save a few hours in getting to New York when recovering from the journey takes more than the time saved?

In considering the future of design nothing seems to me so vital as the attitude of the ordinary man and woman to CHANGE itself. At present this attitude ranges through the whole gamut from the dyed-in-the-wool preservationists, who resist change of any kind at all, to those ardent anarchists who feel in their bones that the mere fact that anything has been shown to work or has been on the market for more than a week proves that it is clearly obsolete. Both these extreme groups have a stultifying effect on design. The first, by discouraging experiments of every kind, build up a situation in which there is no experience to cope with a radical change which, though held up till the very last moment, eventually becomes essential. A really bad solution is then likely to be accepted, in a great hurry. 'Change and decay in all around I see': the writer of the hymn evidently took the view that the two were linked. The plain fact is, however, that history shows many examples of peoples whose thinking became so crystallized that they could not adapt themselves to conditions which had changed in spite of them and so failed to survive. At the other end of the scale, constant change merely for its own sake means that no design ever has enough thought put into it and novelty becomes the sole criterion. To some letter cutters, for instance, a round o is now 'square'! I think there is little doubt that if more research and thought were put into new designs, so that the products satisfied the consumer's real needs rather than his supposed preferences, the articles would then be perfectly adequate, in most cases, for considerably longer periods and the public would get better value for money. The great pressure of advertising today with its exploitation of snob appeal creating a fear of being left behind, of having the wrong car and so on, inevitably builds up the idea of any change as progress in order to increase sales. This is bound to affect the retailer, who knows that new goods are news and consequently exerts great pressure on the manufacturer to produce ever more patterns—not necessarily good patterns but new ones. This not only means that the public often gets poor quality anyway but also that in many cases replacements cannot be obtained and the uneconomic runs make production costs higher than they should be. It is obvious, too, that journalists are bound to be interested in the latest thing ever and consequently to give a most powerful push in the same direction, although it is only fair to admit that the Press has also done much to bring better designs to the notice of the public. However, it would be silly for anyone in Britain today to pretend that he is not influenced by advertising one way or another. Recently action has been taken to try to prevent juries in criminal cases being influenced by Press reports, but selection juries of every kind are bound to be influenced in some degree and it isn't practicable to segregate them all.

Between these two extremes of approach there are many gradations, but the balanced point of view is uncommon. This surely must accept change as inevitable. It therefore seems reasonable to plan ahead, taking account of change so far as it can be foreseen but allowing flexibility so as to be able to meet completely altered circumstances. The discovery of North Sea gas, for instance, must affect every aspect of fuel planning previously laid down. At the same time, it also seems reasonable to be wary of scrapping irreplaceable buildings, open spaces, ways of doing things, customs or even goods unless careful investigation shows it to be essential. It is clear that new techniques and materials need constant examination and testing but, generally speaking, should they not be regarded as increasing the designer's range of choice rather than entirely replacing well-tried ones? Much is bound to depend on the quantities required and it is greatly to be hoped that a way will be found of using handwork for the many small production jobs for special purposes for which it is admirably adapted. But this could hardly happen if designing for obsolescence becomes our sole concern, and the world-wide pressure of American advertising points in that direction. So I repeat that the future of design depends, in my opinion, on people's reaction to change.

The complete shift in our status as a world power during this century is leading to a radical reassessment of what we can best do. In a world where so many have lost their bearings we can at least set an example by holding on to some of the qualities we have fought for in the past—standards of justice, honesty, decency and commonsense. Are these, too, to be subject to change, or even to be scrapped, as they have been in some places? As one who has spent his life trying to do something equivalent to pushing a tank uphill I have discovered that there are occasions when holding one's own can count as progress.

INDEX